KU-467-962

IS DIGITAL DIFFERENT?

How information creation, capture, preservation and discovery are being transformed

Every purchase of a Facet book helps to fund CILIP's
advocacy, awareness and accreditation programmes
for information professionals.

IS DIGITAL DIFFERENT?

How information creation, capture, preservation and discovery are being transformed

Edited by

Michael Moss and **Barbara Endicott-Popovsky**
With **Marc J. Dupuis**

facet publishing

© This compilation: Michael Moss, Barbara Endicott-Popovsky
and Marc J. Dupuis 2015
The chapters: the contributors 2015

Published by Facet Publishing,
7 Ridgmount Street, London WC1E 7AE
www.facetpublishing.co.uk

Facet Publishing is wholly owned by CILIP: the Chartered Institute of Library
and Information Professionals.

The editor and authors of the individual chapters assert their moral right to be
identified as such in accordance with the terms of the Copyright,
Designs and Patents Act 1988.

Except as otherwise permitted under the Copyright, Designs and Patents Act 1988
this publication may only be reproduced, stored or transmitted in any form or by
any means, with the prior permission of the publisher, or, in the case of
reprographic reproduction, in accordance with the terms of a licence
issued by The Copyright Licensing Agency. Enquiries concerning reproduction
outside those terms should be sent to Facet Publishing, 7 Ridgmount Street,
London WC1E 7AE.

British Library Cataloguing in Publication Data
A catalogue record for this book is available from the British Library.

ISBN 978-1-85604-854-5

First published 2015

Text printed on FSC accredited material.

Typeset from editors' files by Facet Publishing Production
in 11.5/14 pt Garamond and Myriad Pro.
Printed and made in Great Britain by CPI Group (UK) Ltd, Croydon, CR0 4YY.

WITHDRAWN

Contents

Contributors

Emma Bayne

Emma Bayne is Head of Systems Development and Search at The National Archives, UK. She is responsible for leading the design and build of technical solutions to improve access to the vast collection of records. She has worked in a variety of technology roles over the last 15 years. Recently, her focus has been on developing Discovery, an integrated search tool which pulls together archival content and improves findability, through user-centred design, for the collections of over 2500 archives across the UK and beyond.

Ylva Berglund Prytz

Ylva Berglund Prytz works for the University of Oxford and is based within the Academic IT Services, where she manages the RunCoCo service. RunCoCo looks at new ways of working with the public for impact, outreach and engagement and has a particular remit to provide advice, training and support to crowdsourcing and community collection projects.

Ylva's role is to liaise with and support those planning or running crowdsourcing and community collection projects. She also produces teaching and support material and runs training and coaching sessions for project managers and staff. She has been actively involved in a number of local, national and international initiatives using crowdsourcing to engage audiences and enhance or create digital collections. She has also worked on a range of other digital projects concerned with the creation, use and preservation of digital resources.

Ylva is a member of the Faculty of Linguistics. She also teaches for the English Faculty and serves on the Committee for Library Provision and Strategy in English. She has a PhD in English from Uppsala University, Sweden and has published in the areas of corpus linguistics, English language and computer-assisted language learning.

David Clark

David Clark, Director, CIBER Research, has worked in publishing and related industries for 40 years, as data processor, information manager and analyst. He has a master's degree in Knowledge Engineering. His PhD, from the University of Warwick, concerns the history and establishment of computing as a distinct academic discipline.

Scott David

Scott David works at the intersections of law and technology, where theory informs practice. For 27 years he worked in large law practices (first at Simpson Thacher in New York City and then with K&L Gates in Seattle), with organizations at the front edge of science, technology, business and financial innovation such as Microsoft, TMobile, Gates Foundation, Google, AT&T and many others. Several years ago, Scott joined academia, first as Executive Director of the Law, Technology and Arts programme at the University of Washington Law School, and more recently with the University of Washington Center for Information Assurance and Cybersecurity, creating programmes that provide students and faculty with new opportunities to engage where technology and people meet.

Scott is deeply involved in global data policy work with multiple organizations, including as a member of the World Economic Forum's Global Agenda Council on Data Driven Development, the advisory boards for the MIT Kerberos and Internet Trust initiative and the Open Identity Exchange, and as a senior analyst for the German consultancy KuppingerCole. Through these and other engagements Scott is actively involved with multiple initiatives of various governments, companies, universities and nongovernmental organizations that are developing policy standards and scalable, distributed legal structures that can help to create unique opportunities for system stakeholders to reduce risk and enhance leverage, security, privacy and value in networked information systems.

Marc J. Dupuis

Marc J. Dupuis, PhD, is a researcher and lecturer with the University of Washington as well as the Director of Human Factors for the Center for Information Assurance and Cybersecurity (CIAC). His main focus is on understanding the information security behaviour of individuals, including issues related to decision making and the user experience. This has included research on the role of trait affect, personality, self-efficacy and risk evaluation on information security decisions made by individuals, as well as an examination of the various security and privacy concerns related to social computing.

In 2014 he started a research group called SPROG – Security and Privacy Research and Outreach Group. The purpose of this group is to provide an environment for innovative research on issues related to security and privacy, as well as to identify opportunities for outreach in these areas with the local community.

Marc earned a PhD and MS in Information Science, in addition to an MPA (Master of Public Administration) from the University of Washington. He has also earned an MA and BA from Western Washington University. He has taught courses on cybersecurity, organizational information assurance, risk management, information assurance strategies, human computer interaction, web design and programming, and research methods.

Barbara Endicott-Popovsky

Professor Barbara Endicott-Popovsky, PhD, is Executive Director of the Center for Information Assurance and Cybersecurity at the University of Washington, designated by the National Security Agency/Department for Homeland Security as a Center of Academic Excellence in Information Assurance Education and Research; Director of the Master of Cybersecurity and Leadership programme; Academic Director for the Masters in Infrastructure Planning and Management in the Urban Planning Department of the School of Built Environments; holds a faculty appointment with the

Institute of Technology in Tacoma; and was named Department Fellow at Aberystwyth University, Wales, (2012). Her academic career follows a 20-year career in industry marked by executive and consulting positions in IT architecture and project management.

Her research interests include enterprise-wide information systems security and compliance management, forensic-readiness, the science of security, cybersecurity education and secure coding practices. For her work in the relevance of archival sciences to digital forensics, she is a member of the American Academy of Forensic Scientists. Barbara earned her PhD in Computer Science/Computer Security from the University of Idaho Center for Secure and Dependable Systems (2007) and holds an MSc in Information Systems Engineering from Seattle Pacific University (1987), an MBA from the University of Washington (1985) and a BA from the University of Pittsburgh.

Tim Gollins

Tim Gollins is currently Head of Digital Archiving at The National Records of Scotland and, as programme director, leads their Digital Preservation Programme. He started his career in the UK civil service in 1987. Since then he has worked on information assurance, user requirements, systems development, systems design, information management, and high-assurance information security, on numerous government IT projects. Tim joined The National Archives in April 2008 and as Head of Digital Preservation led The National Archives' work on digital preservation and cataloguing. He recently worked on the design and implementation of a new digital records infrastructure at The National Archives, which embodies the new parsimonious (digital) preservation approach that he developed.

He recently completed a secondment from The National Archives as an honorary research fellow in the School of Computing Science at the University of Glasgow, where he studied the challenges of digital sensitivity review. Tim remains an honorary research associate in the School of Physics and Astronomy at the University of Glasgow. He holds a BSc in Chemistry (Exeter), MSc in Computing (UCL), and MSc in Information Management (Sheffield). He was a director of the Digital Preservation Coalition for six years and is a member of the University of Sheffield I-School's Advisory Panel.

Norman Gray

Norman Gray (School of Physics and Astronomy, University of Glasgow) studies the development of next-generation scientific data management. He has been directly involved with scientific data-management software since 1997, working with the Euro-VO project (VOTECH) and Astrogrid in Glasgow and Leicester, and has more recently been the Principal Investigator (PI) of a number of (broadly) astroinformatics projects funded by the Engineering and Physical Sciences Research Council (EPSRC) and Jisc in the UK. Between 2012 and 2015 he was the chair of the International Virtual Observatory Alliance's (IVOA) Semantics Working Group and is the co-author of a number of IVOA Recommendations.

Valerie Johnson

Dr Valerie Johnson is the Interim Director of Research and Collections at The National Archives, having previously held the role of Head of Research. Prior to this, she worked on a funded history project based at the University of Cambridge History Faculty. She holds an MA with Distinction in Archive Administration and was awarded the Alexander R. Myers Memorial Prize for Archive Administration. She also has a PhD in History for her thesis, 'British Multinationals, Culture and Empire in the Early Twentieth Century', for which she won the Coleman Prize. She is a Registered Member of the Society of Archivists, a Trustee and member of the Executive Committee of the Business Archives Council, a Fellow of the Royal Historical Society and a Fellow of the Society of Antiquaries. She has worked as an archivist and a historian in the academic, corporate and public sectors.

Gavan McCarthy

Associate Professor Gavan McCarthy is Director of the University of Melbourne eScholarship Research Centre in the University Library, founded in 2007. His research is in the discipline of social and cultural informatics, with expertise in archival science and a long-standing interest in the history of Australian science. He contributes to research in information infrastructure development within the University and his projects highlight strong engagement with community. His distinctive cross-disciplinary research reaches into other fields such as education, social work, linguistics, anthropology, population health and history. He re-examines theoretical foundations and tests new theories through practical interventions with a focus on public knowledge domains, contextual information frameworks and knowledge archives.

Helen Morgan

Helen Morgan is a Melbourne writer and archivist. She is a research fellow in the area of cultural informatics at the University of Melbourne eScholarship Research Centre, having significant experience of working in collaborative research teams using digital technologies, with particular emphasis on building resilient contextual information frameworks, exploring the challenges and requirements of mapping cultural heritage in digital/networked environments and the transfer of knowledge between researchers, memory institutions and the community. Helen has worked as an information architect and exhibition designer on the Australian Women's Archives Project since its inception in 2000 and is currently a Chief Investigator on the Australian Research Council-funded 'The Trailblazing Women and the Law Project' (2012–15). She is the author of *Blue Mauritius: the hunt for the world's most valuable stamps* (Atlantic Books, 2006).

Michael Moss

Michael Moss is Professor of Archival Science at the University of Northumbria. Previously, he was Research Professor in Archival Studies in the Humanities Advanced Technology and Information Institute (HATII) at the University of Glasgow, where he directed the Information Management and Preservation MSc programme. Prior to being appointed to HATII, he was archivist of the University from 1974 to 2003. He was educated at the University of Oxford and trained in the Bodleian Library. He is a non-executive director of the National Records of Scotland and until 2014 was a member of the Lord Chancellor's Advisory Council on National Archives and Records. In 2015 he was Miegunyah Distinguished Fellow at the University of Melbourne.

Michael researches and writes in the fields of history and the information sciences. His recent publications include: 'Archival research in organisations in a digital age', in David Buchanan and Alan Bryman (eds) *Handbook of*

Organizational Research Methods, Sage, 2009; 'Brussels Sprouts and Empire: putting down roots', in Dan O'Brien (ed.) *The Philosophy of Gardening*, Blackwell Wylie; 'The High Price of Heaven – the 6th Earl of Glasgow and the College of the Holy Spirit on the Isle of Cumbrae', *Journal of the Architectural History Society of Scotland*, 2012; 'Where Have All the Files Gone, Lost in Action Points Every One?' *Journal of Contemporary History*, 2012; and 'From Cannon to Steam Propulsion: the origins of Clyde marine engineering', *Mariner's Mirror*, 2013.

David Nicholas

David Nicholas is a Director of the CIBER research group (http://ciber-research.eu). The group is best known for monitoring behaviours in the virtual space, especially with regard to the virtual scholar and the Google Generation. David holds chairs at the College of Communication and Information Studies, University of Tennessee and at Tomsk University, Russia. Previously he was Head of the Department of Information Studies at University College London (2004–11), and previous to that was Head of the Department of Information Science at City University.

David's interests include the digital consumer, mobile information, e-books, e-journal usage; web analytics and scholarly communication.

David Thomas

David Thomas worked for many years at The National Archives, where he became Director of Technology in 2005. Prior to that he held a variety of posts and from 1999 led The National Archives' pioneering developments of systems to deliver digital copies of records to online users. He is a member of the project board for the Wellcome Trust's digital library and also advised the Globe Theatre on its plans for a digital archive. He is currently a visiting professor at Northumbria University. His current research interests focus on the issues of acquiring, reviewing and delivering digital records.

Introduction and acknowledgements

Michael Moss and Barbara Endicott-Popovsky

The purpose of this book is to introduce students, particularly but not exclusively those on information studies programmes, to the issues surrounding the transition from an analogue to a digital environment. The contributors strip away much of the e-hype that surrounds the digital environment and focus on the opportunities and challenges afforded by this new environment that is transforming the information landscape in ways that were scarcely imaginable even a decade ago. Contributors examine whether analogue practices and procedure that are largely handicraft are still valid and if they shape or distort those in the digital, which can best be characterized as industrial and requiring engineering solutions.

By drawing on examples of the impact of other new and emerging technologies on the information sciences in the past, such as the printing press in the 15th century, the wet-copy process in the 18th century and the typewriter in the late 19th century, the book emphasizes that information systems have always been shaped by available technologies that have transformed the creation, capture, preservation and discovery of content. Whilst seeking to avoid techno-determinism, the contributions illustrate the ways in which the digital environment has the potential to transform scholarship across the disciplines at all levels, even if it has not done so yet, and to break down barriers between the academy and the wider community through social networks and crowdsourcing. There are analogies here with the way in which the reordering of libraries pioneered by Martin Schrettinger in the early 19th century helped to transform scholarly enterprise that came to be described in all disciplines as 'scientific'.

From the different perspectives of each chapter the contributors explore the role, as they see it, of information professionals in this rapidly changing digital landscape, which is challenging the very existence of the traditional library and archive as more and more resources become available online and as computers and supporting networks become more and more powerful. Users expect to be able to work at their screens from home, however unrealistic this may seem to many traditional curators.

The authors alert the readers to the perils and pitfalls of the digital world with its ever-present risks of breaches in security and unwitting infringement of copyright, data protection and other regulatory constraints. They argue for the need for new ways and models of working and emphasize the importance of information professionals from different disciplinary perspectives working with the grain of societal expectations through a critical encounter with the emerging technologies and mechanisms. Attention is given to the long-term curation and preservation of both born-digital and digitized content and, importantly, to modes of access. Given the broad scope of this book, it has been possible only to introduce the reader to the salient features of the topics covered by each chapter and provide pointers to further reading.

The editors would like to thank all the contributors for their help and support in the preparation of this book, particularly Marc J. Dupuis for formatting the text. Norman Gray would like to thank Susan Stuart for exacting and detailed comments on the drafts of his chapter, members of the semantic-web@w3.org list for 'in-use' references and Chris Bizer for making available an early copy of the 2014 Linked Data cloud. Valerie Johnson and David Thomas wish to thank the following librarians who kindly agreed to be interviewed and provide generous insights for their chapter: Simon Chaplin, Helen O'Neill, Darlene Maxwell, John Tuck, Amy Warner, Dace Rozenberga and Jane Winters.

The editors would like to thank Helen Carley and her team at Facet Publishing for being so understanding. This book has been a long time in the making.

CHAPTER 1

What is the same and what is different

Michael Moss

Screens have become so ubiquitous and so much part of our daily lives that it is easy to forget that they are simply rendering content that is familiar in the analogue world and which still surrounds us. When we buy goods in a store we are usually handed a receipt which is the evidence of a transaction, even if we have paid for the goods electronically with a card. When we use a word processor we render words on a screen in much the same way as we render words on a piece of paper when we use a typewriter or a pen. It is easier, as we can delete and redraft much more readily, but the process is more or less the same. We are rendering or inscribing content on another medium. However, there are things that are different, as processes are happening between the keyboard and the screen which allow the content to be rendered in the typeface and point size we have chosen. With a typewriter we were confined to the typeface and point size provided and the only choice we had was between capitals and lower case. If we wanted the content rendered in another typeface or, for example, in italics, then this had to be done by resorting to a typesetter. What word processing has done is to bring together the typewriter with the skills of the typesetter and cut out many intermediate processes. The quality of the output has improved and a great deal of frustration has been removed, but on the whole content has remained stable. We can do more with the content apart from changing the typeface and point size: we can easily change the layout and we can insert pictures, graphs and tables simply by 'cutting and pasting'. This is a term borrowed directly from the analogue world of printing and describes precisely what we do in the digital environment. We identify something we want to insert in a text, cut it out using a cursor (not a pair of scissors) and insert it into the text. The final product looks much as before, but we have done it ourselves without resorting to either a designer to create the layout or a typesetter to set the text. It might look better if we had done so, but the final product is essentially the same. It is very easy when addressing the digital, which is nearly always bracketed with the term 'new technology' to assume without thinking that it represents a discontinuity with the past and makes possible radically new ways of doing things. It may allow us to do things more quickly, but it may not necessarily do things differently. This is a theme that will recur regularly in this book.

The speed of the digital depends only in part on the ease with which content can be rendered on the screen, but critically on the tractability of the world wide web and associated communication systems. I can type a message on my computer in the United Kingdom and within seconds it has been delivered to a recipient on the other side of the world. What is different about this is the speed, not the ability to send a message half way around the world. I could do that before by using postal services, which might have taken several weeks but nonetheless depended on technology to get the message there, at first on sailing ships, later by steam ship and finally by aeroplane. Each of these represented a step change in technology and, as a consequence, in the speed of transmission. Even when communication was very slow it was possible to both build and maintain relationships. How otherwise could business have been conducted? From the earliest times all bureaucracies have depended on letter writing. From at least the early Middle Ages the Vatican received a swelling tide of supplications to the Holy See from every Catholic country, which were registered in the registers of the Penitentiary and survive to this days (see, for example, Clarke and Zutshi, 2014). Two great European banking families, the Corsinis of Florence and the Fuggers of Augsburg, have left behind vast collections of correspondence dating from the mid-16th century (Beale, Almond and Archer, 2011)[1]. Almost every archival collection is full of evidence of extensive correspondence and other transactions, particularly accounts, from every part of the known world. From the beginning, efforts were made to speed up communications: by the Romans with their networks of roads and beacons, much later by Napoleon with his manual semaphore telegraph system, in the late 19th century with the telephone and cable telegraph and in the late 20th century with the fax machine (Coppersmith, 2015). Speed is needed to unify administration and to improve the efficiency of markets. These are the arguments advanced for the high-speed Atlantic cable that will transfer data in nanoseconds. It is claimed that stock trading will get 5.2 milliseconds faster, which allegedly will be worth billions to those who have access to the cable.[2] Much the same could have been said for the Borromeo family's network of post horses that crisscrossed Europe in the 16th century to bring market intelligence to its bank's headquarters in Milan.[3]

What might be missing from such rapid transactions is time for the reflection and reflexivity that characterized communication at a slower pace in the analogue environment. This absence has preoccupied some scholars, who are critical of the digital environment we now inhabit. The neuroscientist Susan Greenfield argues in her latest book, *Mind Change: how digital technologies are leaving their mark on our brains*, that it is changing the way our brains work (Greenfield, 2014); Marc Prensky, the educationalist who coined the terms 'digital natives' and 'digital immigrants', holds much the same opinion but from a different perspective:

> A really big *discontinuity* has taken place. One might even call it a 'singularity' – an event which changes things so fundamentally that there is absolutely no going back. This so-called 'singularity' is the arrival and rapid dissemination of digital technology in the last decades of the 20th century.
>
> (Prensky, 2001, 1)

Andrew Keen, Nicholas Carr and Jaron Lanier all hold similar opinions. Tara Brabazon – whose book *The University of Google: education in a (post) information age* attracted a great deal of attention when it was published in 2007 for its forthright attack on the impact of the digital on higher education – seems to have shifted her ground, partly, it would seem, because most of these authors have extreme views and do not see, as she does, that 'Life and learning are not filed into analogue and digital folders. They spark and dialogue' (Brabazon, 2014). Other authors fail to look back to previous examples of transition in communication technologies, most obviously the coming of printing. This is often mistakenly linked to the Protestant Reformation – as Marshall McLuhan would have had us believe – but in fact evidence suggests that the Counter-Reformation made more effective use of it. The shift from patient copying by hand to mass production and distribution resulted in precisely the same 'singularity' that Prensky describes, from which 'there [was] absolutely no going back', but it is arguable that it did not change things in the way that some of the alarmist critics of the digital environment suggest, and this is borne out by some of the contributions to this book. Brabazon is nearer the mark when she suggests that the analogue and the digital interact with each other in much the same way that when printing first began it imitated script to ensure a seamless connectivity with the past. Only later were new fonts created that made both printing and reading easier. It was never imagined that printing would suddenly replace script in a binary exchange.

There may, however, be some loss of reflection, that moment staring at the wall or the screen, lost in thought, and of reflexivity; as Julia Gillen put it, 'how we come to interpret and reflect upon our own actions and experiences and communicate these to others in specific language practices' (Gillen, 1999). The screen does not intrinsically prevent or inhibit either of these, apart from its apparent insistence on the shortening of time. There is no reason to strike a deal in nanoseconds or to respond immediately to an e-mail any more than there was to settle accounts in three days or to reply to a letter the day it was received. These are all matters of personal choice and there are many practices designed to inhibit such behaviour by emphasizing the importance of reflection – such as 'mindfulness' – that take us back to that old aphorism, 'stop and think'. What might be different may be the sheer tractability of the web that is the handmaid of the systemic risk that lay at the heart of so much of the trouble in the 2008 financial crisis. It is a truism to say that the insurance group AIG could not have bet the whole of the world's Gross Domestic Product without the internet. The same could be said of the part played by the postal service, or the telegraph or the cable in other financial catastrophes. In fact, when communications were poor or non-existent, greater trust was needed to prevent fraud or ill-timed transactions. When exchange rates were much more unstable than they are today or news took a long time to reach a market, transactions were much riskier, as we know from Shakespeare's play *The Merchant of Venice*. This is why it was not until the coming of the submarine cables to the Far East that futures trading became possible in the commodity markets. Merchants in London need access to local market intelligence before fixing the prices of goods that may take several months to arrive.

Behind all these arguments lies the question that has troubled philosophers since classical times, of how we conceive of technology. Do we conceive of it as neutral, in the Platonist tradition, or do we endow it with 'agency', as McLuhan did in his much-quoted catchphrase 'The medium is the message', a form of technical determinism that shaped 'the scale and form of human association and action' (McLuhan, 1964, 9). In doing so he was endowing inanimate 'objects' with agency in what has come to be known as the 'linguistic turn'. The debate he sparked still has currency. Greenfield echoes McLuhan when she suggests that digital technology can in some ill-defined way shape the pattern of the neurons in our brains. Peter-Paul Verbeek, the Dutch philosopher of technology, has sought to navigate a path between these two opposing perspectives by introducing the concept of mediation, which, he argues, 'helps to show that technologies actively shape the character of human world relations'. He continues: 'Technologies do not control processes of mediation all by themselves, for forms of mediation are always context dependent – otherwise we would be back at the technological determinist view' (Verbeek, 2010, 11). Although there are many other authors who have contributed to this debate, such as Albert Borgmann, Don Ihde and Bruno Latour, Verbeek's analysis helps us to grapple with the question at the heart of this chapter, as all communication, in whatever form, is mediated by technology and, as all archivists know, is 'context dependent'.

For the information manager and the archivist, context in the digital environment is complex, not because it needs to be but because practices that were second nature in the analogue world have been abandoned. For example, a letter written on a piece of paper had a form and properties that unambiguously provided the recipient with context: there was a letterhead declaring where it had been written, a date, the name of the person to whom it was addressed, and a salutation and a valediction. These features often themselves conveyed information; a formal or informal salutation or valediction told a reader something about the relationship of the writer and the recipient. In business correspondence the header often included a reference that located the letter in a file plan that, once the document was filed, would give it further context. All these practices were built up over centuries, beginning with dockets, which were transformed over time into manila files held together with bits of string, known as tags. In many organizations, but particularly government bureaucracies, discussions and correspondence were usually summarized in what were known as minutes, often developed over time as policy was developed (Moss, 2015). Accounting records mostly followed double-entry principles, first systematized by the Italian Franciscan Luca Pacioli (1494) in the late 15th century in his famous book *Summa de Arithmetica, Geometria, Proportioni et Proportionalita*. Receipts and invoices were referenced and entered carefully into a journal or organizer and posted to a ledger. In the ledger, balances were struck with suppliers and customers and, more often than not, the balance sheet and profit and loss account was calculated. Taken together, all these practices recorded context and provided an unambiguous audit trail which was easy to follow. As technology developed and organizations grew and became more complex these practices were simply transferred to the new environment. The appearance of the typewriter in the early 19th century changed little, except that it made copying more straightforward, as did the invention of the photocopier (Kittler, 1999).

Change came first with the introduction of mechanized accounting systems, which meant there was no longer any need for journals and ledgers, as receipts and invoices could simply be coded and aggregated and disaggregated at will. In other words a balance could be struck at the press of a button. Although the result was exactly the same as it had been in the analogue environment, the working was no longer visible. There was still an audit trail, but the context changed in the transition to the digital environment, leaving a much impoverished record for the archive to capture. It is possible to link individual entries in the accounting database with individual receipts and invoices, but it is unrealistic to expect archives to keep them. Given the way that the digital system works, this transition was probably inevitable. Less to be expected are the consequences of the introduction of the networked personal computer and the emergence of the internet, which coincided with the need to make organizations more competitive by stripping out costs. This resulted in the disappearance of secretaries (who typed letters), managers now typing their own communications (largely e-mails), the closure of registries where files were maintained and stored, the closure of libraries and the takeover of information systems by computer scientists. The outcome is not only the disappearance of systematic filing, but also a fundamental change in the way business is transacted. This can be seen very obviously in the layout and features of e-mails, which have lost much of the form and structure of a letter. The recipient's name is now simply an e-mail address that may or may not have much to say about the identity of the person, the title of the e-mail is usually less than informative and the date is simply captured from the system. The content of the message usually lacks the salutations and valedictions of a letter and it may only open with 'Hi' or 'Hello' and end with a name or nothing at all. The other feature is the ease with which people can be copied in, either explicitly (visibly) or implicitly (invisibly – blind copying). Moreover, the default of most e-mail systems is to store everything, and, as we all know, even when it has been deleted it can be resurrected. In many organizations the minute or memorandum has disappeared and been replaced by an e-mail thread, the stuff of mosaics. Although digital output is stored in what are called 'files' these bear no resemblance to files in the analogue world. It is the context of the technology that has led to this state of affairs, but the context of the content, which was inherent in analogue practice, has vanished (Moss, 2013).

Information managers and archivists imagined that they could overcome this state of affairs by intervening in the records-creation process. Continuum thinking, which was developed at Monash University in Australia by Sue McKemmish and Frank Upward, is predicated on this assumption:

> Archival documents first and foremost provide evidence of the transactions of which they are a part – from this they derive their meanings and informational value. The effective creation and management of archival documents are critical to their use and the role they play in governing relationships in society over time and space. Their effective creation and management are also preconditions of an information-rich society and underpin the public accountability of government and non-government organisations, freedom of information and privacy legislation, protection of people's rights and entitlements, and the quality of the archival heritage, made up of documents of continuing value. The concept of the archival document can provide a framework for a greater shared understanding of the nature of recorded information, and of the importance of transactional records to the continuing functioning of a society.
>
> (McKemmish, 1997)

This all sounds very neat, but attempts to implement such policies have failed. The underlying premise was an attempt to recreate in the digital environment, through the imposition of what are termed Electronic Document and Records Management Systems (EDRMS), the registry systems that had been swept away by its advent (see, for example, The National Archives, 2010). Such systems are resented by management, as they impose additional burdens without contributing to efficiency, which from the outset was the main purpose of all registry systems. Busy staff who can see no added value or benefit in following prescriptive rules will not be bothered to file documents, particularly the plethora of e-mails that may or may not be important (Currall et al., 2002). In many organizations IT support is contracted out against tight budgets, and any attempt to add further utilities – and therefore costs – will be resisted. Contrary to continuum thinking, the function of information and records management is not to create an archive, which may or may not be a consequence of the process. Despite evidence that EDRMS have been a failure, there are those who still cling to the idea that records management that will yield records for deposit in the archive can be mandated, particularly across government. They are mistaken and, as such, they divert attention away from the important question of what it is that the archive is likely to receive, which can best be characterized simply as 'stuff' with no discernible structure.

This is very different from the analogue paradigm, where archivists could expect to accession records in some semblance of order and where the context was discernible by simply looking at the content and, where possible, its place in the file plan or registry system. This is no longer the case. It is possible using various computational techniques to parse the content so that different genres can be separated, but, in the absence of the familiar files of the analogue world and in face of the fact that so much more survives than before, that still leaves open the question of how to select what should be kept. As a rule of thumb, archivists would claim only to keep some 5% of content in the analogue world, selecting only records that related to policy and discarding the bulk of records relating to individual cases, often referred to as 'particular instance papers'. There were exceptions, such as records relating to major contracts. As historical scholarship has changed and with the growth in demand from genealogists there has been pressure to keep more, particularly big collections rich in genealogical material – for example, records of all the military who served in the wars of the 20th century. It could be argued that, rather than trying to disentangle the content, everything should be kept, but that would impose a considerable cost burden downstream. Irrespective of the interests of family historians, the volume kept is likely to increase to an estimated 20% because the way of transacting business in the digital environment has changed. It is difficult to be precise, because most of the evidence we have is either anecdotal or what can be observed from individual case studies. Processing and curatorial costs will add significantly to downstream costs. We should be able to develop tools that will help us to identify records that relate to policy by tracing e-mail threads, searching for key words or elements and reviewing the length of documents, but we do not yet have those tools (see, for example, Allen, Connelly and Immerman, 2015).

Once content has been selected for preservation, the expectation is that it will become publicly accessible sometime in the future. For records produced by the public administration this is not the same as Freedom of Information, which normally relates to access to records relating to specific topics, but the opening of all records unless there is some legal reason for them to remain closed, such as the disclosure of personal information or records that might contravene international agreements, such as the Geneva Convention. In the United Kingdom public records are opened with these conditions after 20 years; in some jurisdictions the periods are even shorter. Reviewing content for information that must remain closed, usually termed sensitivity review, is of necessity labour intensive. In the analogue world reviewers look through the papers that are to be preserved and either redact information, such as personal information, or remove individual pieces (pages) if redaction is impractical because too much content needs to remain closed. Only rarely in the United Kingdom today are whole files closed. Inevitably, mistakes are made, but for researchers to find them is like looking for needles in haystacks. This will not be the case when digital content is made available online, as ubiquitous search engines will index the content and make it relatively simple to identify information that should not have been released. This presents the archive with a major obstacle in granting access to born-digital content against a background of tightening privacy regimes and hardening public attitudes to inappropriate disclosure. The US Council of Library and Information Resources (CLIR) has warned collecting archives not to take digital content unless it has been reviewed for such sensitive content because, once deposited, it exposes the archives to contingent liability and can be 'discovered' for litigation. This is very different from the paper world, because the risk of discovery is so much greater (Redwine et al., 2013).

It is impossible to completely automate the process of review, as sensitivity is nearly always context dependent. For example, if you sign off a document with your name and your role in an organization this is unlikely to be sensitive, but if you are referred to by name in a document this could be sensitive. The problem becomes more acute in the digital world when, by piecing together an e-mail thread in what is termed a 'mosaic', it might be possible to identify sensitive content. However, manually reviewing an enormous quantity of digital content in no logical order would clearly be too expensive and impractical. One response, to which some commentators have already drawn attention, is the precautionary closure of records for a long time (Erdos, 2013). Most sensitive content is personal information, which is now closed in most European countries for between 100 and 110 years, less the age of the individual if known. If the age is not known, for minors it is closed for the whole period; for those deemed to be over the age of 16, for 84 or 94 years. There are good reasons for such long closure periods. They safeguard the individual, particularly if the material might affect their health and well-being, and they also help to prevent identity theft – used by criminals and, unfortunately, by law-enforcement agents. These are the longest mandatory closure periods and, inevitably, precautionary closure could be expected to be for a similar time. This is unacceptable in an open democracy, where records are the means by which the executive can be called to account.

Ways need to be found to identify content that might contain sensitive information. This can be done using sophisticated information retrieval protocols that employ techniques which are similar to those used by archivists and documentary scholars, known as diplomatics. What information retrieval protocols do is look for names that might be sensitive, such as those of presidents and kings, or combinations of entities that could identify individuals, such as a name and a date of birth or a role, for example police inspector, a place and so on. They might also look for specific words, such as terrorist, informer and so on, or the length of a document, the number of words used and so on. All these attributes can be bundled together as significant properties. These tools do not yet exist, but there are utilities under development such as Project Abacá at Glasgow and Northumbria universities in the United Kingdom and the Mellon-funded Bit-Curator at the universities of Maryland and North Carolina in the United States.[4] These utilities will be able to distinguish sensitive information at only the most simplistic level, such as an insurance number or details of a bank account; all other instances that are flagged will need to be reviewed. They will be able to rank sensitivity, prioritizing instances of possibly the highest sensitivity. Inevitably there will be errors, as there were in the analogue environment, but they will be easier to detect and the owners of the information will need to be satisfied that the level of risk is acceptable. This will vary from one organization to another. For example, in the United Kingdom, the Foreign and Commonwealth Office and the Ministry of Defence, which handle a great deal of sensitive information, will be much more risk adverse than, say, the Department of Energy and Climate Change. Of course, sensitivity does not just apply to public records, but to all records. Given the risks associated with inappropriate disclosure in the digital environment, information needs to find a place on risks registers. This is new territory for information services and archives, which have often seen themselves as the final arbiters of what should be selected for deposit and, in many jurisdictions, of the terms of access. If risk is overlooked, then the archive or library will be exposed unnecessarily to contingent liabilities. Although this is new territory, these developments are as much a consequence of changing public attitudes to privacy as of the digital environment itself, which has enabled the so-called 'surveillance society'. These issues are explored by Scott David and Barbara Endicott-Popovsky in Chapter 5.

Once content has been reviewed for sensitive information and decisions have been taken regarding what content should not be released immediately, there is a further problem that makes the digital environment very different from the analogue. In the analogue environment content can be listed easily, down to item level (a file or a volume of assorted material) and sometimes an individual object (a letter, a telegram, a memorandum, and so on). This will not be possible for a large blob of 'stuff', and for two reasons: there will be too much of it and the listing would not be particularly useful. It would be possible mechanically to capture details of objects from what is called ambient metadata; crucially, its date and some indication of the author and to whom an object may have been addressed, and possibly the subject. It would also be possible to link objects together using graphs and digital forensic techniques. Such techniques would allow the user to navigate pathways through the content and avoid blind alleys leading nowhere, for example to people who were copied in just for the sake of it. The user's experience would not be the same as for records in the analogue environment, where the reader can follow the order of documents from a register or a file, nor would it be like using commercial search engines that yield results randomly ranked. Just like the software that needs to be developed for appraisal and sensitivity review, information-retrieval utilities will need to navigate a sequential logical route through a maze of 'stuff', which, to satisfy users, will need to be as precise as possible. One of the challenges of information retrieval even in the analogue world is that objects often relate to one or more entity, usually referred to as a one-to-many relationship. This was resolved in the analogue world by filing copies of a document in several places or by elaborate cross-referencing. In the digital environment navigational tools will need to have the flexibility to chart multiple routes, possibly across several collections. For example, in the United Kingdom all government policy involves expenditure that, if it is large enough, requires the approval of the Treasury, so there will inevitably be interaction between the Treasury and the sponsoring department. This will require, as Norman Gray, Tim Gollins and Emma Bayne discuss, in Chapters 3 and 6, the re-engineering of cataloguing.

Using technologically dependent tools to interrogate a large blob of heterogeneous 'stuff' in order to discover information may seem at first sight to be different from using conventional analogue finding aids; but will it? In the analogue world users are very dependent on what the cataloguer has chosen to catalogue; they do not have the luxury of free-text searching. Before online catalogues were introduced, users were equally dependent on the way in which indexes were constructed. However much archivists and librarians liked to pretend that cataloguing was objective, it inevitably reflected contemporary preoccupations and the individual interests of the cataloguer. This is what Clifford Lynch, director of the Coalition of Networked Information, dubbed as 'the haphazard historical gerrymandering of knowledge into institutional collections belonging to communities' (Lynch, 2001).

Users will need to become familiar with new utilities that are now only in development, in the same way that they have got used to using online catalogues and search engines to find useful stuff. What may make the new utilities different is the precision with which they should be able to locate and visualize relevant content, which is why the risk of inadvertent disclosure is so much higher. The lack of utilities helps to explain why the digital world has as yet made little impact on scholarship in the humanities, as Valerie Johnson and David Thomas argue in Chapter 9. Referencing should be straightforward, as there should be sufficient ambient metadata to make it possible to identify individual objects within the overall aggregation. What of course is very different is ubiquitous access from the desktop that brings with it all sorts of intellectual property rights and copyright issues, which are addressed by Helen Morgan and Gavan McCarthy in Chapter 8. No longer will it be necessary to visit an archive or a library to access material. This does not mean that archives and libraries as we know them will cease to exist; this will not be the case, the same as online shopping will not extinguish shops. But there will be fewer of them and they will have to reinvent themselves so as to deliver a range of online offerings and services (Hernon and Matthews, 2013).

Finally, there is the issue of preservation. In the analogue world records survive for a very long time, quite often in less than ideal conditions, provided that they do not get wet or eaten by rodents. Archivists and librarians store them in strongrooms to which they have the keys. The digital world is different, as the content on our screens is rendered from a binary bit pattern consisting of ones and zeros. Bit patterns are notoriously logically unstable. Every time they are opened, their logical structure changes, and so does some of the ambient metadata, for example the date (Allison et al. 2005). This is a formidable obstacle to preservation, but utilities are being developed, such as the Forensic Tool Kit (FTK) which can capture bit patterns without disturbing the logical structure.[5] The actual process of preservation is relatively simple compared with the other challenges of the transition to the digital environment, but – and it is a big but – it will require much more monitoring and surveillance than equivalent analogue content (Gollins, 2009). No one knows quite how much, but, as with everything to do with the digital environment, however much costs appear to come down, it will be much more expensive and require specialist staff with the necessary technical skills to ensure not just that a digital object is preserved and is what it purports to be, but also that it is held as securely as in the analogue world. As we have learned from WikiLeaks and Edward Snowden, digital repositories without the right safeguards are exposed to the theft and distribution of information on an unimaginable scale. What is the same here is the human factor; what is different is the power of the internet as a distribution channel. Security is Barbara Endicott-Popovsky's subject in Chapter 7.

Because preservation of born-digital content requires intervention, the digitization of analogue content, for all its advantages, is not considered to be an appropriate preservation medium. In other words, analogue content should not be destroyed once it has been digitized, but it can be shrink-wrapped and put into deep storage. There are also other factors: the quality of digital cameras and scanners is improving all the time, as are techniques for compressing high-resolution images. The digitization of records needs careful thought as it presents issues, often overlooked, that make them different from the analogue form, largely because the principal motive is to make content available on the web. This is not an issue with printed books, as they can simply be 'hung off' a content management system and, if the content has been OCRed, then it can be indexed by search engines. The same is not the case when single objects are digitized, because the only way they can be linked together is through the descriptive metadata. Conventional cataloguing practices are not fit for purpose, as search engines search only the substantive textual element and not the rest. Conventional catalogues also work hierarchically and are often difficult to navigate. Digital consumers navigate content in multiple directions, in much the same way that users of archives and libraries explore collections serendipitously, as David Clark and David Nicholas explain in Chapter 2. It is possible to hang digitized content off an archival catalogue, but then, because only occasionally will it be OCRed, it is just an extension of the catalogue.

The expectation of suppliers (archivists, librarians and their funders) is that digitization will add value to a collection or the objects within it. This is much more difficult than it would seem, largely because the curatorial professions notoriously do not focus on customers in ways that publishers in the print culture must do in order to survive. The first thing that has to be grasped, which should be self-evident, is that consumers can enter a site exposed to the internet at any level, and if they are going to stay they must be able to navigate easily within it. This means being able to move between analogous objects and to discover information that gives context to an object. Most objects have one-to-many relationships and will have multiple contexts and form elements in multiple narratives, which may not be known to those who described them. Well-designed websites that are built around such collections need to be open ended, otherwise they can in no sense be described as a learning resource. They need to embed the concept of co-creation, so that users are empowered to contribute content to the descriptive metadata and can incorporate links into their own collections. This is the subject of Chapter 4 by Ylva Berglund Prytz. All of this demands that a great deal of thought be given to the architecture of a site and how content is going to be selected, described and contextualized, and who the potential customers are, before digitization begins. If sites are to be co-created, then they have of necessity to be dynamic, in other words there must be someone at the other end of the line to respond to queries and to add new content. Although none of this should be new or different, it is regularly overlooked, largely because it is assumed that analogue practice has nothing to tell the digital.

In practice, from the perspective of archivists and librarians there is more that is the same in the digital environment than is different. Much of the argument that the digital is different came from technologists who have never troubled to learn what it is that archivists, librarians and records managers do. They think that money can be saved by jettisoning what, to their eyes, seemed wasteful practices. Managers, particularly in the public sector where there is pressure to reduce expenditure, are easily persuaded. As a result, practices that have been developed over hundreds of years are being lost and a binary opposition has opened up between the technologists and the curatorial professions. Matters were made worse by those who made an industry out of digital preservation and failed to address substantive issues surrounding content, such as the ingrained problems of appraisal, sensitive content, in particular data protection, and navigation. The chapters in this book are intended to help to breach the binary divide and raise issues that can be resolved only through collaboration.

References

Allen, D., Connelly, M. and Immerman, R. (2015) Crisis in the Archives, Is It the End of History as We Know It?, https://www.gov.uk/government/uploads/system/uploads/attachment_data/file/370930/RECORDS_REVIEW-Sir_Allex_Allan.pdf.

Allison, A., Currall, J., Moss, M. and Stuart, S. (2005) Digital Identity Matters, *JASIST*, **56** (4), 364–72.

Beale, P., Almond, A. and Archer, M. S. (eds) (2011) *The Corsini Letters*, Amberley.

Brabazon, T. (2007) *The University of Google: education in the (post) information age*, Ashgate.

Brabazon, T. (2014) Review of *Mind Change: how digital technologies are leaving their mark on our brains*, by Susan Greenfield, *Times Higher Education Supplement*, 28 August.

Clarke, P. and Zutshi, P. N. R. (eds) (2014) *Supplications from England and Wales in the Registers of the Apostolic Penitentiary, 1410–1503*, Boydell & Brewer.

Coppersmith, J. (2015) *Faxed: the rise and fall of the fax machine*, Johns Hopkins

University Press.

Currall, J., Johnson, C., Johnston, P., Moss, M. and Richmond, L. (2002) *No Going Back? The final report of the Effective Records Management Project*, https://dspace.gla.ac.uk/handle/1905/19.

Erdos, D. (2013) Mustn't Ask, Mustn't Tell: could new EU data laws ban historical and legal research? UK Constitutional Law Blog, http://ukconstitutionallaw.org.

Gillen, J. (1999) Reflexivity, Consciousness and Linguistic Relativity: an attempted link, http://www.did.stu.mmu.ac.uk/cme/Chreods/Issue_13/JGillen.html.

Gollins, T. (2009) Parsimonious Preservation: preventing pointless processes! (The small simple steps that take digital preservation a long way forward), http://www.nationalarchives.gov.uk/documents/information-management/parsimonious-preservation.pdf.

Greenfield, S. (2014) *Mind Change: how digital technologies are leaving their mark on our brains*, Rider Books, Random House.

Hernon, P. and Matthews, J. R. (2013) *Reflecting on the Future of Academic and Public Libraries*, Facet Publishing.

Kittler, F. (1999) *Gramophone, Film, Typewriter*, Stanford University Press.

Lynch, C. A. (2001) Colliding with the Real World: heresies and unexplored questions about audience, economics, and control of digital libraries. In Bishop, A., Butterfield, B. and Van House, N. (eds), *Digital Library Use: social practice in design and evaluation*, MIT Press.

McKemmish, S. (1997) Yesterday, Today and Tomorrow: a continuum of responsibility. In *Proceedings of the Records Management Association of Australia 14th National Convention, 15–17 September 1997*, Records Management Association of Australia.

McLuhan, M. (1964) *Understanding Media: the extensions of man*, McGraw-Hill.

Moss, M. (2013) Where Have All the Files Gone? Lost in action points every one? *Journal of Contemporary History*, **7** (4), 860–75.

Moss, M. (2015) Understanding Core Business Records. In Turton, A. (ed.), *International Handbook of Business Archives Handbook*, Ashgate.

Pacioli, L. (1494) *Summa de Arithmetica, Geometria, Proportioni et Proportionalita* (Venice).

Prensky, M. (2001) Digital Natives, Digital Immigrants, *On the Horizon*, MCB University Press, **9** (5), 1–6.

Redwine, G., Barnard, M., Donovan, K., Farr, E., Forstrom, M., Hansen, W., John, J., Kuhl, N., Shaw, S. and Thomas, S. (2013) *Born Digital: guidance for donors, dealers, and archival repositories*, CLIR Publication 159.

The National Archives (2010) *Migrating Information between EDRMS*, TNA, Kew, http://nationalarchives.gov.uk/documents/information-management/edrms.pdf.

Verbeek, P.-P. (2010) *What Things Do: philosophical reflections on technology, agency, and design*, Penn State University Press.

Notes

1 www.fugger.de/en/business/organisational-chart.html.
2 www.telegraph.co.uk/technology/news/8753784/The-300m-cable-that-will-save-traders-milliseconds.html.
3 www.queenmaryhistoricalresearch.org/roundhouse/default.aspx.
4 https://projectabaca.wordpress.com/publications/ and www.bitcurator.net/.
5 http://accessdata.com/solutions/digital-forensics/forensic-toolkit-ftk.

CHAPTER 2

Finding stuff

David Nicholas and David Clark

Introduction

Admit it, today, finding stuff is very easy, maybe too easy. The senior author of this chapter should know because he has spent half his working life teaching students how to find information using Boolean operators, word proximity, field markers, nesting and all the rest of the paraphernalia associated with conducting an online search in the 'old days', and then only to retrieve an abstract. No need any longer; now you simply bung a word or two into an empty box, which thoughtfully corrects your spelling, and low and behold, thanks to a kindly algorithm or two, you get a huge, ranked list of annotated hits – fortunately, with the most relevant at the top. And while you might get an abstract as part of the search you will also get the whole thing and a lot more than text (hence our use of the word 'stuff'), there and then, usually for free – but if not, there is always a digital friend from an online community who will give it to you. If that is the case, why then devote a whole chapter to finding stuff in the digital environment? The answer is that this revolutionary form of searching and finding has naturally enough led to a revolution in the way we seek information and consume it and commentators (and parents and teachers) are split as to whether this leads to better or worse outcomes as a consequence. Equally important for this book's core readership – information professionals, libraries and, to a certain extent, publishers, once the holders of the keys to the information hoard – they have become bit-part players in the digital searching and finding business. How can that be? Surely information retrieval has long been a central part of a librarian's expertise and professional canon? Read on for the answer.

Today people do all their searching on the web, and this should come as no surprise because everything they might ever want to look for (and loads of other stuff too) is there and it is all easy to find, despite what the naysayers say, at any time of the day or night. We have all come a very long way in a relatively short period of time; after all, it is barely 20 years since most searching was conducted in the library, frequently by a librarian on the user's behalf. For many young people there has never been another way to search: they were born digital, they are the Google Generation and, as we shall learn, it shows (Rowlands et al., 2008).

This chapter, then, is all about how people search the web; how they navigate the digital environment to meet their need for information and, particularly, how they employ search engines, notably Google, which they all love, to help them do this. It also assesses the role and position of librarians, once dominant in matters of searching and now clearly side-lined (Nicholas, 2012).

The chapter may appear to be futuristic and controversial in tone, but in reality it describes what is widely going on now and what will become even more widespread in the near future. We are all becoming conditioned, young and old, to the new ways of searching and consuming information and have forgotten or turned our backs on the old ways. But information professionals, and publishers to a lesser extent, have been slow to wake up to this. In short, they are in denial. There is a marked reluctance to accept that searching is universally thought to be easy, and this reluctance stems largely from the fact that librarians make capital out of portraying it as difficult. This chapter, therefore, identifies and describes a trend that we will all have to live with. While what is described here will prove challenging and controversial for some readers, it should act as a wake-up call for information professionals and policy makers who mistakenly believe that what we are witnessing is a deviant form of behaviour, a dumbing down that, with sufficient dollops of information literacy, can be put right. In fact, neurologists tell us that it is rewiring our brains. And with the avalanche of billions of smartphone users, information-seeking behaviour will become even further removed from the nostalgic ideal of many information professionals.

What is provided here is an accurate and truthful representation of how people search for information in the digital age, built on an enormous and robust evidence-base produced by CIBER over more than a decade of researching the virtual scholar (CIBER, 2014; Nicholas and Rowlands, 2008a). Indeed, thanks to techniques such as digital-footprint analysis we have never known so much about information-seeking behaviour (Nicholas and Clark, 2012). Moreover – and this is very important in the fast-changing environment of the web, where it is said that an internet year is just seven weeks – much of the data presented is very recent indeed, coming as it does from an international research project on scholarly communication in the digital age conducted during 2012 (University of Tennessee, 2014), with much of the data yet to be fully published at the time of writing. So this chapter is built not upon the personal views of the authors, but on the views and behaviours of tens of thousands of people, mainly but not exclusively academics, researchers and students whom we have studied over a decade.

It follows, then, that this chapter is consumer driven; it is all about how people *actually* find stuff in a digital environment, not how they are *supposed* to find stuff; it is about what they *do* and not what is thought best for them to do by information literacy advocates. It is not prescriptive and preaching and we shall avoid technical jargon, such as metadata, discovery and federated search engines, as far as we can. It is about the evidence that CIBER has on everyday finding in the digital environment, in all subjects or professional contexts, and for any 'stuff' – journal articles, books, videos, sound, film, paintings, photographs and people.

Five CIBER research projects in particular contribute the evidence upon which the chapter is based:

1 The Behaviour of the Researcher of the Future (Google Generation). Funded by the British Library and JISC, 2007.
2 Evaluating the usage and impact of e-journals in the UK. Funded by the Research Information Network (RIN), 2008–10.
3 User driven development for Europeana. Funded by the European Commission, 2009–10.
4 Europeana: usage evaluation and analysis, 2011–13. Funded by Europeana, 2012–13.
5 Trust and authority in scholarly communications in the light of the digital transition. Funded by the Alfred P. Sloan Foundation, 2012–13.

More information and publications from these projects can be found at http://ciber-research.eu/CIBER_projects.html.

Digital information seeking

The internet has fundamentally and irrevocably changed the way we search for and find things, although, as we have already indicated, not everyone fully understands or accepts this, despite the weight and robustness of the evidence accrued. Searching for and consuming information in the digital environment is wholly different from doing the same things in the physical environment of a library. The digital transition has changed the paradigm and the game: we are all librarians now and it shows in the way we search.

Let us now take a long and hard look at how people, in this case academics, behave in the virtual environment. When research academics in the UK and USA, in the most recent study on scholarly communications in the digital age (University of Tennessee, 2014), were asked whether the digital transition had resulted in changes in their behaviour, the response was a unanimous 'yes it has', and the biggest change for them was that it all had become 'easier': it was easy to discover stuff and, also, easier to disseminate stuff. In fact researchers said that they were influenced in what they used or read by ease of access and, significantly, young researchers were the most influenced. This, of course, explains the widespread popularity of Google Scholar and the Google search engine among researchers. While librarians and scholarly policy makers like Jisc (the Joint Information Systems Committee) argue that the scholarly information terrain is becoming increasingly complex and difficult, what with Open Access publishing, institutional repositories and social media, it seems that researchers do not think so, largely, perhaps, because search engines appear to iron out the differences and difficulties. This is surely a classic case of policy makers and professionals talking up the difficulties for their own benefit.

Amazingly, very few researchers of the hundreds spoken to as part of the study complained that they could not find the information they wanted, when they wanted it. Twenty years earlier, access, delays in supply and overload would have been their biggest complaints; we have moved on. Easiness is unquestionably what everyone wants and this explains a very interesting characteristic of searching in the digital environment – the popularity and dominance of that empty, but inviting search box, which holds centre stage in all our searching. It follows that nobody really uses the advanced search facility that all websites advertise. When told of this phenomenon, publishers defend themselves by saying that librarians asked them for it! The reason why users prefer to search simply is obvious: (a) it is faster that way, and in today's fast and furious world speed is everything; (b) the search terms they use tend to be so specialized that a simple search retrieves a manageable number of hits; (c) it is relatively easy to narrow the search down after an initial hit list is generated, especially if you, as most people do, look at only the first page; (d) it is easy to scroll through even big hit lists, especially since researchers (notably in the science-based disciplines) tend to make nearly all their relevance judgements at the top level, on titles, journal names and authors; (e) the first few entries generated by simple searches are generally found to include all that is needed to obtain the information required. The proof is in the pudding.

Connectivity

The second-biggest change is probably the massive information choice now on offer, courtesy of the web. Thanks to huge advances in connectivity (e.g. wireless) and expanding Open Access publishing, virtually everyone is connected to the 'big fat information pipe' supplying information 24/7, 365 days a year. In addition, the playing field has been levelled and privileged access is becoming a thing of the past. The average user today in a rural location or on a train now has, in many respects, almost as good access as a national or research-intensive university library user. Whatever some commentators may say, people, many of whom are new to digital searching, certainly avail themselves of that fat pipe. In fact, the astonishing level of access has made us drunk in information terms, because the usage logs of publishers' websites show that the digital user is hyperactive. All this means that few people spend much time on any one thing for long, always minded to move on to something else more interesting; the digital grass always seems greener on the other side of the hill.

Users would rather do many things lightly than do one thing deeply; we are all becoming web foxes (Nicholas, Rowlands and Williams, 2011). In other words, multi-tasking is the nature of the game. People bounce around the digital domain with gusto. This results in lots of fast and abbreviated searching and viewing. Most people view only one or two pages on a visit to a website, from the thousands available to them, and three is a lot of pages viewed. Users are also promiscuous, with around 40% not coming back to a website. They tend to 'bounce' the digital terrain. One-shots – one visit, one page – are the dominant user group. Lots of activity, then, but seemingly with little obvious reward, other than, perhaps, the thrill of the chase and the prized possession of one snippet of information. From all this it would be easy to jump to the conclusion that a good number of users do not like what they find because of its bad/mediocre quality (as one academic we interviewed explained, 'There is a lot of rubbish out there'), that much of it is irrelevant or simply that there is a surfeit of information. This is a consequence of: (a) the huge reach of the web and the great expansion in content, which naturally enough has brought about much more content, but also a lowering in overall quality; (b) the shotgun and gaming methods of search engines, which inevitably create many false hits, and this is something we shall return to. Having said this, a lot of search traffic will inevitably lead to 'dead ends'. This can be considered, more or less, a sub-category of 'bouncing': many searches lead to a page that is clearly not what is required, and the visit will bounce. It is foolish to assume that the site has somehow failed to capture or retain an audience in all such cases. Seventy per cent bounce rates are normal; this is the way the web works.

There are some other possible explanations for widespread bouncing behaviour:

a) Search engine lists and embedded web links constantly enjoin users to move on and cross-compare; there is always a spur.
b) The continuous refreshing of the digital environment causes churn; there is always something appearing in the shop window.
c) The limited retrieval skills of digital consumers, many of whom are untutored or relative novices to online searching, mean that they do not always find what they are looking for. Thus, on average 2.2 words are used per query (to search the whole world of information!), frequently mis-spelt (but, hopefully, corrected by Google), and most people only ever look at the first page of Google results. What we have on show here is risk-taking on an enormous scale or, possibly, breath-taking pragmatism.
d) Users leave their memories in cyberspace, assigning their memory to the likes of Google, which means that they easily forget what they did previously and have to start all over again (sometimes compounding errors previously made).
e) It is a direct result of end-user checking because in a disintermediated environment, remote from the library and its sheltered/safe environment, users make trust and authority decisions themselves, and

they commonly do this by sampling hit lists and then cross-checking.

f) Users do not have the time to wade through the information that all too easily envelops them at every turn they make.

g) It is a function of easy and always-on information access, which engenders a topping-up or 'snacking' form of information feeding.

It follows from all this that nobody dwells or does much reading, or certainly not what is traditionally thought to be reading (that is, reading whole 'things', such as documents or chapters). Today a 'read' typically involves a paragraph rather than a page or article. Only a few minutes are spent on a typical web visit, and 15 minutes is a very long time to spend on a visit. If it is an article that the user is interested in, three to four minutes will be spent on it, and shorter articles have a much greater statistical chance of being viewed. Abstracts, because of their brevity, the condensation they offer and their navigational qualities, so crucial for the bouncer, have never been so popular, and ironically perhaps, in a world chock full of full text, some of which you have to pay for (abstracts are free after all). Importantly also, abstracts are the places where users go to cross-check and compare. This is not to say that people do not read offline, but long and deep reading is increasingly being elbowed out in an environment where we spend so much time online and have so many things to do.

A third change is that in the overcrowded and busy digital environment in which we find ourselves, searching and navigating is proving so attractive and rewarding that people spend much more time on looking than they do in consuming what they find. We were told by one academic that they went online to avoid reading; viewing has replaced reading. The fact that, in a recent study, usage logs show that only around 3% of visits to a publisher's website result in a download bears this out. People like looking, especially now that things are so accessible and searching is so easy. Finding things by happy accident has always been the most rewarding form of searching and the difference now is that it happens all the time. Neurologists tell us that this is because the brain gets an endorphin rush for finding information – but not, it appears, for reading what has been found.

A fourth change is that the 'trusted' big fat information pipe that people are connected to for usage purposes is, of course, not the library or publisher's platform; it is the internet. This means that assessing the trustworthiness and authority of content is much more difficult and users have to do it for themselves. There is so much content to deal with, so many players responsible for it, most of whom are unfamiliar. You do not even know whose information it is. As with the case of all digital consumers, generally they either choose the first one up on the search list, trusting the search engine to have made the decision for them, or seek refuge in trusted brands, although the brands now trusted are not the ones that were originally trusted. Thus, for instance, today the brand is Wikipedia and not Encyclopaedia Britannica. The rise of trust proxy metrics (citation and usage counts) and altmetrics (e.g. social media mentions and likes), together with the wisdom of the crowd (personal recommendations), has provided some relief for the confused searcher.

A fifth change – and this is very recent – is that most people today search the web via a mobile device, a smartphone or tablet. This means not only that most searching is conducted in the digital environment, but that the physical place where searching is conducted has also changed. Searching is now undertaken from the home or on the go (train, plane or bus), rather than in a library or office; this has wrought big changes in how and when we search. We no longer search in a dedicated space; we tend to search outside office hours (late at night is now the searching rush hour) and in the social space (home, coffee bar or pub). Not surprisingly, then, this searching is proving to be different. We can best describe it as being information 'lite'. Compared to PC/laptop searching in an office or library, it is typically much shorter and less interactive, less content is consumed and it is less likely to lead to satisfaction and a return visit. There are many more one-shots – one page viewed and one visit made (Nicholas, Clark and Rowlands, 2013).

The sixth change is that we now have the searching equivalent of the Holy Grail, the one-stop shop. Thanks to the digital transition and the web, all types of information and objects (stuff) can be found together. Information seeking is no longer associated only with text. Indeed, a recent evaluation of Europeana (www.europeana.eu/), the multi-media gateway to cultural objects in museums, libraries and galleries in Europe, shows that film and video are the most sought-after and visited media.

The last change is one that nobody talks about. Now, surely, as the argument goes, the result of connecting the consumer directly to the big fat information pipe is that they will drown in the information flood. Wrong; because users do not even mention information overload, unless prompted to, and then they explain that they have no problems in this respect. The sheer benefits of unparalleled and unlimited access to information are so great that they more than compensate for any problems that arise from an over abundance of irrelevant, poor or mediocre information. The general view was summarized by an academic researcher who said they preferred 'to have problems with information management rather than problems with information retrieval'. Finding things is relatively easy; managing/filtering the information flood is more difficult, requiring experience and skill, which, of course, established researchers have in buckets, and which early-career researchers compensate for by utilizing and maximizing their personal networks – something that is much easier to do now with the likes of ResearchGate and Academia.edu, and something they are very good at.

Searching tools

The vast amount of searching that takes place on the web is conducted through search engines, and specifically one search engine, Google. So dominant a force is it that according to the *Sunday Times* (Duke, 2014) Google accounts for more than 90% of web enquiries in Europe. Search engines are brokers of access; they are the gateways to content and keys to the web door. In a nutshell, they are the strategic link in the communications process. They are the ultimate one-stop shops and they have massive shop windows with displays of a whole world of information. And search engines are not just popular with the general public and young people (the younger the person, the more likely they are to use search engines), they are also very popular with academics, even among physicists.

Google and its handmaiden, Google Scholar, are by some considerable margin the most popular and trusted finding tools for academics, regardless of discipline and age, although among younger academics and students they are even more popular and trustworthy. Library websites (more on this later), federated search engines and publishers' platforms are rarely ever mentioned by the academics we have interviewed. Subject gateway sites, such as PubMed Central, are mentioned positively, but not frequently. It seems as though search engines and gateway sites are preferred for discovery, and publishers' platforms are used for full-text pick-up, should that be needed. Researchers use gateway services such as Google and Google Scholar, PubMed, Scopus and Web of Knowledge because they are typically seeking a wide search horizon (Nicholas, Rowlands and Williams, 2011).

This has to be a real turn up for the books, because, unlike most other user communities, academics are familiar with retrieval systems, have choices and have access to their own library systems and many publishers' platforms too, and are very picky because of their particular trustworthiness concerns. If they are convinced of the value of search engines, then everyone else should be too.

Further evidence of Google's popularity and trustworthiness among academics can be found in the referral logs of publishers' websites. Thus, take the typical case of a medium-sized, international scholarly publisher: 22% of traffic comes into the site from Google, another 13% from Google Scholar and another 1–2% from other search engines. These are followed by subject gateways, such as PubMed Central and The National Center for Biotechnology Information. Significantly, by comparison, relatively little traffic comes from academic institutions and their libraries. Even physicists are smitten by Google, and they are richly endowed with powerful information services such as SPIRES and ArXiv. Thus, just four months after Science Direct content was opened to Google indexing, a third of traffic to the physics journals on the site came via that route, and that from a standing start.

A very different case study, but one that tells a very similar story, is that of Europeana. In order to increase usage, Europeana, ironically originally established as a European alternative to Google, which at the time was thought by the French to be too English-centric, allowed Google robots deep into the website in order to index content (previously it had been restricted to indexing the home page). The impact was huge, with usage growing by some 400% in a very short period of time. At the time of writing (2013) 70% of the 4.5 million visits to Europeana in 2012 were search referrals, nearly all (97%) from Google. By contrast, runner-up Bing, Microsoft's engine, accounted for just 0.5%.

Google's popularity

The relatively quick take-up and popularity of Google among academics (Jamali and Asadi, 2009) can be put down to a number of factors:

1   Usage is a scholarly activity in which researchers have relatively more freedom to experiment and be more innovative because it is less regulated – much less so than citing, or where you publish. It is also the

area where there has been the most change and innovation as a result of the digital transition, especially since the scope and use of commercial search engines has increased so markedly, incorporating a wider range of information sources and so providing even greater choices.

2 Citation data and indices (supplied by Google Scholar) are much more accessible and, as a consequence, it is much easier to determine quality and to establish trustworthiness in a disintermediated environment. If an academic is unfamiliar with an author they will 'Google' the author for previous work, university affiliations and other credentials.

3 Academics find Google a very useful pathfinder for navigating unfamiliar fields. This is when hit counts are most beneficial. Many researchers start with Google or Google Scholar and then switch to a more specialized database, such as PubMed Central, when they have a more defined search query.

4 There are occasions when authority or ranking are of only secondary concern in determining what to read. This is especially true when researchers are looking for something new, fresh and creative and are as likely to find this in low-ranked ('dodgy') journals as in higher ones – arguably, more likely to. In these cases a 'quick and dirty' search in Google or Google Scholar can be productive, especially in delivering interdisciplinary material.

5 It provides the highly prized ease of access in buckets and the widest information horizons of all. Google Scholar was thought to be surprisingly good by senior research academics; surprisingly, because researchers did not expect a quality scholarly product from such a commercial organization that has so many (commercial) fingers in so many pies.

6 Google provides access to 'unknown unknowns'. In general, there is a belief that one is able to identify more of the relevant sources for one's research than was possible before improved methods of searching were available. Despite this, however, it is admitted that the new ease of searching has led to laziness and that hard-to-find documents are less likely to be used.

What is really interesting is that the hugely popular Google search interface is simplicity itself and seems to fit the no-nonsense, smash-and-grab, in-and-out approach of today's digital-information seeker. Of course, it also helps to promote this type of behaviour: a classic chicken-and-egg situation. What is perhaps surprising is that it has none of the functions that 'experts' recommend. There is no wisdom-of-the-crowd stuff here; it is not immersive and the user has to do all the work, which is to peruse an extensive hit list. But it is fast and effective, and that is its trump card.

Search engines, with their empty search boxes, massive reach and (endless) ranked hit lists have shaped information-seeking behaviour so much that it is barely recognizable from the descriptions you find in the standard texts on information-seeking behaviour. Search engine users have a highly identifiable way of searching that marks them out from other online communities. They are typically what we call bouncers, people who view one page in a visit, spend very little time on it and do not always come back. They have followed a direct link to the article text or its abstract, it is of interest or maybe not. In either case it is probable that the next action will be to move on to another reference or new search rather than stay to browse the website. They tend not to be loyal or sticky – except, that is, to the search engine. Search engine users are also more likely not to arrive at the home page; the engine takes them direct to content. They do not come in by the front door – web designers please note. They also tend to be smartphone users.

It is common wisdom that users look at only the first few results of the hit display, but this is not always the case and images can be the exception: the explanation for this lies in the fact that the eye can quickly scan a lot of images with a lot less effort than it takes to read and assess the relevance of a text-search result. Information seeking related to non-textual objects is clearly different; we have already mentioned the longer dwell times associated with images.

Libraries (and publishers)

Libraries have been disintermediated and marginalized as a result of the digital transition. Information do-it-yourself has become the norm and Google and the like have helped to accelerate the process by providing the consumer with a search facility par excellence (Nicholas and Rowlands, 2008b). When you talk to academic researchers – clearly a core academic library community – about scholarly information, libraries, if mentioned at all, are mentioned generally in a negative or nostalgic fashion. They clearly do not go near them, in terms of physically visiting them, anymore. This probably comes as no surprise to anyone, but what surely comes as a big surprise is that neither do they appear to use them remotely and digitally. They just do not see libraries as the main point of entry to the knowledge/information/ideas they are looking for. Even though they do use e-journals (sometimes unknowingly) courtesy of library subscriptions it could be the human resources department or the research office that provides them, as far as they are concerned. Furthermore – and this could be part of the explanation – academic researchers do not feel the need to search very often because anything that they might be interested in comes to them through their personal networks and circles of trust, and increasingly they are alerted through social media channels. Libraries, once the key to the information door and the guardians of quality, seemingly have little role to play today in helping users to find things.

Nor do academics talk about publishers' platforms in respect of their information-seeking behaviour. Yet libraries and publishers think they are very important. Publishers' platforms are used as warehouses, places to obtain the full text. This, together with the fact that academics tend to obtain much of their reading material from colleagues and, as we have heard, do use and trust Google and the main subject gateways to navigate, might well explain the short visits so characteristically found in the usage logs of publishers' and library websites. After all, if you know what you are looking for already, you are not going to dwell long in the publishers'/library space. An information case of fast bag pick-up.

For librarians, the mobile device is a big challenge, taking disintermediation to another level. The library's information horizon has not expanded as fast as everyone else's. Scholars' information horizons were once bounded by the library, but not anymore. Google has opened their information horizons, and they like big ones. Libraries are increasingly seen as *incomplete* sources of information, with users not trusting librarians to make the critical decisions on their behalf on what is and what is not in the walled garden. Librarians have not developed good policies and practices to deal with a borderless and mobile information world. In fact, the term 'walled garden' is a put-off to many searchers.

What libraries have generally failed to understand is something we learnt very early on in our research. Users, young and old, like it easy. Thus, in a focus group PhD students from a number of research-intensive universities told us something that threw us all initially. They said that they could not understand why they had to do all the work in getting something from library and publishers' websites. At first this was attributed to laziness, but it turned out not to be that. They felt that the content was locked, submerged, and they had to dig a lot to see it, when maybe the service could make some things available automatically – the data coming to them, rather than having to chase it. They also said something else that was very interesting. They said that the websites were quiet, it was as if nobody was there; there were no signs of anyone else using the service, they left no clues. A quick inspection of library and publishers' websites will confirm the truth of what they said; and of course they did not say this about Google, because it is easy to use and the work you have to do, the sifting, they don't mind doing.

Conclusions

Maybe Marshall McLuhan's (1962) universe of linear exposition, quiet contemplation, disciplined reading and study (and we can add in 'advanced searching') is an ideal which librarians, scholars and society readily bought into and developed services around. However, maybe we always wanted to bounce, skitter, power-browse, grab snippets and view rather than read, but in the batch-processed, analogue, narrow and heavily regulated world of the physical library it was just not possible. The difference now is that opportunities for skittering and for grabbing information snippets are legion and in our own backyard (in our pocket even), and the opportunities are increasing as we write; there appears to be no let-up; just consider the march of Twitter and smartphones.

Maybe, just maybe, bouncing or skittering is an effective, but different, learning approach, and better suited to the crowded and dynamic digital world and our low attention spans. That is the optimistic take on the evidence, but there is a small possibility that we are heading for a plane crash; after all, the Google Generation are about to land in a university or office near you (Rowlands et al., 2008; Nicholas et al., 2011). They are, of course, the born-digital, the ones who know no better or other way; technology has conditioned them. According to some commentators, Nicholas Carr (2010) among them, skittering will impact negatively on traditional learning skills as it chips away at the capacity to concentrate and contemplate. He argues that the digital is making us stupid and depriving us of our memories. We are with him in part, because there is plenty of evidence that we have moved to a fast-information society, in the way that we have become a fast-food society, and the consequences will probably be similar. The propensity to rush, rely on point-and-click, first-up-on-Google answers, along with unwillingness to wrestle with uncertainties and an inability to evaluate information, could indeed keep young people (and eventually the whole of society) stuck on the surface of the 'information age', not fully benefiting from 'always-on' information. The writing has been on the wall for years about the lack of reflective reading, but we have been lulled into complacency by the sheer amount of 'activity' taking place in cyberspace, much of it, of course, traffic noise. The smartphone, shortly to be the platform of choice for searching the web and the purveyor of information 'lite', could be the straw that breaks the camel's back. It could just be the end of civilization as we know it.

And what then of Google, in a way the architect of much of the behaviour we have been agonizing over? Well, Google is a classic case of the tail wagging the dog. Who would have ever have thought that a retrieval, rather than content, service (although Google is in fact changing its portfolio) would conquer the world and become one of the world's most profitable businesses and biggest brands? Of course, finding is at the heart of everything we do today, even shopping; it's just the nature of the digital environment. So maybe we should not be so surprised. Thanks to Google, people are discovering that searching and finding (navigating) can be very pleasurable indeed. How, then, do we explain the perilous position libraries currently find themselves in, side-lined and largely anonymous in the digital world? After all, until Google came along, libraries had a monopoly on searching and finding, but never attracted much of a following; they really majored as warehouses, and that is how they are largely seen in today's digital environment. Google trail-blazed when libraries should have done so – certainly in the scholarly field – so why did it not happen for them?:

- Users probably do not like delegating searching to a third person because it is personal and time consuming; they also do not like delaying it, husbanding it to do it later in dedicated spaces.
- The information systems that libraries provide as a gateway to internal and external sources are designed more for the use and benefit of librarians. They are never easy to use.
- Library collections are perceived to be largely local and limited in scope, and this brush also tars the provision of access to external sources.

- Knowledge about library services is poor and this leads to a lack of trust on the part of the user.
- Until Google came along, all search and retrieval services were heading in the wrong direction, a direction that was too complex for the rapidly expanding population of digital consumers and searchers.

References

Carr, N. (2010) *The Shallows: how the internet is changing the way we think, read and remember*, W. W. Norton and Co.

CIBER (2014) http://ciber-research.eu/.

Duke, S. (2014) Brussels Threatens a War on Google, *Sunday Times*, 5 January, p. 3.

Jamali, H. R. and Asadi, S. (2009) Google and the Scholar: the role of Google in scientists' information-seeking behaviour, *Online Information Review*, **34** (2), 282–94.

McLuhan, M. (1962) *The Gutenberg Galaxy*, University of Toronto Press.

Nicholas, D. (2012) Dis-intermediated, Decoupled and Down: future of the library profession, *CILIP Update*, (March), 29–31.

Nicholas, D. and Clark, D. (2012) Evidence of User Behaviour: deep log analysis. In Dobreva, M., O'Dwyer, A. and Feliciati, P. (eds), *User Studies for Digital Library Development*, Facet Publishing.

Nicholas, D. and Rowlands, I. (eds) (2008a) *Digital Consumers*, Facet Publishing.

Nicholas, D. and Rowlands, I. (2008b) In Praise of Google, *Library and Information Update*, (December), 44–5.

Nicholas, D., Clark, D. and Rowlands, I. (2013) Information on the Go: case study of Europeana mobile users, *Journal of the American Society of Information Science*, **64** (7), 1311–22.

Nicholas, D., Rowlands, I. and Williams, P. (2011) E-journals, Researchers and the New Librarians, *Learned Publishing*, **24** (1), 15–27.

Nicholas, D., Rowlands, I., Clark, D. and Williams, P. (2011) Google Generation II: web behaviour experiments with the BBC, *Aslib Proceedings*, **63** (1), 28–45.

Rowlands, I., Nicholas, D., Williams, P., Huntington, P., Fieldhouse, M., Gunter, B., Withey, R., Jamali, H. R., Dobrowolski, T. and Tenopir, C. (2008) The Google Generation: the information behaviour of the researcher of the future, *Aslib Proceedings*, **60** (4), 290–310.

University of Tennessee (2014) http://cics.cci.utk.edu/cicsprojects/Sloan.

CHAPTER 3

RDF, the Semantic Web, Jordan, Jordan and Jordan

Norman Gray

This chapter is about the key novelties of the Semantic Web – the novel ideas, and the novel opportunities. But we will discuss these digital novelties in the context of the Semantic Web's *continuities* with other features of the information world.

Our most obvious antecedent is not that old – the (non-semantic) web didn't exist before the 1990s – and we will learn about the very close technical overlap between the Semantic Web and the 'textual web' of our now-usual experience. The Semantic Web is – closer than a cousin – the sibling of the textual web.

Other antecedents have a history as old as the first library index. The Semantic Web has, we might say, a 'logical wing' and an 'information wing'. These are primarily distinguished not by their technical or organizational features but by the largely disjoint research questions they address, and by their motivations. While the 'logical wing' is characterized by a concern for formal logic and its implementations, rich in the theory of computing science,[1] the 'information wing', with a sturdily pragmatic focus, can be regarded as continuous with the information-organizing goals of the world of library science, sharing its aspiration to systematize and share information and its acknowledgement that such sharing is always approximate and never unmediated and that one must aim for a balance between faithfulness to sources and what is actually usable by the information's actual audience.

Below, we will start with a broad introduction to the Semantic Web. From there we can move briskly on to practice and the question of where, how and whether the Semantic Web might appear in technological fact. Our goal is to indicate the continuities with the textual web and thus to indicate the novelties of the Semantic Web, and so to suggest why they are important. After a brief parenthesis on 'Web 2.0', we describe 'linked data'.

What is the Semantic Web?

The Semantic Web is simple, in summary:

> The Semantic Web is the emerging next stage of the web, designed to transmit machine-processable meaning, through a logical framework named RDF [Resource Description Framework], enhanced by machine inference based on OWL [Web Ontology Language] and other ontologies.

Though I assert that this modest statement is plausible, and the outcome desirable, the reader may be disinclined to agree, on the grounds that the statement is, on the face of things, gobbledegook. Over the course of this chapter I intend to explain each component of this remark, step by step, in the hope that it is a short hop from there to plausibility.

The Semantic Web ...

First, a general lament.

The term 'Semantic Web' is an unfortunate one, since it makes the topic sound much more arcane than it really is. It is, arguably, simple: the next stage in a long-term vision of the web, originally formulated by Tim Berners-Lee and elaborated by the World Wide Web Consortium (W3C), which he was instrumental in founding.

... is the emerging next stage of the web ...

Before we can fully understand the Semantic Web, we need a clear idea of what the world wide web is, even though, nowadays, such a question may seem as odd as asking what air is.

The web is *remarkably* homogeneous: it consists of *one* protocol, *one* bit of glue and markup.

Everything on the web is connected by the Hypertext Transport Protocol

(HTTP) (Fielding et al., 1999), and if you look at a web page, update a podcast, talk on Jabber or download videos, on a computer or on a mobile phone, the bytes come to your device via HTTP. Indeed, a debatable but plausible definition of the web is as the set of things reachable through an HTTP request. The only bit of that protocol that you ever notice is '404', which is the HTTP error code meaning 'I don't have anything by that name'.

The bit of glue is the Uniform Resource Identifier (URI) (Berners-Lee, Fielding and Masinter, 2005). That's a uniform *naming* scheme for things on the web and beyond. Everything on the web has a URI, and most URIs refer to things on the web.[2]

The markup is mostly Hypertext Markup Language (HTML), the angle-brackets which indicate how web pages should be formatted. But it's also RSS and Atom feeds (i.e. blogs and podcasts), wiki syntax, PDFs, and a few other, more obscure, alternatives.

These components come together when you click on a link in a web page (the following explanation of how the web works is probably not new to you, but I'm spelling it out in order to make clear how the various components work together). The web browser program on your computer, tablet or phone is a *client*, which displays a page previously sent to it by a program sitting on a *server* somewhere in the internet (we will use these latter terms repeatedly below). The page (typically) arrives at your computer in the form of HTML, which the browser knows how to format and display as headings, sidebars, images and links. The link associates some text on the page with a URI, and clicking on it tells the browser 'go and look at this page instead'. The browser then examines the URI to discover which web server is providing that page, then immediately makes another HTTP request to that server to retrieve the page, display it to you and start the cycle once more.

Before we go on, I should (parenthetically) be careful to distinguish the web from the *internet*. The internet is a set of protocols (plural) for exchanging material between networked computers. When you send an e-mail or retrieve a web page, the material travels over the internet, but under the control of different programs – an e-mail client and a web browser – using a combination of lower- and higher-level protocols, or languages.[3] Internet telephony (such as Skype) and time services are two reasonably visible internet services that are distinct from the web. The key point is that the web – and this includes the Semantic Web – is a notably simple structure sitting atop the internet.

There are a few key dates in the history of the web:

- 1990: Tim Berners-Lee and Robert Caillau first proposed the system which became the world wide web (Berners-Lee and Caillau, 1990).[4] The first server and client implementations appeared as CERN-internal services later that year.
- August 1991: First public web server. Initially, users interacted with the server by using Telnet (another non-web internet protocol) to connect directly to a client program at CERN, and thence to the server.
- December 1991: First web server outside Europe, at the Stanford Linear Accelerator Center (SLAC, like CERN, an experimental high-energy physics laboratory).
- April 1993: Mosaic, from the (US) National Center for Supercomputing Applications (NCSA), was the first graphical browser. Mosaic led to Mozilla, which led to today's Firefox; Mozilla also led to the Netscape browser. About the same time, NCSA released its 'httpd' web server, which eventually mutated into the now-ubiquitous Apache.[5]
- October 1994: The World Wide Web Consortium (W3C) was founded, with Berners-Lee as its director, to act as the standards body of the emerging system. Early standards included HTML 3.2 (1997),[6] the first version of XML (Bray, Paoli and Sperberg-McQueen, 1998), and the first model and syntax for RDF (Lassila and Swick, 1999).
- 2006: Lolcats (and other 'user-generated content'). We return to this below.

Although it may seem a slight tangent, it is worthwhile briefly discussing what it is that makes the web so special, and so very successful, since the Semantic Web is in protocol terms identical to the web we are familiar with and so shares the same special features.

The web is not the first hypertext system (Vannevar Bush's hypothetical *Memex* system (Bush, 1945), and Ted Nelson's *Xanadu* system[7] can probably lay claim to that), and it's not the first distributed hypertext system (VAX Notes and Lotus Notes can probably claim that), but it is the first truly successful worldwide distributed hypertext system.

The web gets some things right:

- It is distributed, or decentralized, so that there is no *centre* to the web – there is no single point which can fail, or be co-opted, or which can grant or refuse permission.

- It is non-proprietary, or open: the protocols which define the web are free to obtain, and may be implemented without any inhibitions from licences. Also, the web's governing body (which the W3C is, in effect) does its work through an open process.
- The web is simple, in the sense that it is architecturally simple (the notion of the web, as servers plus browsers plus links, is easy to comprehend), and straightforward in protocol terms (the core protocol of the web, HTTP, is such that a crude server or client implementation can be developed in a relatively short time).
- It's easy to join in: this is to a large extent a consequence of the simplicity and openness.
- You can waste hours on Wikipedia.

One sense of 'easy to join in' is that the web has *always* been read-write: Berners-Lee conceived it as a read-write medium, the first browsers could write to the web as well as read it, and 'anyone' can put up a web page. Now, 'anyone' here meant 'anyone with access to a Unix box connected to the internet, who can build, configure and install a web server'; so not quite everyone's 'anyone', but the key point is that it was usability that stopped you from putting up a web page, not the need for permission. Thus the (genuinely) big innovation of what became known as 'Web 2.0', or 'the read/write web', was that it was 'Web 1.0' for everyone else.

The last point in the list is not frivolous, but is the point that, on the web, you can link to *anything else on the web*, and that this is both culturally acceptable and encouraged. You can wander through a lot of web servers by starting at one page and 'following your nose'. This is a consequence of the simplicity and openness, which together mean that there are very many web servers, from very heterogeneous sources, serving web pages written by experts and non-experts, and that linking between these is not inhibited by any requirement for pre-co-ordination.

The web's success is also partly due to getting some things *wrong*:

1 links can break, and pages disappear
2 links are *all* 'see also' (as opposed to 'parent', 'next', 'author' or anything more informative)
3 everything is a string – the information on the web is, fundamentally, communicated through text.[8]

One might also say that 'no quality control' is a vice, but since one can simultaneously claim that 'no control at all' is a virtue, this is at least debatable.

Xanadu, for example, guaranteed link integrity, had typed links and tried to develop a new intellectual property model, all at the same time. Berners-Lee and Caillau's insight (Berners-Lee and Caillau, 1990) was that these are simply ignorable problems – it's acceptable for things to break, and occasional 404s are a price worth paying to avoid the need for pre-coordination or registration; and the web's type-less and one-directional link is such a powerful notion that its intrinsic vagueness is only a detail. The point of the Semantic Web is that it starts to address the second and third problems.

Why is 'everything is a string' a problem? If you search on the web for 'jordan', you get links about the country, the river, the glamour model, the breakfast cereal, the brand of shoes, various small businesses, the basketball player, the mathematician and more. These are not all the same thing.

This doesn't matter, however, because we, as humans, know they're different things and we're not likely to get confused (and if we are, briefly, confused we think it's our fault, rather than Google's). We can, in other words, add the semantics ourselves, in exactly the same way that we do so when reading text anywhere else. But this means that computers are flying blind when they try to perform actions on the web on our behalf. They have no idea what all these strings mean, nor (more importantly) how they relate to one another.

The web works very well for many things, and search engines of course work spookily well in many cases.[9] But it only really works when there's a human in the loop, or where there are a lot of statistics to build on – and you wouldn't want to let your computer unsupervised onto the web with your credit card.

But in fact you *do* want to let your computer onto the web with your credit card. In a famous and seminal paper, Berners-Lee, Hendler and Lassila (2001) describe an extended scenario in which computers are able to interact with each other to organize travel and other appointments. This scenario has come about to some extent: price-comparison websites now routinely interact with other websites to extract price data; and sites like tripit.com work by parsing the confirmation e-mails from travel websites such as Expedia to extract the details of flights and hotel stays. The problem is that these services work by painfully scanning the content of web pages or e-mails directed at humans (this is known as 'screenscraping'), heuristically parsing them and acting on what may or may not be the intended meaning.

This is hard work for limited results, but (at least until computers somehow manage to understand text) it is a fundamental limitation of the *web of strings*.

... *designed* ...

I have stressed that Berners-Lee and Caillau's original conception is architecturally still very close to the web we see now, 25 years later. Berners-Lee went on to form the W3C, and it is this body which by general consent – for no compulsion is possible here – still shepherds the development of the collection of standards which underlies the web (other bodies, most notably the IETF (Internet Engineering Task Force), are responsible for the technical governance and development of the internet by a similar process of general consent). Although the core standards are easily identified – HTTP, URI and HTML – these are accompanied by a blizzard of other agreements, major and minor, ranging from the syntax of XML (eXtensible Markup Language) to consensus on the formatting of dates. These agreements take the form of 'W3C Recommendations',[10] collaboratively authored by W3C Working Groups formally drawn from academic and commercial W3C member organizations, but with wide and occasionally noisy participation from interested individuals worldwide.

Much of the development work for the Semantic Web, in particular, has come from universities and a small number of research-active commercial organizations, often with quite close links to academia. There is a strong inheritance from preceding decades of research on Artificial Intelligence (AI); this inheritance included crucial experience of the logical underpinnings of what became RDF (below) and experience with related technologies, which meant that the first RDF standards were remarkably self-consistent and well developed. However, this same process meant that these first standards were rather hermetic, which will have contributed to their early reputation for incomprehensibility.

However comprehensible these standards are – and we will touch on the core ideas below – it is important to stress that it does not require some foundational understanding of the mathematico-logical foundations of RDF in order to describe, for example, a book's bibliographic details. In recent years the 'linked data' paradigm has emerged, again with both academic and industry backing, with a focus on the practical steps to bring about the immediate-term payoffs of the Semantic Web. We discuss this in a little more detail below.

...to transmit machine processable meaning ...

The Semantic Web has some family relationships with the world of AI, and indeed has suffered, in marketing terms, from its association with that discipline's repeated postponements of its great promises. The Semantic Web is not concerned with machine understanding, or with machines' creation of meaning, but instead with the more modest goal of transmitting meaning across the web in a more reliable way than is possible with the web of strings.

Our confusion, above, about the different things called 'jordan' arises because these various very different things all share a single label – 'jordan' – and it is only our ability to understand the context, and our knowledge of the structure of the world, that allows us in practical fact to distinguish the various denotations (we do not get confused when the term 'jordan' appears on a news website's politics and celebrity pages, denoting different things). Faced with the same text, computers can do little more than (be programmed to) rely on statistics and heuristics. Search engines show that this approach is more successful than one might expect, but until computers do finally manage to 'understand' things (if they ever do), there is little more that we can do if we stick with just the text.

Semantic Web technologies allow us to step beyond these limitations, by:

- providing a foundation with which to define more specific labels for the concepts and categories which make up our world; and
- allowing us to manipulate these labels (and by analogy manipulate the concepts and categories) in a more or less simple calculus of relationships.

An example is useful here.

One name for the River Jordan is http://dbpedia.org/resource/Jordan_River. This derives from DBPedia (Lehmann et al., 2014), which is a collection of Semantic Web names derived directly from Wikipedia. The name http://sws.geonames.org/7874114/ is another one, which derives from the GeoNames database.[11] The resemblance of these 'names' to ordinary web URIs is not a coincidence – all the names within the Semantic Web are syntactically of this form. One of the reasons for this is that it preserves the 'decentred' property of the (text) web: the owners of the geonames.org domain can create what names they like within that domain, since 'creating a name' in this context consists solely of deciding that a particular URI should act as such a persistent name, and providing RDF (see next sub-section) to describe it. This has the immediate attractive property that (usually) one can find more about a particular name by typing the name into an ordinary web browser; although it's not a requirement, the usual good practice is for such a URI to produce a human-readable description of some type.

Anyone can create such a name: I own the domain nxg.me.uk and decided, by personal fiat, that http://nxg.me.uk/norman/ should be my 'name' in this context. After a short bit of website configuration, it was so.

Once we have names, we can start to describe the things so named.[12]

Since anyone can – and many do – create online names for things, one of the first things we might want to do is to address the apparent problem of duplication. So, for example, we might want to say that http://dbpedia.org/resource/Jordan_River is the same thing as http://sws.geonames.org/7874114/. This will be true in some contexts, but false in others. In this case, it turns out that the geonames.org designers have decided that http://sws.geonames.org/7874114/ refers to the River Jordan *in Jordan*, and that the 'same' river in Israel is named http://sws.geonames.org/294624/. Therefore, in some contexts, it would be simply false (and importantly false) to state that http://dbpedia.org/resource/Jordan_River is 'the same as' one or the other, and we might find it better to say that http://sws.geonames.org/294624/ is 'part of' http://dbpedia.org/resource/Jordan_River. This sort of (often barely consistent) subtlety is something which we are comfortable with in human conversation, but which we have to spell out in pedantic detail as soon as computers are involved.[13]

Other things we might want to say are that http://dbpedia.org/resource/Jordan_River has a certain length, that it is a member of the category of 'rivers', that 'rivers' are a type of geographical feature, that the river is *located within* (as opposed to being a component part of) both Israel and Jordan; we might want a computer to 'know' that the categories of 'rivers' and (for example) 'cats' are disjoint (computers are *very* ignorant).

Here, the term 'know' does not of course refer to any cognition on the part of a machine. Instead, it refers to a calculus of manipulations which would allow it to detect that a statement that 'http://dbpedia.org/resource/Jordan_River is a cat' is inconsistent with what it has already stored, or that a search for 'things labelled "jordan" which are geographical features' should not return any basketball players.

This last point indicates one fragment of where the applications of the Semantic Web might lie. We know how to store and manipulate *facts* on computer – we can match an employee number with a name and department, or a star at particular co-ordinates with brightness and colour – but often these facts lack the real-world structure and interrelationships that are so important to how we, as humans, want to handle them. Even when such knowledge is structured in some contexts, so that the internal structure of a library catalogue might reflect the real-world structure of the organization that maintains it, this structuring is not shareable without close prior co-operation. If I e-mailed you a copy of such a catalogue as a spreadsheet, you, as a human, would swiftly work out what this document was and what some of the columns meant, though you might (for example) have difficulty in telling apart the columns containing publication year, acquisition year and, say, the year when the book was first borrowed. I would have to talk to you to tell you which column was which; neither of us would expect the spreadsheet to be usable on a computer without this human-to-human interaction.

The goal of the Semantic Web is to make this sort of structured knowledge – about geography, stars, people or retail opportunities – generally shareable and manipulable by computers, while preserving as many as possible of the (text) web's properties of decentralization (there is no permission or co-ordination required), openness (what we can communicate is not limited *a priori*) and simplicity (there is still only one protocol, HTTP).

That is, the Semantic Web is not about machine *understanding*, but about the technology required to let computers manipulate these URI-based names in ways which are, as far as possible, not inconsistent with the properties of the real-world objects for which they are analogues. This analogy – the functional consistency between the behaviour of real-world objects and the declared rules for manipulating their names in the machine – is the 'semantics' in the Semantic Web.

... through a logical framework named RDF ...

So far, so abstract. How do we actually *write down* the statement that 'http://dbpedia.org/resource/Jordan_River is a river'? For this, we must examine the Resource Description Framework (RDF).

RDF is a *framework* for describing things and their mutual relations. It's a rather abstract framework for thinking about the mechanics, and is not a specific data *format* or language (though there are formats and languages intimately associated with it).

In the logical language in which it was first described, RDF is rather simple (or at least compact, which is not necessarily the same thing). It seems best, therefore, to follow the overall plan of this section and give the compact explanation first, and subsequently gloss it at a little more length. We will omit a few details which are unimportant at this point.

- The world is described by a mixture of *resources* and *literals*.
- *Literals* are simply strings, such as 'River Jordan' or 'Río Jordán'.
- *Resources* are things in the world such as individuals, categories of things (such as people or rivers), abstract concepts ('world peace'), things on the web or off it, or indeed *anything that can be given a name*.
- Resources are given *names* which are all syntactically URIs.
- One can make *statements* about resources, all of which are of the form of a *'triple'* of subject (the resource in question), predicate and object. Subjects and predicates are always resources; objects may be resources or literals.

RDF version 1.1 is formally described in RDF 1.1 Concepts and Abstract Syntax (2014).[14]

To say more, we will have to write down RDF. There is no single RDF syntax; we will pick the syntax Turtle (RDF 1.1 Turtle, 2014) from the available options. In this syntax, we can write

```
<http://nxg.me.uk/norman/>
    <http://www.w3.org/1999/02/22-rdf-syntax-ns#type>
        <http://xmlns.com/foaf/0.1/Person>.

<http://nxg.me.uk/norman/>
    <http://xmlns.com/foaf/0.1/name>
        "Norman Gray".
```

There are two statements (i.e. triples) here, one stating that http://nxg.me.uk/norman/ is a Person, and the other stating that resource's name. In each case we can see the structure of the subject-predicate-object triple, with the resource http://nxg.me.uk/norman/ being the *subject* in both cases, and the resource http://xmlns.com/foaf/0.1/Person and literal "Norman Gray" being two *objects*. The first predicate – stating the type of the resource – is one of the predicates defined in the W3C's RDF 'Schema' standard (RDFS) (RDF Schema 1.1, 2014); the type in question is one defined by the independently defined Friend of a Friend (FOAF) schema (which we will return to below). The FOAF schema also defines a 'name' predicate, which gives the literal, conventional name of the resource that is its subject.

This notation is obviously rather cumbersome. The Turtle syntax states that we can abbreviate the 'type' predicate by just 'a', that we can collapse repeated subjects and that we can provide abbreviations for cumbersomely long URIs; as a result, the more idiomatic way of representing the statements above is just

```
@prefix foaf: <http://xmlns.com/foaf/0.1/>.

<http://nxg.me.uk/norman/>
    a foaf:Person;
    foaf:name "Norman Gray".
```

There are a few more subtleties to this notation, which can be found in RDF 1.1 Turtle (2014), but they need not detain us, since our goal here is simply to concretize the generalities of earlier sections and to allow us to use this notation in examples below.

You may object that this seems a terribly long-winded way to indicate someone's name, and you would be right. There is another notation, called RDF/XML (RDF 1.1 XML Syntax, 2014), which is even more long-winded – which only its mother could love – and which we will pass over in silence. And there is yet another RDF notation, called RDFa,[15] which is concerned with embedding RDF statements within other documents, and most particularly within human-readable HTML pages; the intention is that the same document that a human reads, describing for example a library book or a 'retail opportunity', is at the same time reliably interpretable by machine. But we must not allow ourselves to be distracted by syntax.

The central goal of RDF is not to provide a data-transport format (and now is a good point at which to emphasize that the 'F' in RDF stands for 'framework', and not 'format'), but to provide a set of primitive notions with which we can represent a wide breadth of knowledge. Those notions are sufficiently simple that it is feasible to translate a wide variety of other, possibly more natural, formats into RDF – for example, the rows in a database table or the elements in an XML file; and they are sufficiently well defined that we can use logical tools to process the results and draw out their implications, while standing a good chance of preserving their real-world meanings (see below).

Saying that we need not store or transport knowledge in this form is not to say that we should not do so, and it is perfectly reasonable to store and transport RDF if that is what is convenient. The databases in which one stores RDF are called a 'triplestore', after the subject-predicate-object triples they contain; they are architecturally different from the relational databases of tables, rows and columns, with which you may be more familiar, and although they are not quite as technically mature as relational databases they are steadily improving.

As a final point, the statements of RDF are not required to be true, consistent or even meaningful (you can say 'Truth smells of muesli' if you want to, or 'the present King of France is bald'). Anxieties about such statements are for the higher levels of inference and ontologies that we will come to shortly.

A brief logical excursion, for the enthusiast: RDF by itself has an exceedingly simple core semantics. The link between a name (in the form of a URI) and its reference (in RDF terms, a 'resource') is made in natural language and is not expected to be meaningful to a machine. RDF does not distinguish between, for example, sense and denotation (in Frege's terminology) and is uncommitted about the identity or otherwise of resources; thus it is possible to name both Mark Twain and Samuel Clemens with URIs, and it is not possible, within RDF alone, to make statements about their mutual identity or otherwise. OWL ontologies (see below) are able to make statements about equivalence, but even here the framework is uncommitted about what equivalence means (it does not, for example, distinguish sense and denotation), and in one context it may, and in another may not, be useful for the author of a statement/triple to state that Mark Twain and Samuel Clemens are 'equivalent resources', or that the model Jordan and the écrivaine Katie Price are equivalents, or that the GeoNames and DBPedia names for the River Jordan are equivalents. Once an association has been made between a name and a referent, the goal of RDF is to allow this association to be preserved across machines and networks and to allow machines provided with both RDF statements and ontologies (which may come from different sources) to discover the statements entailed by the ontologies, which have the same truth values as the initial RDF. For further detailed logical discussion, see RDF 1.1 Semantics (2014).

... enhanced by machine inference ...

In the Turtle example above I 'described' the resource http://nxg.me.uk/ norman/ by saying that the thing with that name is a foaf:Person, whose foaf:name is "Norman Gray" (Figure 3.1). These are two terms from a simple *ontology* (see below) called FOAF.[16] The FOAF ontology has a *namespace* http://xmlns.com/foaf/0.1/, meaning that all of its types and predicates start with that URI. It includes a number of types such as 'Person' and 'Project', and a number of relations such as 'name', 'mbox' (e-mail address), 'publications' and so on. Another ontology, well known in the library community, is Dublin Core (DC). This is described authoritatively in http://dublincore. org/documents/dcmi-terms/, and the RDF expression of this vocabulary describes the namespace http://purl.org/dc/terms/, so that the DC 'title' predicate is, in full, http://purl.org/dc/terms/title, which is most often seen abbreviated to just dc:title. The DC ontology is focused,

```
<http://nxg.me.uk/norman/>
    foaf:name "Norman Gray";
    foaf:mbox <mailto:norman@astro.gla.ac.uk>.

<http://example.org/a.n.other>
    a foaf:Person;
    foaf:name "Aloysius Naismythe Other".

<http://someone.org/ping>
    foaf:mbox <mailto:norman@astro.gla.ac.uk>.

<isbn:9781856048545>
    dc:title "Is Digital Different?";
    dc:contributor <http://someone.org/ping>.
```

Figure 3.1 Some statements about people

at least initially, on metadata for bibliographic and archival resources and includes relations such as 'title', 'creator' and so on.

Importantly, these various terms have no intrinsic meaning and RDF places no restrictions on the predicates attached to a resource, nor on who attaches them. Thus if you wish to say

```
<http://nxg.me.uk/norman/>
        foaf:name "Capitania General Bernardo O' Higgins";
        myprops:shirtType "class C".
```

then you are at perfect liberty to do so, even though the first statement (stating that my name is Bernardo O'Higgins) is false and the second (apparently saying something about my shirt) is meaningless to me, although doubtless it is somehow useful to you.

The primary goal of these various relations is to describe a relationship sufficiently unambiguously that even a machine can process it. Thus a 'title' in the DC sense – that is, the object of the dc:title predicate – is always a bibliographic title, such as dc:title "Is Digital Different". The FOAF ontology also has a 'title' predicate, but in this case it is always and only a person's honorific: <http://nxg.me.uk/norman/> foaf:title "Dr".

But we can do more than this.

Consider Figure 3.1: this provides an FOAF name and e-mail address for http://nxg.me.uk/norman/, states that http://example.org/a.n.other is a (FOAF) Person and provides an e-mail address for an otherwise unidentified something named http://someone.org/ping. You may already have a picture of the entities being described here, in terms of their number and type.

If you were to put the descriptions in Figure 3.1 into a triplestore and then query it to retrieve all of the Persons described, you would obtain only a single Person, namely http://example.org/a.n.other, because this is the only resource which has been explicitly stated to be of type foaf:Person. However, it is obvious to us, as humans, that if something has a name and an e-mail address then it's almost certainly human, and the FOAF specification indeed makes this stipulation, that an foaf:mbox property can be attached only to a foaf:Person. In formal language, we can say that foaf:Person is the 'domain' of the foaf:mbox and foaf:name predicates, meaning that only things of type foaf:Person are permitted to have those predicates (this is distinct from the use of 'domain' to name a collection of machines on the internet, as in, for

example, www.w3.org); similarly, we can say that dc:Agent is the 'range' of
the dc:contributor predicate, meaning that any object of this predicate can
be deduced to be a dc:Agent. In consequence, an RDF triplestore with this
extra information (more precisely, a triplestore possessed of basic inferencing
capabilities) can *deduce* that /norman/ and /ping are Persons, and so would
give three answers when asked to list the Persons it knows about.

A further thing that humans know is that, while individuals may have
multiple e-mail addresses, an address is usually owned by a single person.
FOAF agrees: only a single foaf:Person can be the subject of a foaf:mbox
property. But both /norman/ and /ping have this property with the same
value. The resolution is straightforward: these two URIs can be deduced to
be merely different names for the same Person. Primed with this extra
information about the domain of foaf:mbox, a triplestore, when asked how
many Persons were represented in Figure 3.1, would answer 'two'. Such a
triplestore can answer more complicated queries without getting confused.
Asked for the titles of things to which the person named "Norman Gray"
has contributed, a triplestore provided with Figure 3.1 could answer "Is
Digital Different?", by following the chain of allowed *inferences* – it synthesizes
statements, such as 'http://nxg.me.uk/norman/ is a foaf:Person' and
'/norman/ sameAs /ping', which are only implicit in the original set of
statements.

The end result, as may now be clear, is that a triplestore can aggregate
information from multiple sources: the information in Figure 3.1 may have
been gathered from a publisher's website, a membership database and an
individual's home page, and may have started off in any or all of RDFa, XML
or a relational database. Once it is gathered, the triplestore can draw the
conclusions which are not apparent from any data source by itself.

Before going on to describe briefly just how these various relations are
articulated, we have a few final remarks to make. Firstly, when we say, above,
that 'an foaf:mbox property can be attached only to a foaf:Person', we are
saying something different from the apparently similar statement which we
might find in an XML schema. In XML, such a statement is a syntactical one,
saying that an 'mbox' element (in that example) is *permitted* to be attached
only to a Person, so that if it is attached to something which isn't a Person,
or at least isn't known to be a Person, then this is an error. In RDF, in
contrast, the statement means that anything to which the foaf:mbox property
is attached must be *deduced* to be a Person. It is not even illegitimate (although

it is in fact untrue) to say that

```
<http://nxg.me.uk/norman/>   foaf:name "Norman Gray";
    dc:bibliographicCitation "Gray (2014)".
```

even though the domain of dc:bibliographicCitation allows a triplestore to deduce that /norman/ is of type dc:BibliographicResource (that is, something, like a book, that can have 'Gray (2014)' as its citation). Only if the store is subsequently told that foaf:Person and dc:BibliographicResource are *disjoint* will it raise any objection, and that objection will not be a syntactic one, but the announcement of a logical inconsistency.[17]

Secondly, we might reasonably object that, in the real world, a library (which is not a foaf:Person) might have an e-mail address for enquiries and that a role-based e-mail address might in fact be shared by multiple people. This is accurate, but the restrictions we placed on the foaf:mbox property above are part of the approximation to the real world that we must make when we describe that world in terms simple enough for a computer. The library's e-mail address is therefore not the object of any foaf:mbox property, for precisely the reason that a library is not a foaf:Person; and similarly for the role-based address, for precisely the reason that it is incompatible with the definition of foaf:mbox for an e-mail address to have multiple owners. A different 'people' ontology might have different restrictions, and so permit different implications.

Another logical excursion: Above, we mentioned the idea that (some of) the River Jordan is located within Jordan, as opposed to being part of it. The truth of this statement depends in part on what, precisely, 'is part of' means, and so potentially drags in a set of philosophical consequences, and indeed political and cultural ones; but the only ones that matter to the computer are the logical consequences: given the information that 'A is part of B', what other statements is it permitted to synthesize? That is a largely technical problem concerning what isPartOf or sameAs is intended to mean in a particular system, and it corresponds to the human problem of articulating what one knows within a formal system in a way which allows the machine to draw the conclusions one expects. It is possible to spend a good deal of work-day effort arguing about what 'is' is. These questions are what permit an ontology to have sufficient structure to make inferences possible and useful, and working out the necessary balance between approximation and expressiveness is what makes the design of ontologies challenging. All that said, such exotic questions are largely irrelevant to the *users* of an ontology, as long as they are broadly aware of the potential dislocation between statements in the formal language and timeless statements about the real world.

Thus we can see that RDF statements, and the ontologies which structure them, are not really, or not only, about *truth*, other than in the abstract logical sense that valid arguments must preserve the truth values of their inputs. Similarly, we are not concerned with developing a single true ontology of the world, or even with the claim that an ontology which is useful in one context will be useful or even meaningful in another, or that two ontologies describing one object will necessarily be commensurable.

Developing ontologies is a type of programming activity, and the types and predicates, and the relationships between them, must be chosen to match the things being modelled, to accept the precision of what can be said about them and to support the range of conclusions one may hope to draw.

FOAF and DC are relatively simple ontologies, with rather lightweight constraints; they are therefore very widely applicable for describing people and artefacts, respectively, and, in consequence, are very useful for integrating otherwise rather disconnected input datasets. In contrast, a large ontology such as the Gene Ontology (Ashburner et al., 2000; Bada et al., 2004) is concerned with a logical structure which is sufficiently intricate, and sufficiently closely mapped to nature, that the ontology can draw scientifically valid conclusions – at the cost of being considerably harder to use.

In the examples above, we have talked of various ways of adding structure to the list of types and predicates in an ontology; now is the time to discuss briefly how this actually happens.

... based on OWL and other ontologies.

The internal structure of ontologies is the most technically intricate part of our story. Fortunately, it is not necessary to discuss that structure in deep detail: our goal in this section is simply to concretize the rather general statements about ontology structure above and to give general pointers towards more detailed advice.

There's a well-known description of an ontology by Thomas Gruber (Gruber, 1993)[18] in which he declares that an ontology is a formal specification of a shared conceptualization

That appears opaque at first glance, but in fact it *very* concisely pulls together all of the key concepts. That is to say, an ontology is

conceptualization: a set of concepts
shared... which at least two people agree about
specification... and which has been written down
formal... in a machine-readable way.

Like 'semantics', the term 'ontology' has a forbidding aspect. In this context, however, it simply labels one end of a spectrum of ways of structuring information. In Deborah McGuinness's 'semantic spectrum' (in McGuinness (2003) and redrawn in Figure 3.2) she illustrates a range of 'shared conceptualizations' and suggests that the term 'ontology' is most naturally restricted to those more formal structures to the right of the central line, dividing informal from formal 'is-a' relations; Gruber's definition applies to most of this spectrum.

First, at the extreme left, simply listing identifiers for a set of objects is a sort of primitive shared conceptualization. Next, and marginally more formally, a *controlled vocabulary* is simply a deliberate restriction of the terms we use to describe the world in some context. In the same general category, a *folksonomy* might be defined as a 'collaboratively' or 'loosely' controlled vocabulary in which, ideally, some consensus emerges on the terms to use to describe some universe of resources. In both cases, though, there is no real structure to (the relationship between) the terms.

A *thesaurus* is a controlled vocabulary representing concepts, plus some

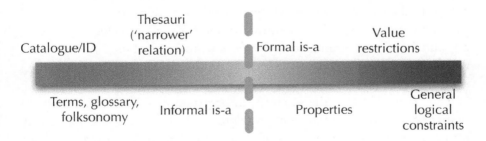

Figure 3.2 The semantic spectrum, simplified from (McGuinness, 2003)

declared relationship between the concepts. Most typically, a thesaurus is used for, or at least associated with, information retrieval: you might go into a library and ask to be directed to books about cats, or what we might call the concept of 'Cats', and a librarian might be able to take you to a shelf of useful books. If you're specifically interested in 'domestic cats', they're on a smaller part of the shelf; if you're actually interested in 'mammals' in general, they might be spread over a few shelves. The relationships between these *broader* and *narrower* terms – for this is the most common structural relation in thesauri – is a practical one: any information retrieved by use of a given concept will also be retrieved by use of the 'broader' concept. These are 'is-a' relations, in the sense that every domestic cat *is a* cat, and each cat *is a* mammal; but this is an 'informal is-a', in the sense of Figure 3.2, since in the layout of a pet shop, for example, or the layout of its supplier's catalogue, 'cat collars' may reasonably be a 'narrower' concept with respect to 'cat', without any suggestion that a cat collar is a type of cat, and a library book about cats may be labelled 'cat' (or, for example, with the Dewey notation 636.8) without anyone or anything being entitled to conclude that the book itself would be improved by the insertion of fish.

The W3C standard for thesauri is the Simple Knowledge Organization System (SKOS),[19] which formalizes these broader/narrower relations and a very small set of further ones in a deliberately simple framework which is designed to be broadly deployable.

Next, and stepping over the dividing line of Figure 3.2, the simplest *ontologies* are those where this hierarchy of 'is-a' relations is indeed expected to hold in a logically useful sense, and where labelling something with an ontology term is indeed an assertion that that thing is an instance of the labelled type, and therefore of any supertype. For example, the Linnaean name for cat is *Felis catus*; this is a species of the genus *Felis* in the family *Felidae*, in the order *Carnivora*, all the way up to the kingdom *Animalia*; and this hierarchy is explicitly intended to allow me to conclude, on being presented with something labelled *Felis catus*, that that thing is indeed a cat rather than a book about cats, and that the (by now indignantly wriggling) subject is a carnivorous animal with claws.

This 'formal is-a' is the intended interpretation – that is, the intended 'semantics' – of the statement in Figure 3.1 that the thing named by http://example.org/a.n.other is of 'type' foaf:Person. The usual word for the type in this context is *class*, and the (FOAF) URI http://xmlns.com/

foaf/0.1/Person (usually abbreviated to just foaf:Person) is the name of the abstract class of persons; individual people are *instances* of this class.

The next step along the semantic spectrum is to be able to declare that instances of some classes may possess *properties* (the term *predicates* is generally interchangeable) such as foaf:name. An ontology of this type may declare the domain and range of a predicate, restricting the type of subject or object that the predicate may have. A triplestore can then use this information to make certain deductions, as we illustrated above. However, there is no way, in this type of simple ontology, to *require* that an instance of a class must have a particular property (I can be a foaf:Person without having an e-mail address, for example, bizarrely Victorian though that notion may seem), and a reasoner which does not know my e-mail address, because it hasn't been provided with an foaf:mbox property for me, is not entitled to conclude that I therefore don't have one.[20]

The simple ontological framework represented by RDFS is capable of expressing no more than this: that classes exist and that some classes are subclasses of others, that resources can be instances (or members) of classes, that properties exist and have classes as domain and range. The payoff is that reasoners[21] which implement this logic can be simpler and faster than a reasoner capable of more intricacy. Referring back to the discussion around Figure 3.1, such a reasoner would be capable of concluding that http://nxg.me.uk/norman/ is a foaf:Person (because that resource is asserted to have an foaf:name, implying that http://nxg.me.uk/norman/ is in that property's domain), and it could conclude that http://someone.org/ping is a dc:Agent; but it could not use the identity of the foaf:mbox properties to conclude that these are the same person, and it could not detect any inconsistency in a subsequent assertion or discovery that http://nxg.me.uk/norman/ is a dc:BibliographicResource. To get such extra reasoning power, it is necessary to go beyond RDFS, to the right-hand side of the ontology spectrum, towards more elaborate frameworks such as OWL. The Web Ontology Language (OWL[22]) comes in several standard varieties – OWL Lite, OWL DL and OWL Full – and further varieties associated with particular implementations (see W3C OWL Working Group, 2012 and references at http://www.w3.org/standards/techs/owl). The difference between these varieties is that some are more *expressive*, in the sense that it is possible to articulate more complicated relationships between resources; the practical trade-off is that the more expressive variants are harder or more expensive to implement. It is in OWL, and not RDFS, that it is possible to say

```
dc:Agent owl:disjointWith dc:BibliographicResource.
```

This asserts that the class of Dublin Core Agents (that is, people and organizations), and the class of BibliographicResource instances, have no members in common. A reasoner, once programmed to calculate the logical implications of the owl:disjointWith predicate, can thereafter conclude that if a resource such as http://nxg.me.uk/norman/ has been asserted or discovered to be in both classes, then it has detected a logical inconsistency. This may form part of a longer chain of reasoning, or it may be practically useful for discovering latent errors in a database: if a mapping database discovers a feature that is marked as both a river deep and mountain high, then its curators can thereby discover that they have some repairing to do.

So what, briefly, is the Semantic Web?

What we have ended up with is this: in RDF we have a flexible model for representing relatively simple statements about the world in a primitive subject-predicate-object pattern. This framework has a number of syntaxes which are more or less suitable in particular contexts; these are most prominently RDF/XML, Turtle and RDFa, but other syntaxes can be, and have been, used when they are a more natural match to the intended users' expectations. Despite this abundance of syntax, it is the simplicity and very broad applicability of the primitive triples that is key, since almost any reasonably structured data source can be wrangled into RDF form, one way or another, and this makes RDF an excellent mechanism for combining heterogeneous data sources.

An important step in this combining mechanism is the carefully struck balance between, on the one hand, the logical precision of the calculus of resources which ontologies express (given a set of RDF triples, what further triples are logically entailed?), and on the other hand (i) the flexible *im*precision of the natural-language link between URIs and their denotations, and (ii) the variable precision of ontological designs, which may range from the broad-brush utility of FOAF ('only Persons have e-mail addresses') to the intricacy of the Gene Ontology.

Furthermore, the very close technical analogy between the Semantic Web and the web of strings reassures us that the properties which made the web successful (its openness, fault tolerance and so on, as discussed above) will support the Semantic Web too.

Once information is in RDF form and stored in a 'triplestore' it can be queried[23] either directly or with the assistance of a 'reasoner', which synthesizes extra triples based on the inferences obtained from the originally asserted triples, in the presence of the extra structure provided by a simple or a complex *ontology*.

We could say more about the Semantic Web. We could talk about some of the details of triplestores and query engines, but that would very quickly immerse us in a level of technical detail which can verge on the impenetrable, and which is in any case still in active research-level development. We could introduce some of the features of ontology design: though this is now largely stable, it would take several more chapters to cover, without immediate intellectual profit. We could talk about deployment, but many of the main deployments of Semantic Web technology are in back-end systems supporting complicated data-integration projects and do not make for vivid illustration.

Instead, the goal of this chapter has been to provide an introduction to the core concepts of the Semantic Web, at a level and to an extent that will allow the reader to understand the goals and starting point of a project using these technologies and to understand the way in which the Semantic Web relates to the web of strings of our last two decades' familiar experience. For more details, the W3C's 'Data Activity'[24] provides useful links to further reading; and for some practical details, including a rather more sceptical account of the Semantic Web than I have produced here, see Swartz (2013).

Where is the Semantic Web?

It is harder to point to the Semantic Web than to the textual web. Although we encounter the text web whenever we look at Wikipedia, book a flight or search for cat videos, the semantic version remains in the background.

The French National Library (BnF) has a large catalogue, split into multiple heterogeneous parts, using various standards (such as Encoded Archival Description and MAchine Readable Cataloging) and making links to a dozen or so external sites. A Semantic Web approach has made this information available through a homogeneous interface which provides intelligibility and syntactical consistency without sacrificing the open-endedness which is necessary if such a complicated and long-accumulated information source is to be made fully available (Simon et al., 2013). This catalogue is now in use by various applications and smaller libraries, or enhanced and expanded by more specialized catalogues elsewhere. Going from the catalogue to the instance, Castro, McLaughlin and Garcia (2013) describe a system which makes available, in machine-readable form, elements of the semantic content of papers in PubMed Central. Simon et al.'s account (2013) is in the 'in-use' track of that year's European Semantic Web Conference (ESWC) conference proceedings, where you can find other illustrative examples; there are further illustrations in the collection of open datasets maintained by the *Semantic Web Journal.*[25]

At the time of writing (2014), it is not yet clear, at least to me, just when the Semantic Web will be manifestly 'working', nor how it will get there; it is not even transparently clear what 'working' would mean. The highly integrated scenario of Berners-Lee, Hendler and Lassila (2001) is still in the future, not because it is infeasible, but most likely because it is predicated on a good deal of large-scale co-ordination which is difficult to force on a decentred web. Linked Data (see below) shows a path into the future but is not an end-point. But perhaps we are asking too much for a grand design. The evolution from web pages to blogs, to Twitter is obvious only in retrospect; the fact that (for example) Instagram, Facebook, Twitter, Flickr and up-to-date conference organizers all use hashtags is explicable, but could never have been predicted; conversely, it is rather surprising that we are still using SMTP-based e-mail 32 years after it was first standardized, and in the face of numerous claims for killer alternatives. Perhaps the most likely future for the Semantic Web matches that of AI research, even though the former community has always been nervous of the comparison: AI never obviously delivered its grand promises – it never 'worked' – but in a world of self-driving cars, face recognition and pocket-sized machine-translation devices, it's clear that it's been quietly engineering its way into successful deployment for decades.

The two final remarks to be made concern, in the first place, Web 2.0, which is sometimes linked to the Semantic Web, but which in fact has almost nothing to do with it; and, in the second place, the Linked Data paradigm, which is arguably the first appearance of the Semantic Web in more nearly everyday experience.

Web 2.0

The term 'Web 2.0' has disorientingly many meanings. To some, it refers to the cluster of mid-level technologies which let services such as Google Maps or Facebook act as an 'application inside a web page'; to others it has meanings which can be grouped under the slogan 'the read/write web'; another camp sees it as a marketing expression and is divided about whether this is an obviously good or an obviously bad thing; and for yet others it is a proxy for a broad change in society towards a more decentred, or engaged, or empowered, or open-licensed, or otherwise utopian future. These terms are not remotely equivalent: in some cases they may not even intersect, so something as obviously next-generation as Wikipedia is Web 2.0 under some definitions but not others.

The term is really only useful as an adjective, to denote something – anything – that is more than a collection of static web pages. However, even saying that much begs the question: what is it that's so *wrong* with static web pages (which we're now obliged to call Web 1.0)? Indeed, depending on your conception of what 'Web 2.0' means, podcasts are firmly Web 1.0, and if you turn off visitor editing on your wiki pages, or commenting on your blog, then those become Web 1.0 as well.

The term 'Web 2.0' appeared as the title of a conference series run by O'Reilly Media in 2004, and the term spread from there to wider and still vaguer usage. There is no technical difference between 'Web 2.0' and the original version of the web; instead, the term refers to a loose collection of techniques, and even attitudes, which became increasingly popular in the first half of that decade which were heavily oriented towards supporting, encouraging and exploiting user *interactivity* on the web.

Above, I characterized the web as a space where anyone can join in, but admitted that initially this was more true in principle than in fact. The web of the 1990s was, for most, a read-only medium: the web was full of text and images, but the only way to talk back was through e-mail, or a few now-arcane spaces such as Usenet. Though both were effective, and though Usenet is still, in 2014, Not Quite Dead Yet, they are hardly a free-flowing worldwide conversation. In the broadest sense of the term, a blog is a Web 2.0 thing: it's easy to set up for oneself, and if even that is too inconvenient, it's easy to use a blog set up by a service such as WordPress. With that step taken, it's merely a matter of creative diligence to broadcast to the world and to dispute, declaim, decry and generally bicker in comment threads. Broadly blog-like things such as Twitter and Facebook become much easier to conceive, as both provider and consumer, once the idea of a blog service plus comments has become part of the culture.

With that step taken, other technologies were able to collide; 'AJAX' was one such. The 'J' stands for JavaScript, which originally appeared as a language supporting simple scripting within a web browser – providing an element of dynamism in web pages so that they could adjust themselves to the browser's environment rather than appear as a simple block of text sent from a server. This language, and the set of practices which AJAX represents, have grown to the point where a web browser may now be seen as a separate programming ecology. Some web pages, such as a Google Mail page, arrive as a minimal amount of HTML enclosing a JavaScript program which, running entirely within the browser, interrogates a server and synthesizes from scratch the HTML which the browser finally displays. From a protocol point of view, there are minimal differences between the earliest web pages at http://info.cern.ch/hypertext/WWW/TheProject.html (with a 'last modified' date of 3 December 1992) and the twitter.com home page which creates the page programmatically and on the fly in the browser: both use HTTP to transport materials from a server, and both offer HTML for the browser to render.[26]

One of the other long-latent possibilities which were explored in the early 2000s was the idea of uploaded and shared content. Flickr (https://www.flickr.com) was one of the first broadly known services to support users' uploading and sharing of images. At a technical level (again), this is not much different from blogging, but Flickr and the social-bookmarking site delicious.com are interesting for this chapter's purposes because they were among the first widespread services to support *tagging*. Flickr allowed users to add simple labels to pictures and Delicious allowed users to similarly label web pages; there is presumably some indirect link here with the rapid adoption of Twitter hashtags. These tags – which were intended to support both categorization and search – were taken from an unrestricted vocabulary, but with the expectation that users would spontaneously co-operate to choose broadly compatible tags (as we briefly mentioned above) in a lightweight shared semantic environment which was soon labelled a 'folksonomy'. However, this is as far towards the Semantic Web as Web 2.0 has ever moved, and so, despite the suggestion of the 'Web 2.0' name and some of the accompanying rhetoric, Web 2.0 has rather little to do with the Semantic Web.

There's more to explore in the programming ecology but, in web terms, Web 2.0 is rather a dead end.

Linked data

Even acknowledging that the Semantic Web will probably remain somewhat obscure, one can ask how broadly it is deployed, or to what extent its deployments are reachable. As we discussed above, the Semantic Web is still largely used in 'server-side' applications, rather than becoming part of the commerce of the open web as was originally anticipated. Part of the reason for this is that the Semantic Web technology stack is challenging to use: the tools are of varying maturity and use a broad range of underlying technologies, so that deployments are still to a large extent bespoke. Even when simply making data available, rather than attempting to process it, making data web ready may require a quite profound engagement with the Semantic and textual webs' conceptual foundations; many such deployments are still, even now, worthy of an academic paper describing the experience. Few non-specialist projects can make such investments.

An alternative approach is to use the *Linked Data* paradigm.[27] At heart, the Linked Data paradigm *is* the Semantic Web, but with a practical focus on the irreducible minimum required to get data onto the web in a way which is compatible with the goals and practices described above.

To quote Berners-Lee (2006), the linked data principles are:

1   Use URIs as names for things.
2   Use HTTP URIs so that people can look up those names.
3   When someone looks up a URI, provide useful information, using the standards (RDF*, SPARQL).
4   Include links to other URIs so that they can discover more things.

Notably, these principles have more to say about HTTP and URIs – that is, about the *mechanics* of retrieving this information and, by extension, the mechanics of making it available – than they say about the semantics of the information being distributed.

Together, these say (in effect) that the 'linked data web' is just like the web of strings which is familiar to us all, except that the raw materials are not HTML files but files in one or other RDF syntax (so RDF/XML, Turtle or

RDFa). All four points are essentially adaptations of the design principles above and best practices such as Sauermann et al. (2008), which were, as it turned out, so very effective in making the web (of strings) so very successful. The third point states that looking up a URI should provide useful (RDF) information *to a machine*, but is also taken to suggest that putting a resource's URI into a web browser should provide human-readable (HTML) information as well – this provides one bridge between the two webs.

Although the traditional web is generally thought of as delivering human-readable pages, it has from the very beginning been used for delivering machine-readable content, such as data files for analysis or PDF files for printing. This is not the machine-readability we mean in this context. Just as a human might read a Wikipedia article, internalize the results and click on a link for more information, a Linked Data client – typically a component of a larger application – is expected to process the semantic content of the data it finds at one URI and then follow further links for further information. Given the RDF of Figure 3.1, for example, a linked data client might store the information listed and then follow the link http://someone.org/ping to see if there is any further information available there. It is this final step which lets the machine 'follow its nose' that represents the key insight of the linked data paradigm and which is the machine analogue of 'wasting hours on Wikipedia'.

The network of links between 'linked-data'-style data sources is illustrated in Figure 3.3. A large fraction of the data in this cloud is in the form of SKOS vocabularies, or uses the simple FOAF or DC ontologies; but while these are useful for co-ordination between data sources, there is no restriction on the ontologies which are used in fact.

The archetypal Linked Data (client-side) application is a simple application – perhaps even running entirely within a browser – which reads the contents of a URI, interprets and perhaps displays what predicates it recognizes (which will probably include at least FOAF) and lets a user move on to further related information. The archetypal Semantic Web application (if such a thing exists) might use SPARQL to query a large and semantically rich database, possibly requiring a fair amount of inferencing on the part of the service and within itself, and significant effort on the part of its author, to understand the ontology or ontologies in which the information is encoded. Although these will be visibly different applications, and one is a lot easier to implement than the other, it is hard to articulate a fundamental difference between them.

There are further compact details in Bizer, Heath and Berners-Lee (2009),

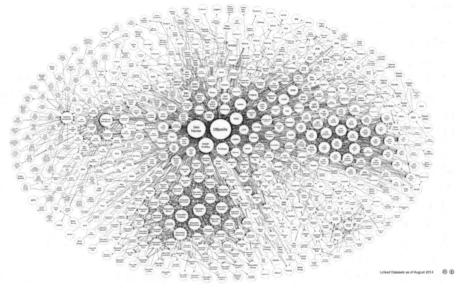

Linked Datasets as of August 2014

Figure 3.3 The Linking Open Data cloud diagram, as of April 2014
Although the text and most of the interconnections are too small to make out at this
scale, the two largest central blobs – which act as rich sources of consensus names for
objects in the world – represent DBPedia and GeoNames. The large clusters on the
middle left and middle right represent government and bibliographic data, respectively;
other clusters represent providers of life sciences, geographic, social networking, media,
user-generated and linguistic data. For a larger-scale image, details and credits, see
http://lod-cloud.net.

a book-length discussion with a practical focus in Heath and Bizer (2011)
and pointers to current information at http://www.w3.org/standards/
semanticweb/data.

Conclusion

One could derive the impression, from the long description in the first section
of this chapter, that the Semantic Web is complicated and arcane. It can be,
but the rude health of the Linked Data cloud shows that that complication
is in the background of a simple and robust means of distributing machine-
intelligible information. While we may not be quite at the stage of letting our
computers run amok with our credit cards, or organize our lives as the vision
of Berners-Lee, Hendler, and Lassila imagines, we have now confidently, if
still rather discreetly, stepped into a web of data.

Glossary

AI Artificial Intelligence.

DC Dublin Core: a set of core metadata terms developed by and for the library community; see http://dublincore.org/.

FOAF Friend of a Friend: a vocabulary for attributes of, and relationships between, people; see http://www.foaf-project.org/.

HTML Hypertext Markup Language; see http://www.w3.org/html/wg/.

HTTP Hypertext Transport Protocol: the underlying language of the web; see Fielding et al. (1999).

RDFS RDF Schemas: lightweight ontologies for RDF; see RDF Schema 1.1 (2014).

RDF Resource Description Framework: see RDF 1.1 Concepts and Abstract Syntax (2014).

triple The triple of subject, predicate and object which is at the heart of the RDF model.

triplestore A database designed to store RDF triples, rather than the tabular data of a more common 'relational' database.

URI Uniform Resource Identifier: the form of a resource name (almost the same as a URL); see Berners-Lee, Fielding and Masinter (2005).

W3C World Wide Web Consortium: the organization which develops and standardizes protocols for the web; see http://www.w3.org.

References

Ashburner, M., Ball, C., Blake, J., Botstein, D., Butler, H., Cherry, J., Davis, A., Dolinski, K., Dwight, S., Eppig, J., Harris, M., Hill, D., Issel-Tarver, L., Kasarskis, A., Lewis, S., Matese, J., Richardson, J., Ringwald, M., Rubin, G. and Sherlock, G. (2000) Gene Ontology: tool for the unification of biology, *Nature Genetics*, **25** (1), 25–9, doi: 10.1038/75556.

Bada, M., Stevens, R., Goble, C., Gil, Y., Ashburner, M., Blake, J., Cherry, J., Harris, M. and Lewis, S. (2004) A Short Study on the Success of the Gene Ontology, *Journal of Web Semantics*, **1** (2), http://www.websemanticsjournal.org/ps/pub/2004-9.

Berners-Lee, T. (1989) Information Management: a proposal, Technical Report, CERN, March, http://info.cern.ch/Proposal.html.

Berners-Lee, T. (2006) Linked Data, Webpage, http://www.w3.org/DesignIssues/LinkedData.html.

Berners-Lee, T. and Caillau, R. (1990) WorldWideWeb: proposal for a hyper-text project, Web page, CERN, November, http://www.w3.org/Proposal.html.

Berners-Lee, T., Fielding, R. and Masinter, L. (2005) Uniform Resource Identifier (URI): generic syntax, RFC3986, January, http://www. ietf.org/rfc/rfc3986.txt.

Berners-Lee, T., Hendler, J. and Lassila, O. (2001) The Semantic Web, *Scientific American*, **284** (5), 34–43, doi: 10.1038/scientificamerican0501-34.

Bizer, C., Heath, T. and Berners-Lee, T. (2009) Linked Data – the Story so Far, *International Journal On Semantic Web and Information Systems*, **5** (3), 1–22, http://tomheath.com/papers/bizer-heath-berners-lee-ijswis-linked-data.pdf, doi:10.4018/jswis.2009081901.

Bray, T., Paoli, J. and Sperberg-McQueen, C. M. (1998) Extensible Markup Language (XML) 1.0, W3C Recommendation, February, first edition of http://www.w3.org/TR/REC-xml/, http://www.w3.org/TR/1998/REC-xml-19980210.

Bush, V. (1945) As We May Think, *The Atlantic Monthly*, July, http://www.theatlantic.com/magazine/archive/1945/07/as-we-may-think/303881/.

Castro, L., McLaughlin, C. and Garcia, A. (2013) Biotea: RDFizing PubMed Central in support for the paper as an interface to the web of data, *Journal of Biomedical Semantics*, **4** (Suppl 1), S5, http://www.jbiomedsem.com/content/4/S1/S5, doi: 10.1186/2041-1480-4-S1-S5.

Fielding, R., Gettys, J., Mogul, J., Frystyk, H., Masinter, L., Leach, P. and Berners-Lee, T. (1999) Hypertext Transfer Protocol – HTTP/1.1, RFC 2616, June, http://www.ietf.org/rfc/rfc2616.txt.

Gruber, T. (1993) A Translation Approach to Portable Ontology Specification, *Knowledge Acquisition*, **5** (2), 199–220, doi: 10.1006/knac.1993.1008.

Heath, T. and Bizer, C. (2011) *Linked Data: evolving the web into a global data space*, Synthesis Lectures on the Semantic Web: Theory and Technology, Morgan & Claypool, http://linkeddatabook.com, doi:10.2200/S00334ED1V01Y201102WBE001.

Lassila, O. and Swick, R. (1999) Resource Description Framework (RDF) Model and Syntax Specification, W3C Recommendation, February, http://www.w3.org/TR/1999/REC-rdf-syntax-19990222/.

Lehmann, J., Isele, R., Jakob, M., Jentzsch, A., Kontokostas, D., Mendes, P., Hellmann, S., Morsey, M., van Kleef, P., Auer, S. and Bizer, C. (2014) DBpedia – a Large-scale, Multilingual Knowledge Base Extracted from Wikipedia, *Semantic Web Journal*, http://content.iospress.com/articles/semantic-web/sw134, doi: 10.3233/SW-140134.

McGuinness, D. (2003) Ontologies Come of Age. In Fensel, D., Hendler, J., Lieberman, H. and Wahlster, W. (eds), *Spinning the Semantic Web: bringing the World Wide Web to its full potential*, MIT Press, http://www-ksl.stanford.edu/people/dlm/papers/ontologies-come-of-age-mit-press-%28with-citation%29.htm.

RDF 1.1 Concepts and Abstract Syntax (2014) W3C Recommendation, February, http://www.w3.org/TR/2014/REC-rdf11-concepts-20140225/.

RDF Schema 1.1 (2014) W3C Recommendation, February, http://www.w3.org/TR/2014/REC-rdf-schema-20140225/.

RDF 1.1 Semantics (2014) W3C Recommendation, http://www.w3.org/TR/rdf11-mt/.

RDF 1.1 Turtle (2014) W3C Recommendation, February, http://www. w3.org/TR/2014/REC-turtle-20140225/.

RDF 1.1 XML Syntax (2014) W3C Recommendation, February, http://www.w3.org/TR/2014/REC-rdf-syntax-grammar-20140225/.

Sauermann, L., Cyganiak, R., Ayers, D. and Völkel, M. (2008) Cool URIs for the Semantic Web, W3C Interest Group Note, December, http://www.w3.org/TR/2008/NOTE-cooluris-20081203/.

Simon, A., Wenz, R., Michel, V. and Di Mascio, A. (2013) Publishing Bibliographic Records on the Web of Data: opportunities for the BnF (French National Library). In Cimiano, P., Corcho, O., Presutti, V., Hollink, L. and Rudolph, S. (eds), The Semantic Web: semantics and big data, *Lecture Notes in Computer Science*, **7882**, 563–77, Springer, 10th International Conference, ESWC 2013, Montpellier, France, May 26-30, 2013. URL: http://2013.eswc-conferences.org/program/accepted-papers, doi:10.1007/978-3-642-38288-8_38.

Swartz, A. (2013) *A Programmable Web: an unfinished work*, Synthesis Lectures on the Semantic Web: Theory and Technology. Morgan & Claypool. doi:10.2200/S00481ED1V01Y201302WBE005.

W3C OWL Working Group (2012) OWL 2 Web Ontology Language Document Overview (second edition), W3C Recommendation, December, http://www. w3.org/TR/owl2-overview/.

W3C SPARQL Working Group (2013) SPARQL 1.1 Overview, W3C Recommendation, March, http://www.w3.org/TR/sparql11-overview/.

Notes

1   This strand can with at least a little justice be regarded as the most recent last

hurrah of AI, a tradition pronounced dead more often than *South Park's* Kenny.

2 That's a sort of 'mindspace' most: this statement probably isn't numerically true if you go by numbers of objects or volume of data.

3 This point is rather muddied by the observation that many people now read e-mail messages in a web browser; nonetheless the e-mail is still transported between systems, in the background, using the decades-old e-mail protocols.

4 This 1990 document came about 18 months after Berners-Lee (1989), which is a broad discussion of information management in the context of 'the management of general information about accelerators and experiments at CERN. This document – on which Berners-Lee's manager wrote 'vague, but exciting' – is clearly ancestral both to the web and to Berners-Lee and Caillou (1990), but it is particularly interesting from the point of view of this chapter, because in hindsight it more closely prefigures the structure and potential of RDF and the *Semantic* Web. One could almost call the textual web 'Semantic Web 0.1'.

5 Apache originally consisted of a set of software 'patches' to National Center for Supercomputing Applications (NCSA) httpd, hence the (unfortunately apocryphal, it seems) etymology of its name as 'a patchy server'.

6 HTML 2.0 was an IETF standard; earlier versions were not formally standardized.

7 http://xanadu.com/.

8 The HTTP protocol can be, and is, used to transport digital media of all types – plain text, images, PDFs, audio and other data; for our present purposes, I take the term 'the web' to refer to the global hypertext system of Berners-Lee's original conception; this does not affect the essential point.

9 If you actually search for 'jordan' in, for example, Google, Bing and DuckDuckGo, you will find that *several* of these distinct senses appear on the first page, so that there is more variety than would result from simply listing the most popular pages with that string in them. This is because search engines can *statistically* identify that there are multiple clusters of related pages and thus, for example, display one hit from each cluster in a situation like this. The search engines are understood to improve their performance here with some lightweight semantics, but the core work of a search engine is at present still probabilistic rather than logical.

10 http://www.w3.org/standards/.

11 http://www.geonames.org.

12 I note parenthetically – for there is a *very, very long* distraction possible here –

that the URIs http://dbpedia.org/resource/Jordan_River and
http://nxg.me.uk/norman/ are names for the physical things themselves, and
not for any online resource describing the things; in the same sense, a DOI is a
digital identifier for an object such as an article, and not for the record
describing the article. This is true even though both of them have the form of
a URI which is retrievable (or '*dereferenceable*') in the sense that a web browser
can retrieve something from that address. If you retrieve either of those URIs
by typing it into a browser, you are redirected to another web page which
describes the resource (that is, a resource with a different name, which *is* a web
page rather than a person or concept); in neither case do you get me, or a river
of water, delivered to your computer. If you are interested, and have a day or
so to burn, search for 'httprange-14'.

13 We make some extra remarks about the logic of RDF, and identity, below.

14 This replaces the original version 1.0; there are further documents, including
links to primers at different technical levels, at
http://www.w3.org/standards/techs/rdf, and a broader collection of
resources at http://www.w3.org/RDF/. The RDF suite of documents was
comprehensively refreshed in February 2014 with the release of new versions
of many of the standards which had accumulated over the previous 15 years.

15 https://www.w3.org/standards/techs/rdfa.

16 The 'Friend of a Friend' ontology was originally conceived of as a way of
creating a peer-to-peer social network.

17 Saying that the two classes are *disjoint* is to say that there are no objects which
are in both classes; this is incompatible with the deduction, above, that
/norman/ *is* in both classes, and it is this inconsistency that machines will
object to.

18 This is the by now apparently traditional slight misquotation of Gruber's
'explicit specification' as 'formal specification'.

19 http://www.w3.org/2004/02/skos/intro.

20 This 'permission for ignorance' is known as the 'open world assumption'. It is
terribly important for the mathematical logic which a reasoner implements, but
most non-specialist users of RDF can be forgiven for feeling it to be a rather
abstract detail. It is in contrast to the 'closed world assumption' built in to
more traditional relational databases: if there is no salary beside my name in
the personnel department's database, then the system will conclude that I am a
person without a salary, as opposed to a person whose salary is unknown
(which is the only conclusion possible in an RDF analogue of this database); in

this case, the personnel office is certain they're not going to pay me.

21 A 'reasoner' in this context is a piece of software which can implement the logical calculus indicated by an ontology.

22 Yes, the standard is indeed cracking a Winnie-the-Pooh joke here.

23 The standard W3C query language for RDF is called SPARQL (W3C SPARQL Working Group, 2013), which is to a triplestore what SQL is to a relational database.

24 http://www.w3.org/2013/data/.

25 http://www.semantic-web-journal.net/accepted-datasets.

26 Indeed there is something of a paradox here: the web of 2010 and the web of 2000 look hugely different, to the extent that they seem to come from different worlds. But these differences are to do with new social possibilities and with browsers' new and almost entirely unpredicted programming ecology, rather than arising from any change in the underlying nuts and bolts; and the closer we look at Web 2.0, the more out of focus it seems to become.

27 The word 'paradigm' is probably the best term in general, to the extent that it represents the result of accepting the insight of a set of rather high-level principles. However, making these principles concrete is sufficiently intricate that 'Linked Data Best Practices' sometimes seems more descriptive; and when defending the principles against other approaches, the word 'dogma' springs quickly to mind.

CHAPTER 4

Crowdsourcing

Ylva Berglund Prytz

What is crowdsourcing?
Introducing crowdsourcing

Crowdsourcing is increasingly emerging as a viable approach in a number of areas. It can be used to source labour for a repetitive task that needs to be done a large number of times, but is also employed to find innovative solutions to problems or to perform tasks that would be beyond one single individual to accomplish.

Crowdsourcing can take many forms but one common feature is that a task or set of tasks is performed by a number of people ('volunteers') who have agreed to take part. Each task can be small and quick to do, but through the input of a large number of people ('crowd'), the combined effort and output will be considerable.

Crowdsourcing is particularly useful for tasks where the human brain and eye cannot be replaced by machines. Some crowdsourcing tasks can seem fairly uncomplicated and menial, and farming out these mind-numbing activities to a crowd may seem like a charitable approach. As will be shown below, however, many crowdsourcing projects offer stimulating and challenging tasks, providing access to material that is interesting and captivating in a context where participants can engage with the material and see the value of their contribution.

A common feature of many crowdsourcing initiatives is that volunteers are presented with some existing material and asked to perform a task or series of tasks, for example, extract information from the material, improve it or make it easier to access and share. Tasks may involve proofreading and correcting text (for example, material that has been scanned and automatically converted to text), transcribing material (for example, typing the text of a letter which is presented as an image), providing metadata (for example, identifying and keying in title and author from the title page of a digitized book) or identifying or classifying objects in different ways (for example, identifying animals in pictures, classifying galaxies by shape or adding tags to describe the content of a painting).

In some crowdsourcing projects the task of the volunteer is to share their own material, rather than to work on material provided by the project. Examples of tasks performed in such cases include uploading family letters from World War 1 or educational material about the Anglo-Saxon period, identifying and submitting interesting uses of words or recording stories, anecdotes or recollections in writing or as audio/video files.

Definition

Various definitions of the term 'crowdsourcing' exist. There are many examples of projects and initiatives that are using crowdsourcing in one way or another and their diversity and variation lend further nuance to the term. Dunn and Hedges suggest that: '[t]he term crowdsourcing is frequently used as a convenient label for a diverse range of activities and projects involving the public doing something to, or with, content' (Dunn and Hedges, 2014, 231).

The term 'crowdsourcing' is generally considered to have been coined by Jeff Howe and Mark Robinson in 2006 (Howe, 2006a). In a 2006 feature, Howe writes: 'Simply defined, crowdsourcing represents the act of a company or institution taking a function once performed by employees and outsourcing it to an undefined (and generally large) network of people in the form of an open call' (Howe, 2006b). Mia Ridge (Ridge, 2014a) gives a simpler definition, glossing crowdsourcing as 'asking the general public to help contribute to shared goals'. Estellés-Arolas and González-Ladrón-de-Guevara present a discussion of crowdsourcing characteristics and classifications. They conclude that '[t]he adaptability of crowdsourcing allows it to be an effective and powerful practice, but makes it difficult to define and categorize' (Estellés-Arolas and González-Ladrón-de-Guevara, 2012).

The aim of this chapter is not to give a precise definition of crowdsourcing. Nor does it purport to cover all aspects of work that may or may not be found under the 'crowdsourcing' heading, but it mainly offers an introduction to the area and provides an insight into some aspects of what may be involved when talking about crowdsourcing.

The next section will introduce some reasons for using crowdsourcing. This is followed by an overview of key factors to think through when considering or planning a crowdsourcing project. Examples from past and current crowdsourcing projects are offered as illustrations, with a selection of projects briefly introduced in a separate section.

Why crowdsource?

There are many reasons why someone may consider using crowdsourcing for a project. Most crowdsourcing projects can be loosely placed into one of four main categories, based on the primary purpose of the exercise, as briefly presented here (more information about the example projects can be found in the 'Illustrations' section below):

- **Collect research data/retrieve information.** Used for research projects which need to extract information from large datasets and where the human eye and brain is more successful than computers. An essential component of 'citizen science'. Examples: Galaxy Zoo, Old Weather, Bat Detective.
- **Correct/improve digital material.** Used to improve the output of previous efforts or automated methods to create a good digital version of material, for example to correct text that has been processed by automatic text recognition software or to crop pictures so as to remove borders and empty space. Examples: Digitised Newspapers (National Library of Australia), Search the Collections (Victoria and Albert Museum).
- **Improve discoverability.** Used to improve access to digital material by making texts searchable or providing relevant metadata. This can be achieved by transcribing texts or providing tags, metadata and classifications. Examples: Your Paintings, Transcribe Bentham, What's on the Menu?, What's the Score at the Bodleian?
- **Collect material.** Used to create digital collections of material

contributed by the crowd. Examples of community collections include Great War Archive, Woruldhord, Oxford English Dictionary.

These are not the only reasons why someone would be interested in using crowdsourcing. Among factors that may influence the decision to run a crowdsourcing project, the economic aspect cannot be disregarded. Crowdsourcing can be used for sourcing labour in a cost-efficient way; for example, for very small tasks that need to be performed many times. Participants may be rewarded with micro-payments (a very small sum for each completed task) or other rewards. One such example is Mechanical Turk, run by Amazon.

A comparison of the crowdsourced Great War Archive (where the general public digitized and uploaded their World War 1 memorabilia) and its traditionally run sister project First World War Poetry Digital Archive (where project staff digitized and uploaded material held in various repositories) showed that the cost per digital item added to the collection was lower for the crowdsourced data (Lindsay, 2009, 21). However, calculations like these may not show the whole picture. It may, for example, be difficult to take factors into consideration that cannot be measured in economic terms, such as the fact that the material digitized for the Poetry Archive was held in dispersed locations with restricted access; it could not practically be accessed and digitized by a crowd and the work had to be done by project staff in collaboration with the repositories. On the other hand, in the case of the Great War Archive, the material to be digitized could be found among the general public, which is how the task of digitizing and uploading the material could be performed by the crowd.

When trying to assess the potential for a crowdsourcing project in economic terms, it is important to consider the effort (and associated cost) needed for the project as such, but also to take into account the impact and potential savings that the project may generate in the long run. For example, the time that a subject librarian has to spend identifying suitable resources to include in a crowdsourcing project may turn out to be compensated for by savings when users regularly require less help to find and retrieve the information they need. The Louisville Leader project (transcribing historical newspapers) found that preparing the material for crowdsourcing and processing the transcripts had considerable demands for staff input, but that there were many positive sides to running the project. 'While this project involved more work for staff members and students than initially anticipated, there were many benefits' (Daniels et al., 2014, 46). Listed among the benefits are positive publicity and increased awareness and appreciation of the work of the library, something which may be difficult to define in economic terms.

As has been shown by several projects (Ridge, 2014b), an important feature and driver of crowdsourcing initiatives is the positive outcomes resulting from engagement with the crowd. A project may initially be perceived as an exercise to improve access to a collection, but lead to the recruitment of dedicated volunteers who will support the institution well beyond the project phase, or draw in new users of both digital and physical collections. The opportunity to reach new audiences, engage with users and raise the profile of an institution have been listed as some of the most valuable outcomes of crowdsourcing initiatives, outcomes that alone may motivate the investment of time and money in a crowdsourcing project.

How to crowdsource

Irrespective of the reasons for embarking on a crowdsourcing project, there are a number of aspects that need to be considered. The kind and amount of resources required, where to base the project and when to run it are obvious questions to be answered. Other key factors to be considered at a very early stage in the planning are presented below. These include:

- the material that will be used or collected
- the task(s) of the volunteers
- who is in the crowd (and how to reach them)
- technical solutions
- quality control
- communicating with volunteers.

Material

A key consideration for any crowdsourcing project is the material to be worked on or collected. In many initiatives the source material is held by the institution setting up the project. This can be material that is digitized or collected specifically for the project or existing digital content, like pictures of galaxies, scanned images of manuscripts or text retrieved by automatic text-recognition processes.

The choice of material is central to a project and its existence may be the primary motivation for running the project. There are, however, examples where the material has been selected not because it is in the greatest need of the attention of the crowd but because it is considered something that would be of interest to many people and encourage participation. That this is a valid approach can be illustrated with the example of the What's on the Menu? project run by the New York Public Library (Lascarides and Vershbow, 2014). The project, where volunteers are invited to transcribe the content of menus from the library's specialist collection, was set up in part to evaluate the potential of the crowdsourcing approach. The material was selected based on considerations including the perceived public interest. As it happened, the result of the project surpassed expectations and a number of unexpected side-effects have been observed – for example, local restaurants creating themed menus based on the content of the collection.

Tasks

Despite the differences in purpose and approach of different crowdsourcing projects, the tasks allocated to the crowd can be broadly defined as a few general categories. Some projects will involve only one kind of task, while others employ a combination; for example, asking volunteers to identify a particular object in an image and then provide more information about it.

Breaking down a complex task into several smaller components is a good way to ensure that a large number of participants will be able to take part, even if they lack expert knowledge about a specific area or are unable to commit to spending much time on a task. Asking volunteers to simply match one Greek letter at the time to a key, or note down the information found in one field of a form means that even those who do not know Ancient Greek, or those who can spare but a couple of minutes of their time, can make a valuable contribution to the Ancient Lives project or record weather observations for Old Weather. It is, of course, possible to run a crowdsourcing project where volunteers are asked to perform larger and more time-consuming or complex tasks. Here, the Transcribe Bentham project can serve as an illustration. Volunteers are not only asked to transcribe the text from Bentham's papers but also to add information about certain features by using XML markup. Although some may find this too demanding, others appreciate the challenge it presents and are happy to devote the time and effort needed to master the process.

Classify

Volunteers classify what they see according to a specific scheme; for example, identifying a galaxy as having a round or spiral form, or identifying an animal by answering a series of questions about its type, colour, kind of antlers, etc. Classification tasks are often found in citizen science projects, where the result of the crowdsourcing will be a set of data that is used to inform science.

Identify

Volunteers examine the data presented and identify particular objects or features; for example, marking bright spots of light in an image (to identify stars) or mention of troop movements in a war diary. Identification is often combined with other tasks, so volunteers may, for example, identify the area of a manuscript where particular information is provided and then transcribe that information.

Tag

In tagging tasks volunteers are asked to assign tags from a pre-existing set or to devise their own. The tags can then be used to group the objects or facilitate search and retrieval. Tagging can be considered a kind of classification, but the sets of tags used are usually larger than the classifications available in classification tasks. Tagging may also be seen as a more creative approach where users are invited to invent the tags that are assigned.

Transcribe

Textual data that is captured as an image cannot be easily searched or processed. By converting such material into keyed-in text the material can be used in new ways. Despite progress in the area of automatic text recognition, humans are still better than machines when it comes to reading handwritten or smudged text, or text that is rendered in graphically challenging ways, which is one reason why crowdsourced transcription projects are becoming popular in a number of areas.

Proofread and correct

It is not unusual to find errors in material that has been automatically processed, for example, in text generated by text recognition software. Crowdsourcing can be an effective means to find and correct such errors. Proofreading and correction can also be used to improve other types of data, such as metadata records, classifications or other descriptive information.

Add metadata

Like objects in physical collections, digital objects are easier to find and retrieve if appropriate metadata exists. Crowdsourcing can be used to generate metadata for an object or record. The actions involved may be similar to tagging or classification (for example, if assigning a subject keyword) or transcription (recording title and author from the cover of a book) and may involve more than one kind of task.

Share material

Some crowdsourcing projects focus on material contributed by the crowd rather than existing or project-related collections. Volunteers are asked to contribute material to a collection which is then archived, published online, researched or used for other purposes. The material gathered for such a collection can be images, letters or documents, personal stories and observations, or any material in digital format. Collections that are built through crowdsourcing projects are known as 'community collections' (Berglund Prytz, 2013).

Identifying and engaging with 'the crowd'

No matter what kind of material or tasks a crowdsourcing project uses, it will not work if there is no crowd contributing. Without volunteers, the material will remain unclassified or the collection will be empty. It is therefore central to the project to identify the relevant crowd at a very early stage and to devise methods for engaging volunteers and getting them to participate throughout the project's lifecycle.

The crowd does not have to be large. The Woruldhord project collected Anglo-Saxon teaching and learning material. It may be thought that this would engage only a small, specialized community and, as such, not be a suitable crowdsourcing project. It was shown, however, that although the potential crowd was comparatively small, a large proportion were actively engaging with each other and the subject area, and a well-established network for interaction existed online. As the network could be reached through existing channels, such as mailing lists and online groups like Facebook, it was easy to reach the relevant community and share information about the project. Because the project was of direct, central importance and interest to this community, members were further encouraged to participate and share their material.

A project such as Europeana 1914–1918 reaches out to a potential crowd of many millions of people, inviting anyone with stories or material relating to World War 1 or who has links to anyone who lived at that time. However, this crowd is less easy to define and find. There are no existing groups or mailing lists that include them all, or even a large proportion of them. In such a case, it may be more fruitful to try to raise general awareness of the project, for example by featuring it in newspapers and media. The Galaxy Zoo project, which invited people to classify images from outer space, featured in a popular TV show, with the result that a huge number of volunteers started contributing. The Europeana 1914–1918 project regularly sees spikes in interest and participation following major media coverage.

It is not always possible to get the kind of media coverage that results in nation-wide interest and commitment. Approaching special interest groups may be another method, even for a fairly general project. If the task is to work on material with strong local links, or to collect information about a place or point in history, local historians and genealogists may be interested in becoming involved. A project about sports could perhaps benefit from establishing links with the local football club or with sports teachers in a school, while a botany project could be advertised through horticultural societies and garden centres.

Identifying the crowd and managing its expectations (support when needed, appreciation, access to new material and so on) requires a considerable effort. Providing support and answering questions can be time consuming and require input from different people to deal with technical questions, questions relating to the choice of classification, messages about interesting observations and so on. Lewis Dafis, Hughes and James observe that: 'an enormous amount of analogue-human-effort needs to go into the preparation and support of community engagement activities of this nature if they are to be a success' (Lewis Dafis, Hughes and James, 2014, 151). In many cases, some of the support can be taken on by the crowd, by volunteers who have extensive experience of the project and are happy to answer questions, monitor performance or perform other tasks that may be outside what the majority of the crowd would do.

Technical solutions

Of necessity, an online crowdsourcing project will require some technical provision. The project needs an online presence, a way to present the task(s) which volunteers are asked to perform, means to display any material that is to be worked on and a solution for collecting the input from the volunteers. The data that is collected needs to be saved, kept safe and stored in a way that allows for retrieval or display as required by the project. It may be that the classification data is to be analysed by researchers, or the pictures of memorabilia are to be published online, or the collected metadata are to be integrated into the library catalogue. Irrespective of what will happen to the output from the crowdsourcing activities, provisions have to be made to ensure that the information is available in a usable format. A dedicated, custom-built solution can make this easier, but it is possible to perform an online crowdsourcing project using only freely available tools.

One considerable difference between a dedicated technical solution and using existing resources is the effort that is required before, during and after the crowdsourcing phase. Developing and configuring a custom-made solution may require considerable resources. It can, however, be designed to facilitate the crowdsourcing process; for example, by including means to help the volunteers (such as context-sensitive advice and support, a 'magnifying glass' for viewing details in pictures, or a list of tags to choose from) or to automatically monitor and validate the information added. A custom-made application should also make it possible to easily extract the crowdsourced data so that it can be analysed, displayed or used as required without further ado.

However, it is possible to run a crowdsourcing project without a dedicated solution. A non-specialist solution can be useful when it is important to get started quickly, or when no resources are available for anything else. A community collection could, for example, be built from material sent in by e-mail. A project aiming to get images classified could perhaps use an existing web-based photo-sharing service. Obviously, the e-mail solution is easy to set up, with no specialist equipment needed, and an account with a photo-sharing website can be created instantly and without cost. However, the simple e-mail solution would involve considerable effort to extract the relevant information from the e-mails, and it would not be possible to ensure that all necessary information had been provided. Using an existing photo-sharing application is also an easy way to get started, but it may be difficult to retrieve the crowdsourced data in a format suitable for storing, analysis or display.

Quality control

When working with non-traditional data creation a question that will come up is to what degree crowdsourced data can be trusted. Is the quality high enough for it to be used as research data, or be included in an existing cataloguing system where certain standards are maintained by qualified, trained staff? That is a question to which there is no single answer. Many factors will affect the quality of the data collected; whether it is good enough for a particular purpose will depend largely on what that purpose may be. It is important to set out in the early stages of a project what the required standards are, and to devise methods to ensure that they can be met, for example by building quality-control functions into the project process.

There are different approaches to consider in relation to quality control. One option is to have each contribution manually checked by qualified project staff. Disregarding possible 'human error' instances, to have everything checked by experts should mean that any required standard could be met. However, this kind of expert, manual monitoring is usually not feasible. Checking, and possibly correcting, information would not necessarily be much quicker than entering or classifying it in the first place, and one benefit of crowdsourcing the task would be lost. Daniels et al. (2014, 45) observe that 'reviewing each transcription against the original would be nearly as time consuming as doing the transcription in-house'.

It is possible that having trained staff check only certain aspects of a record (for example, the format but not the content of a date field) could make the process slightly less demanding, but this would still require considerable effort. If it is considered necessary for all entries to be manually checked, this task could also be crowdsourced, possibly by assigning the role to selected 'super volunteers', experienced contributors who have been given additional training or guidance.

Some crowdsourcing systems have built-in methods for quality control. Such a feature could be, for example, that each task is performed by a number of volunteers. A task will remain active and be repeated by new volunteers until the same result has been returned a specified number of times. That means each analysis is based on the activities of not one individual but several. Difficult cases (defined as instances where the analysis varies between different volunteers) can be referred to an expert for a definite analysis. Another option is to compare the output of a volunteer with a 'gold standard'. Unbeknown to the volunteer, they are given a certain set of tasks to perform. Their results are compared to those of the same tasks done by experts, and when the correlation is high enough, the volunteer is considered proficient and given previously unclassified material to work on. Their analyses could then be used as the new gold standard, and new volunteers be trained on that standard. Versions of built-in quality control can be found, for example, in Zooniverse projects.

There are situations where manual checking of results or material can be necessary, not least in cases where automatic methods cannot be employed (usually for technical reasons). As it is rarely feasible to check everything, random checks can be performed, or the manual examination can focus on certain aspects, for example adding library classifications to records where the title, author and ISBN have been entered by the crowd.

It is important to consider quality control at an early stage of a project and to trial the considered approach; for example, by checking a set of test records produced by volunteers, or manually comparing a transcription to one that has been done by trained staff.

For community collections, where material is shared by volunteers, it may not be possible to check the correctness of the entered data. For example, if someone claims to have been born on a particular day or says that an uploaded picture shows their paternal grandmother it is not possible to verify this in any practical manner. That does not mean that the material cannot be used. Images and documents can be valuable primary sources also where contextual information about the material is missing or difficult to verify, and personal stories and information can offer a fascinating and rewarding research area to explore.

Crowdsourcing: illustrations

The previous sections have introduced the concept of crowdsourcing and discussed some of the central points to be considered before embarking on a crowdsourcing venture. This section will put these concepts and ideas into context by briefly introducing a selection of crowdsourcing projects. The list of projects is far from complete, nor is it even necessarily representative of the whole landscape of crowdsourcing, but it provides some illustrations of how crowdsourcing can be done and has been done.

Oxford English Dictionary: from slips of paper to online crowdsourcing

The Oxford English Dictionary (OED) has used crowdsourcing to get 'quotations which illustrate how words are used' since 1857 (Oxford University Press, n.d.). In the beginning, these were sent in by volunteers who recorded examples from their reading, mainly of literary works. In 1999 an appeal invited volunteers to contribute online, making the OED an early example of online crowdsourcing (Gilliver, 2012). The OED Appeals now ask volunteers to help find the earliest recorded date of a use of a word by submitting examples of use with information about the source and date (http://public.oed.com/the-oed-appeals/).

Galaxy Zoo and Zooniverse: citizen science on a galactic scale

No discussion of crowdsourcing projects would be complete without including the work performed under the umbrella project Zooniverse (http://zooniverse.org). Zooniverse started as the crowdsourced astronomy project Galaxy Zoo in 2007, when nearly one million pictures of galaxies were put on a website where anyone was welcome to look at them and classify the galaxies according to a simple scheme comprising six defined categories (Lintott et al., 2008). The classifications were collected by the astronomers behind the website and used to inform their research. Over a six-month period the project saw some 100,000 volunteers make 40 million classifications, which by far exceeded expectations with regard to both speed and the number of classifications that were made. The immediate success of the project lay not only in the large number of classifications but also in showing the potential for such citizen science projects.

The project has been followed by others collected under the name Zooniverse, and the list keeps growing. Although Zooniverse projects largely use the same approach (users are presented with images or other material and asked to identify, classify or transcribe what they can see or hear), the types of material and tasks differ greatly. Volunteers are invited to classify images from outer space, transcribe war diaries from World War 1, watch videos of animals, identify Greek letters on fragments of papyrus – and the list keeps growing.

One aspect that makes the Zooniverse approach easy for volunteers to embrace is the use of a dedicated interface that will guide participants, both before they start and while working on the tasks. Projects include training modules that are adapted to each project and may involve videos explaining the project and the tasks, or some training sets of data which the volunteer is invited to go through to become familiar with the process. Tasks are broken down into small, separate actions, which makes it possible for volunteers to contribute even if they have only limited time or if they prefer to focus on certain tasks.

Automatic processes for quality control may be built in, for example regulating the number of times an image is presented for analysis, or making sure that one user is not presented with the same material again.

An important feature of Zooniverse projects is also the user engagement aspect. Forums are used where volunteers are invited to post questions or discuss aspects of their work. The forums may be monitored by project staff or more experienced volunteers who can provide answers and support.

Snapshot Serengeti: animal surveillance

Snapshot Serengeti (www.snapshotserengeti.org) is a Zooniverse project where volunteers are asked to identify animals caught on Serengeti camera-trap images. The interface has been constructed so that volunteers do not have to know the difference between a wildebeest and a gazelle, or even between a zebra and a giraffe. By following a series of questions ('Does the animal have antlers' – yes or no? 'Select the picture which shows the type of antlers the animal has', etc.), the volunteer is not only helped to identify the animal but also has a chance to learn about the animals, allowing them to more easily identify the same species when they next come across it. It also means that the data that is collected is less affected by the level of knowledge of the volunteer.

Your paintings: opening up the gallery

In the Your Paintings project (http://tagger.thepcf.org.uk/) volunteers are invited to look at oil paintings held in UK collections and describe them, based on what they see. The user is not only given a list of descriptive options to choose from but is also free to choose their own tags. Once a particular tag has been used a certain number of times for different paintings and by different users, it is added to a list of 'accepted tags', which is then used for searching and retrieval (Eccles and Greg, 2014).

Your Paintings has a rich selection of displays showing how the project is progressing. Among these are two 'Top ten' lists showing the usernames of the taggers who have tagged most paintings in the last seven days and since the beginning of the project. The provision of two lists means that new volunteers have a chance to appear on the one showing progress over the last week, which solves the problem of new participants losing interest because they can never come up in the numbers achieved by those who have been active for a long time. Another way to encourage new volunteers is the 'our newest taggers' list, displaying the usernames and progress of those who last joined the project, and the assignment of a colour to all taggers who have tagged a certain number of pictures (0–4 = green, 5–49 = yellow and so on). There is also a progress bar, showing overall project process.

Amazon Mechanical Turk

Amazon runs the Amazon Mechanical Turk service linking volunteers and businesses that require help with various tasks (https://www.mturk.com). The tasks, called 'Human Intelligence Tasks', can involve identifying objects in images, transcribing audio recordings, correcting errors and much, much more. Volunteers, here referred to as 'workers', are paid a small sum for each completed task (https://www.mturk.com).

The National Library of Australia: correcting digitized newspapers

The National Library of Australia has digitized a large collection of Australian newspapers. These are available online as page images and 'electronically translated text'. Due to the quality of the old newspapers, the automatic character recognition tools that are used to convert the images to text may not be able to render an accurate version. Users of the archive are invited to identify and correct errors. The corrected versions are used for search and retrieval, improving and facilitating access to the online archive (http://help.nla.gov.au/trove/using-trove/digitised-newspapers).

Old Weather: transcribing ships' logs for weather research and history

The Old Weather project (www.oldweather.org/), part of the Zooniverse family, collects weather observations and other information from old ships' logs. The logs have been digitized and volunteers are invited to look at the images and record the information they can find by typing it into a custom-made interface. The data is then harvested and the weather observations are used in climate research. The transcriptions of the additional information in the logs, such as free-text descriptions of day-to-day activities on board, are used for other kinds of research and applications (Blaser, 2014). One example of how the information in the logs can be used is the animation of all navy traffic during World War 1 (Rogers, 2012).

What's on the Menu? Food in New York

The New York Public Library holds an impressive collection of printed menus, which have also been digitized. A crowdsourcing project What's on the Menu? (http://menus.nypl.org/) was set up to capture the dishes listed on the menus and proved to capture the interest and imagination of a large body of volunteers, leading to unexpected side-effects such as restaurants featuring menus from the project, or cook-books based on them.

A noteworthy aspect of the project is that considerable effort was put into making the project as simple as possible. For example, it does not require volunteers to register or create an account, so it is easy to start contributing (Lascarides and Vershbow, 2014).

Ancient Lives: working with Greek papyri

The Ancient Lives project (www.ancientlives.org) uses the Zooniverse platform to crowdsource transcriptions of Greek text found on ancient papyri. The transcription is done on a character-by-character basis. Volunteers are asked to mark each letter that they can see and then select the corresponding symbol on an on-screen keyboard. This means that it is not necessary for the volunteers to know Greek – they simply have to be able to match one symbol to another. A forum is used to discuss questions or findings and a project blog, available from the transcription site, presents findings and discusses related topics that may be of interest to volunteers or scholars. This means that volunteers can take part in discussions about the project and also see the impact of their efforts in the area of scholarly research.

Louisville Leader: transcribing a historic newspaper

The Louisville Leader transcription project invites volunteers to transcribe articles from the newspaper archive. The material is pre-processed by the project to identify individual articles and allow volunteers to choose the material they are interested in, based on basic metadata (Daniels et al., 2014; http://digital.library.louisville.edu/cdm/landingpage/collection/leader/).

What's the Score at the Bodleian? Metadata for Victorian sheet music

The Bodleian Library in Oxford holds a rich collection of sheet music. However, in a way that is far too familiar to many libraries and archives, parts of the collection are poorly classified and have no item-level metadata. This means that the material is difficult to find, evaluate and use. A pilot project was set up in 2012 to explore the potential for using crowdsourcing to generate descriptive metadata for individual printed scores (http://scores.bodleian.ox.ac.uk/). Material from the Bodleian's collections of sheet music was digitized and uploaded to a custom-built interface (created by the Zooniverse group). Volunteers were invited to browse the collection and capture information they could find, including the title and composer of each piece.

The crowdsourced information is harvested and the processed material is made available through an online interface where the collected metadata is used to make it possible to search or browse the material in different ways. The pilot was run on a specific, small set of material rather than a mixture of different types of scores. This means that an additional outcome of the small project has been to create a digital collection of a specific kind of material (piano music intended for the amateur market in mid-Victorian Britain), which can be of value and use as a research or reference resource in its own right.

The Great War Archive: stories and material from World War 1

The Great War Archive (www.oucs.ox.ac.uk/ww1lit/gwa/) was the first in a row of crowdsourcing projects employing the Oxford Community Collection Model (Berglund Prytz, 2013). The model is used to create a collection by combining large-scale crowdsourcing online with direct, personal, often face-to-face interaction. Over only a few months in 2008, and with limited staff resources and time, a small team at Oxford collected some 6500 digital objects related to World War 1. The collection contains photographs, letters, diaries and memorabilia contributed by the general public. Contributions were made either through a dedicated collection website or at a series of collection events where the project team would record stories and digitize objects brought in by the local community and add these to the collection.

The project showed that not only could a high-quality collection be created in this way, but the cost was also considerably lower than for a traditional digitization project (also see discussion above).

The model has since been used for a number of projects, including the large, international Europeana 1914–1918 project (www.europeana1914-1918.eu) involving teams in some 20 European countries, and Merton@750 (http://share.merton.ox.ac.uk/), where the history of an Oxford college is illustrated in a collection combining archival material with oral histories and material submitted by alumni and staff.

Woruldhord: a hoard of Anglo-Saxon treasures for education

Woruldhord (http://projects.oucs.ox.ac.uk/woruldhord/) is a repository of freely reusable educational resources for anyone studying or teaching 'the period of English history centred on the Anglo-Saxons, or Old

English (literature and language)'. The initial project was run over a summer by one academic at the University of Oxford and shows that community collection projects can be successful even if run with very limited resources.

The project greatly benefited from the availability of an existing, dedicated network with well-used communication channels which could be used to promote the project and reach suitable volunteers.

Transcribe Bentham: transcribing manuscripts

The Transcribe Bentham project (http://blogs.ucl.ac.uk/transcribe-bentham/) invites volunteers to transcribe the handwritten documents created by the philosopher and reformer Jeremy Bentham (1748–1832). In addition to transcribing the text, volunteers are invited to identify various features of the text (headings, line-breaks, paragraphs and more) and add specific codes to these, thereby creating a richer resource that can be searched and displayed in different ways (Causer and Terras, 2014). The project is often used as an illustration of how crowdsourcing can be used for highly specialized topics and complex tasks.

Search the Collections: cropping images for the Victoria and Albert Museum

The Victoria and Albert Museum houses extensive and varied collections and some of this material has been digitized and is available online. However, the digital images that are used to represent each object have been chosen automatically and may not be the best possible views. Volunteers are invited to crop these images so that the square thumbnails that are shown on the website offer a useful view of the object (http://collections.vam.ac.uk/crowdsourcing/).

Bat Detective and Whale FM: sound recordings to identify bat activities

Bat Detective is a Zooniverse project where volunteers are invited to help find sounds generated by bats. The tasks involve include listening to very brief sound recordings and looking at spectrograms visually representing the sound and using that information, in combination with the information presented in the supporting documentation and tutorials, to identify and classify the kind of sound recorded. Whale FM (http://whale.fm) uses a similar approach, but asks volunteers to listen to recordings of whale calls and group together those that sound similar.

Conclusion

There are many reasons for inviting a crowd to take part in research projects or the creation and improving of a digital collection. This chapter has provided a brief introduction to some of the areas where crowdsourcing has been used, with illustrations of how this has been done.

Crowdsourcing may not be the solution to staff-shortage problems, nor provide a cheaper alternative to using paid staff, but it has been shown that inviting the crowd to take part can be a viable way to address tasks that could not be done within the normal day-to-day activities of an institution. Moreover, crowdsourcing is increasingly emerging as a valuable approach to engagement between an institution and the individual users or participants who form the crowd. This engagement is of mutual benefit, not only allowing a project or institution to perform valuable research or improve its collection but also offering the volunteers an opportunity to learn, take part and engage with material in new and inspiring ways. As suggested by Ben Showers: 'Users are no longer happy to be passive consumers of information and content, but instead want to be engaged with, contribute and, most importantly, create content' (Showers, 2010).

Crowdsourcing projects require a considerable investment to set up and run. This investment can be financial (not least where the development of a dedicated interface is involved), but in the long run the greater investment is likely to be the time and effort spent on a project by staff and, not least, by the volunteers performing the tasks which form the basis of any crowdsourcing initiative. That this investment can reap ample rewards cannot be doubted. The fact that the benefits are seen both by those running the projects and by those performing the tasks suggests that crowdsourcing is an approach that will continue to be used.

References and further reading

Berglund Prytz, Y. (2013) The Oxford Community Collection Model, RunCoCo Blog, http://blogs.it.ox.ac.uk/runcoco/2013/06/24/the-oxford-community-collection-model/.

Blaser, L. (2014) Old Weather: approaching collections from a different angle. In M. Ridge (ed.), *Crowdsourcing Our Cultural Heritage*, Ashgate.

Carr, M. E. (2013) Crowdsourcing Content to Promote Community and Collection Development in Public Libraries, *Journal of Electronic Resources Librarianship*, **25** (4), 313–16.

Causer, T. and Terras, M. (2014) 'Many hands make light work. Many hands together make merry work': Transcribe Bentham and crowdsourcing manuscript collections. In M. Ridge (ed.), *Crowdsourcing Our Cultural Heritage*, Ashgate.

Daniels, C., Holtze, T. L., Howard, R. I. and Kuehn, R. (2014) Community as Resource: crowdsourcing transcription of an historic newspaper, *Journal of Electronic Resources Librarianship*, **26** (1), 36–48.

Dunn, S. and Hedges, M. (2014) How the Crowd Can Surprise Us: humanities crowdsourcing and the creation of knowledge. In M. Ridge (ed.), *Crowdsourcing Our Cultural Heritage*, Ashgate.

Dunning, A. (2011) Innovative Use of Crowdsourcing Technology Presents Novel Prospects for Research to Interact with Much Larger Audiences, and Much More Effectively than Ever Before, Impact of Social Sciences, http://blogs.lse.ac.uk/impactofsocialsciences/2011/08/25/ 2014.

Eccles, K. and Greg, A. (2014) Your Paintings Tagger. Crowdsourcing descriptive metadata for a national virtual collection. In Ridge, M. (ed.), *Crowdsourcing Our Cultural Heritage*, Ashgate.

Estellés-Arolas, E. and González-Ladrón-de-Guevara, F. (2012) Towards an Integrated Crowdsourcing Definition, *Journal of Information Science*, **38** (2), 189–200.

Gilliver, P. (2012) 'Your dictionary needs you': a brief history of the OED's appeals to the public, http://public.oed.com/the-oed-appeals/history-of-the-appeals/.

Hopkins, C. (2011) Physical and Online Crowdsourcing Documents the Real First World War, Readwrite (blog), http://readwrite.com/2011/06/16/combining_physical_and_online_crowdsourcing_to_doc 2014.

Howe, J. (2006a) The Rise of Crowdsourcing, *Wired*, 14.06, http://archive.wired.com/wired/archive/14.06/crowds.html.

Howe, J. (2006b) Crowdsourcing: a definition, Crowdsourcing (blog), http://crowdsourcing.typepad.com/cs/2006/06/crowdsourcing_a.html.

Huberman, B. A., Romero, D. M. and Wu, F. (2009) Crowdsourcing, Attention and Productivity, *Journal of Information Science*, **35** (6), 758–65.

Lascarides, M. and Vershbow, B. (2014) What's on the Menu? Crowdsourcing at the New York Public Library. In M. Ridge (ed.), *Crowdsourcing Our Cultural Heritage*, Ashgate.

Lewis Dafis, L., Hughes, L. M. and James, R. (2014) What's Welsh for 'Crowdsourcing'? Citizen science and community engagement at the National Library of Wales. In M. Ridge (ed.), *Crowdsourcing Our Cultural Heritage*, Ashgate.

Lindsay, K. (2009) *JISC Final Report: the First World War Poetry Digital Archive, University of Oxford.*

Lintott, C. J., Schawinski, K., Slosar, A., Land, K., Bamford, S., Thomas, D., Raddick, M. J., Nichol, R. C., Szalay, A., Andreescu, D., Murray, P. and Vandenberg, J. (2008) Galaxy Zoo: morphologies derived from visual inspection of galaxies from the Sloan Digital Sky Survey, *Monthly Notices of the Royal Astronomical Society*, **389** (3), 1179–89.

Macdonald, S. and Osborne, N. (2013) Addressing History – Crowdsourcing a Nation's Past, *Journal of Map and Geography Libraries*, **9** (1–2), 194–214.

Owens, T. (2012) Crowdsourcing Cultural Heritage: the objectives are upside down, Trevor Owens (blog). http://www.trevorowens.org/2012/03/crowdsourcing-cultural-heritage-the-objectives-are-upside-down/.

Oxford University Press (n.d.), History of the OED: reading programme, http://public.oed.com/history-of-the-oed/reading-programme/.

Ridge, M. (2014a) Crowdsourcing Our Cultural Heritage, Mia Ridge (blog), http://www.miaridge.com/crowdsourcing-our-cultural-heritage/.

Ridge, M. (ed.), (2014b) *Crowdsourcing Our Cultural Heritage*, Ashgate.

Ridge, M. (2014c) Crowdsourcing our Cultural Heritage: introduction. In Ridge, M. (ed.), *Crowdsourcing Our Cultural Heritage*, Ashgate.

Rogers, S. (2012) Britain's Royal Navy in the First World War – animated, Datablog, http://www.theguardian.com/news/datablog/interactive/2012/oct/01/first-world-war-royal-navy-ships-mapped.

Shen, X.-L., Lee, M. K. O. and Cheung, C. M. K. (2014) Exploring Online Social Behavior in Crowdsourcing Communities: a relationship management perspective, *Computers in Human Behavior*, **40** (November), 144–51.

Showers, B. (2010) Capturing the Power of the Crowd and the Challenge of Community Collections, http://www.jisc.ac.uk/publications/programmerelated/2010/communitycollections.aspx .

CHAPTER 5

Pathways to integrating technical, legal and economic considerations in the design, development and deployment of trusted IM systems

Scott David and Barbara Endicott-Popovsky

Introduction: the IM problem and solution landscape

This chapter suggests that networked IM (information management) challenges of security, privacy and risk/liability are just symptoms of a single condition. That single condition is the lack of agreement by stakeholders. This condition is acute, since networked IM systems (the 'cloud') operate as distributed, socio-technical systems, i.e. those that simultaneously serve and are constituted from both people and technology acting in concert. However, IM systems are typically designed, developed and deployed as if they were systems composed solely of technology and as if the problems with their operation could be fixed by technology alone. This ignores the people operating IM solutions, causing their destabilization.

Technology solutions are a natural focus because their performance is more readily measurable than that of people and institutions. Unfortunately, like the man who is looking for his lost wristwatch only under the streetlight because that is where the light is better, we are unlikely to find the solutions we are looking for just because they are more readily apparent. The actions of individuals and institutions in networked IM systems, not the technology, are the source of most current security, privacy and risk/liability concerns, and focus on technology alone does not adequately address the system operational variables that arise from human behaviours engaged in by IM system stakeholders. That blind spot is revealed through consideration of the fact that the vast majority of data breaches are the result of human, rather than technological, factors. Technological fixes alone are insufficient for improving socio-technical systems where human negligence and intentional misconduct are the chief causes of lack of system integrity. We all need socio-technical processes to evolve socio-technical systems. Markets and other formal and informal rule-making processes generate enforceable 'agreements' among people that also reduce risk and offer an additional solution space for networked IM.

The big strides in improving security and privacy, and the introduction of measures to mitigate liability will allow stakeholders to develop their own performance standards which can be measured meaningfully and provide feedback that can be used to police both technological and human failure in systems.

The technology 'tools' (set forth in specifications) and legal/policy 'rules' set forth in contracts and laws will be described in hybrid 'trust frameworks' recorded in searchable registries to provide access to solutions in interconnected markets of information risk-reduction ideas.

By integrating solutions for multiple stakeholders simultaneously in referenceable trust frameworks accessible in registries, it becomes possible for stakeholders to create integrated metrics that are relevant to multiple stakeholders with different concerns, allowing system 'cross talk' that enables more informed IM decision making by all stakeholders in various scales from negotiation to purchase and strategic market decisions.

This chapter suggests a pathway to creating more broadly integrated, reliable 'architectures of interaction self governance' for IM systems, mapped by the measurements and standards of economics and law as well as the metrics of technology, through hybrid, interdisciplinary IM systems engineering.

Law and economics are not typically considered at the early stages of system design and development, but instead are most often relegated to after-the-fact roles like enforcement of system rules and return-on-investment analysis of already-deployed systems. Unfortunately, this is too late in the process to yield the full benefit of the insights of these disciplines for IM stakeholders. This chapter narrates some of the emerging ways in which these once-separate disciplines can be gainfully integrated at the design and development stages of networked IM systems.

Effective, engineered IM systems should include a plan to identify, develop and categorize system technical tools and legal/economic rules according to their anticipated use in networked IM systems viewed as socio-technical systems. For example, a technical solution may be appropriate for system security; economic incentives may help to create behavioural predictability across populations for system privacy; or contract and existing public law duties may be applied to coax behaviours consistent with certain system security goals to help mitigate risk and unanticipated liability. Interdisciplinary engineering can help make the system more reliable across multiple vectors of technical, legal and economic intervention, increasing system resiliency and reducing the potential risks implied for each stakeholder in the system.

Unfortunately, focus on this integrated analysis is relatively new in IM and it doesn't yet benefit from referenceable and established conceptual models or measurements. This is the realm of new forms of applied social science. Fortunately, best practices for the integration of technology, economics and law in designing and deploying socio-technical systems (of which IM is a type), can be derived from examination of earlier successes (and failures) in other socio-technical systems which can help to guide IM systems engineering initiatives going forward. This chapter references some of those earlier examples as inspiration for the IM system work to come.

This chapter is organized around four concepts that together constitute the cohesive information feedback loops (and nascent 'rule-making' processes) that help to lend coherence to the behaviours of individuals acting in groups. IM networks are just the latest iteration of group co-ordination, albeit at historically unprecedented scales and levels of refinement that will continue their exponential march as the Internet of Things comes online. Notwithstanding the scales, this chapter suggests that attention to these four concepts can help to crystallize architectural and performance requirements for hybrid tools and rules to render reliable socio-technical systems involved in IM.

Specifically, the four concepts of reliability/trustworthiness, standards, metrics and feedback/UIs (user interfaces) are conceptual crossroads of technology, law and economics that can be gainfully applied to the design, development and deployment of networked IM systems. These four concepts offer useful analytical categories of systems analysis through which technology, economics and law can come together to simultaneously address issues of security, privacy and liability mitigation in massively distributed IM systems.

In particular, since the technologies of IM systems are their most highly developed component, it is helpful to adopt a conceptual framework that can leverage that ubiquity. The concepts of standards, metrics, feedback and reliability are familiar to engineers engaged in any technology system design and analysis. Engineers spend time thinking about each of these concepts, even if they are referenced by other names. This chapter advocates for their application to the people and institutions in socio-technical systems as well.

The four concepts relate to one another and to IM operation in the cloud as follows: engendering user *trust* (of all types of user/stakeholders) can be readily understood as among the fundamental design requirements of IM systems. From an engineering perspective, IM systems can be engineered to be *reliable*, which earns them reputations for being predictable and *trust*worthy. To determine the extent to which a system, including an IM system, is trustworthy, reliable and predictable, it must be evaluated against *standards*. The quantitative evaluation of system performance against standards generates *metrics* of performance. Metrics of performance can be fed back to various IM system stakeholders through tailored *feedback UIs* to enable them to perceive the extent to which IM systems are reliable and predictable, based on metrics that they consider most relevant to inform their system-oriented behaviours. IM systems that present metrics demonstrating system performance within standards of performance can be said to be reliable and trustworthy, which can be said to then satisfy the system design requirement of engendering user *trust*.

Socio-technical feedback loops of the type described above are called 'markets' in economic parlance and 'rule making' or 'politics' in social and political contexts; and indeed markets and politics might be considered to be learning systems, given their weighted inputs and outputs. Those same feedback loops can be 'primed' if any of the four concepts is stabilized, such as where government regulations establish performance *standards* that define markets, or where new technology enables new system *metrics* that launch new markets like fibre-optic communications, or Moore's law's iterations in enabling circuit measurement at ever smaller scales.

Brief reflection reveals that these stakeholder feedback loops inform a variety of emergent communication structures, from the natural standardization of bird-songs in territorial displays to political polling and all other information channels in between. The ubiquity of these feedback loops in developing information systems suggests that the consideration of their four constituent concepts can be fruitfully applied to configuring the system architecture of future IM systems at even larger scales and in a distributed manner.

When the four concepts are brought together in designing, developing and deploying systems that can reliably address these stakeholder needs, they will help to identify shared metrics and standards that can help stakeholders to understand the interdependence of their IM interactions in an increasingly networked world and will form the kernels for new institutions of governance for distributed IM systems: distributed governance for the distributed internet.

Following this introduction, the chapter proceeds in the next section with a review of the problem landscape that also reveals candidate strategies for solutions. The following sections provide a brief introduction to the concept of systems engineering as it might be applied to those problems and a survey of the problem and solution landscape. The four related concepts of trust/reliability, standards, metrics and feedback/UIs are then each developed in separate sections as parts of the solution.

As will become evident in the discussion, when systems engineering with feedback is applied to human and institutional issues, it is often called 'governance'. Indeed, trust frameworks can be thought of as hybrid technology, people and institutional governance documents. Among the goals of these documents of governance structures is the iterated reduction of risk and the creation of leverage for stakeholders as IM systems grow, which helps individuals and institutions to interact with greater confidence through networked IM systems (aka the 'cloud').

Review of the networked IM problem landscape

This introduction surveys the risk and opportunity landscapes in which IM systems currently operate, in an effort to inform future systems engineering requirements for IM systems that might better address security, privacy and risk/liability issues.

Just as physical landscapes can be mapped with different standard perspectives and sets of metrics (consider, for example, topographical maps versus political maps versus average rainfall maps of a given region), so too can IM risk and opportunity landscapes be mapped with different perspectives and metrics. One architectural requirement for sustainable risk-reduction processes is that every stakeholder should have access to relevant metrics to inform their interactions in the system. No metrics = no transparency = no trust. In this chapter, the risk landscapes are mapped with reference to stakeholder concerns as described in each of the separate disciplines of technology, law and economics. Systems engineering approaches will help to integrate these separate perspectives, metrics and maps based on risk profiles of common data actions (like collection, disposal, storage, matching, etc.) which are the quanta of mediated social, economic and other interactions in IM settings.

Each of the disciplines of technology, law and economics generates a story or narrative, told in the language of that discipline, about various types of systems that help people and institutions to design, develop, deploy and deal with those systems. As socio-technical systems, IM systems are amenable to development and evaluation through the combined disciplines and metrics of technology, law and economics. Each discipline has, in its own ways, already affected the organization and operation of current IM systems. However, the design and development process for networked IM is ongoing in each of these domains and additional benefits can be gleaned if the paradigms and models of these separate disciplines can be brought together in a more integrated fashion in hybrid systems of engineered structures to address the unique challenges of distributed IM systems. That is the focus of this chapter.

The unique challenges of IM systems

Before turning to solutions, it is necessary to understand the problems. Current IM systems have developed a variety of unique characteristics that are at the root of current problems with IM. IM systems are: (i) constantly new (and unmeasured), (ii) dynamic, (iii) interdisciplinary, (iv) complex, (v) recursive, (vi) socio-technical, (vii) distributed and (viii) networked. Each of these qualities, taken alone, results in new challenges and opportunities for IM system stakeholders. Taken together, they compound the effects of all the others, creating massive complexity that resists one-dimensional analysis and control. The sum of the overall system complexity is much greater than the parts. Some of these challenges are unprecedented, and others are 'old wine in new bottles', but all are amenable to systems engineering-based solutions integrating technical, legal and economic analyses.

Later sections of this chapter will suggest that each of these problem areas is also a source of solutions when seen through the four lenses of trust/reliability, standards, metrics and feedback UIs. In fact, from an entrepreneurial-risk perspective, each 'problem' reflects an opportunity for finding solutions and charts a path to new value creation for IM stakeholders.

(i) IM is constantly new and unmeasured

New technologies have always had new social implications. As new technologies have taken the lead in creating new capacities, economics and law (and the measurements upon which they rely) have typically more slowly followed, helping to define how those capacities are deployed after the fact. Notwithstanding the lag time, the disciplines of engineering, economics and law have all already contributed to the achievement of successful IM architectures, albeit each through its own, relatively isolated discipline. Today's massively interoperable IM structures have achieved huge successes in advancing IM adoption and reliability, notwithstanding the ongoing concerns of security, privacy, risk/liability, etc., giving us the systems upon which we rely so heavily today. They are far from perfect, but are clearly serviceable.

All of that development has taken place in regulatory and industry economic-model landscapes that are often decades old and are increasingly unable to accommodate new technological capacities and their corresponding new risks and value propositions. Existing disciplines are based on old institutions that reflect old divisions of thinking and old measurements; new technologies invite new interdisciplinary approaches to both.

This lag is not news, but it remains an unaddressed problem. It can be most effectively addressed through new feedback/market/rule-making processes that can generate new interaction-integrity metrics, based on new standards of IM performance, that can enable reliability to turn into trust.

(ii) IM is a dynamic operating environment

The reliability of engineered systems is measured by examining system performance metrics against standards. Where a dynamic environment exceeds the operating parameters assumed in establishing such standards, the reliability of the system cannot be measured and it cannot be governed or controlled, increasing the threat of harm.

Dynamic operating environments therefore make it more difficult to identify and deploy system standards, which in turn makes it more difficult to achieve reliability and risk reduction at large scales. It is clear that IM takes place in a highly dynamic environment from technical, legal and economic perspectives and that it promises to continue to change rapidly into the future. The dynamics of rapidly changing environments (whether physical, economic or social) challenge system standardization, which in turn undermines their reliability and predictability, raising risk. The adoption of standards is based on certain assumptions about the bounding of system performance dynamics.

Massively distributed, networked IM systems operate in highly changeable environments, where operating parameters have not been established in technical, legal or economic domains. In fact, the emergence of social networks and the Internet of Things has the result that the highly dynamic variables of user behaviours, stakeholder context, subjective needs and market considerations of information and identity are now part of IM operating environments, adding to their dynamism. These factors combine to resist generalization and standardization, and depend on real-time feedback loops to maintain optimal system performance.

(iii) IM systems are interdisciplinary

As discussed below, IM systems are socio-technical. This means that their operation depends on both technologies and people (acting alone and in groups). This is increasingly true as the Internet of Things becomes realized. IM systems must be trusted if they are to be adopted, and reliability is a prerequisite to trust. The introduction of people into IM operations as part of social networks, crowdsourcing and data rights markets invites consideration of what causes people and groups to act more or less reliably.

These questions are not comprehensively answered in the engineering or computer science departments of universities, but also are the subject of analysis in disciplines as diverse as law, economics, anthropology, sociology, political science, psychology, sociology, philosophy, religion, language studies, environmental studies and a host of other people-focused disciplines.

Solutions that are informed by those multiple disciplines involving the study of people acting individually and in groups will likely be more familiar and comfortable to individual and institutional stakeholders, and might therefore enjoy the steepest adoption curves.

(iv) IM systems are complex

Engineering solutions are most easily applied to those systems that are characterized by the fewest parameters and which therefore display more predictable, linear behaviours over time. However, most systems in the real world, including networked IM systems, are sufficiently complex that they also display non-linear behaviours (i.e. those outside of periodic or other expected performance and operating parameters – like earthquakes and stock market crashes) that can result in substantial harms if they cause system function to vary from the optimal performance parameters of engineered systems.

Non-linear behaviours are characteristic of complex systems deployed in technology, economic and legal environments and cannot be engineered away. Of course, efforts to engineer solutions to complexity should continue, but it is also possible to achieve system resiliency through other means, such as avoidance of risk, absorption of risk, dissipation of risk, sharing of risk and other strategies. These strategies frequently depend on co-ordination of group behaviours through mechanisms of governance and enforceable promises, both of which help to stabilize interactions through time, which can be analysed and measured through the compound lens of law, economics and other applied social sciences.

(v) IM systems display recursive feedback

Efforts to control systems operating in complex environments sometimes rely on feedback systems that include inputs that are affected by that same system's outputs. A system of a thermostat and a boiler operating in a temperate climate is a good example. The system both detects and reacts to changing environmental conditions and to changes in optimal temperature set by the home-owner. Markets are similarly recursive in their detection and reaction to price and risk environments. IM systems operating in networked settings are similarly recursive at multiple levels of operations among various communities of interest.

Specifically, IM systems are complex, hybrid recursive systems that involve various sorts of technical, economic and legal feedback mechanisms, through which system outputs and metrics in each domain are made available to other system components (including other people in their role as 'system components'), which informs the future behaviour of those components engaging with those same systems. The resulting informed behaviour of those components in turn affects those metrics further, *ad infinitum*. These forms of recursive feedback are both a source of additional complexity and a source of solutions. For example, in acoustics, feedback is typically an irritation for audiences, but rock guitarist Jimi Hendrix frequently used it to create new, positive aesthetic effects.

(vi) IM systems are socio-technical

Modern information and identity management systems are a special class of complex system because they are not merely complex systems involving a large variety of technical inputs but are socio-technical systems. Socio-technical systems are those that operate with both technical and human inputs in the course of normal operation. They are systems the operation of which depends on both technologies and people acting individually and in groups (aka 'institutions').

For example, a hammer is a technology, and a managed construction crew with equipment is a socio-technical system. A car is a technology, and a car and driver is a socio-technical system; as is a city traffic system of drivers, vehicles, traffic signs and police. A credit card is a technology, but the payment card system including cards, card readers, telecommunications equipment, data-processing facilities, banks, retail stores and consumers is a socio-technical system.

Information management has traditionally been viewed as a set of technologies, but the term 'information management' increasingly refers both to the technologies and the people and institutions that produce, consume and handle data. These multiple uses of the term should not be permitted to obscure the roles and value of people acting in socio-technical systems.

In socio-technical systems such as networked IM, the behaviours of both technology and people must be rendered reliable. A question for systems engineers and system stakeholders involved in socio-technical systems such as IM systems is how might this be best accomplished for systems that combine technology and people, and in particular how might it be accomplished in hybrid socio-technical settings such as IM.

Evidence that the systems are only partially engineered, and that the role of people in IM is in need of additional (legal and economic) engineering, is presented by evidence that most or all data-breach events are caused by people, rather than by technology, and by the continuing challenges of transferring data about people across national borders.

(vii) Networked IM is distributed

IM systems are increasingly distributed. In fact, it is increasingly rare to find an IM system that is isolated from other IM systems. This is a result of multiple factors including (i) cost considerations and general trends towards outsourcing, (ii) the enhanced leverage and risk-reduction opportunities from networked IM and (iii) the intrinsic distributed architecture of the internet (as conceived by Paul Baran for the RAND corporation in 1966), which affects the architectures of those IM systems that connect to the internet. Distributed systems do not lend themselves to centralized management and hierarchical governance.

(viii) IM systems are networked

IM systems are heavily networked and interconnected, reflecting the success of technical standards and interoperability. Networked technologies unlock new value and entirely new challenges. Consider, for example, the historical network effects upon the technology of the steam engine (railway networks), the electric dynamo (electrical grids), the internal combustion engine (highway system) and electro-magnetic modulation (telephone and television networks). In each case, the combination of instances of the technology into broad networks ushered in new value propositions, and new challenges.

The same is true of IM; as its network connectivity increases, new opportunities and challenges arise. The challenges include the fact that networking increases interaction points, which increases risk. However, the enhanced leverage of networking creates convenience that leads to dependencies that are hard to overcome. This creates a risk of 'lock-in', where a user is economically (and even socially and emotionally) compelled to continue to use a service.

Systems engineering of hybrid solutions

Engineering, economics and law are typically considered to be separate disciplines that each purport to render different aspects of human needs more reliable and predictable, and they do so in different ways.

Engineering offers reliability in human interactions with physical systems, economics in the economic interactions of market space and law in the interaction risks of social space. Their separate analyses are each based on different conceptions about leverage and risk reduction for individuals and entities, and their practices each manifest in different types of formal institutions that standardize processes to perpetuate those leverage and risk-reduction benefits. Each discipline also relies upon stakeholders to communicate their respective needs in different ways (through specifications, markets and legislation/contracts, respectively) that are applied as 'requirements' and 'goals' to inform the approaches of the respective disciplines.

Networked and distributed IM systems are socio-technical systems that invite stakeholders to simultaneously consider the benefits of engineering, economics and law, but the interaction of these disciplines is not yet structured. Systems engineering approaches, combined with transaction-cost accounting and standard contractual solutions, together offer the promise of providing hybrid solutions that can best address the hybrid challenges of socio-technical systems such as IM.

The systems engineering approach

The term 'systems engineering' generally describes an approach to integrated design and management of complex systems over their entire life cycles, and it is applied loosely here to invite consideration of its interdisciplinary reach. Many current challenges in increasingly complex IM systems might be addressed through systems engineering-type approaches; specifically, those that can incorporate economic and legal analyses for socio-technical systems.

Systems engineering generally

The area of systems engineering has evolved significantly since the 1950s as systems have become increasingly complex. There are a variety of established strategies of systems engineering, for example Quality Function Deployment (QFD), Universal Systems Language (USL), Integrated Definitions (IDEF) and Unified Modeling Language (UML) that offer established techniques for achieving systems engineering goals. This chapter will not attempt to describe or directly apply these strategies but introduces them as having potential value for enhanced system design, development and deployment strategies where complex legal and other social structuring mechanisms need to be integrated into the system design criteria and operations, such as in the case of IM systems.

Who will lead distributed IM systems engineering?

Who will be the 'systems engineers' to engage in the design, development and deployment activity? Where will future 'data governance' structures reside? It is a challenge to identify the institutional actors from within the various silos that can embrace that broader, cross-silo perspective. Simply stated, no one country or company is big enough to fill the role. In fact, the current institutional tendency is to avoid costs for the development of seemingly remote enhancements with benefits across sectors, and instead to free ride on the efforts of others.

This hesitancy to lead (described by game theory and theories of the commons) creates a substantial hurdle, but also an opportunity for those organizations that are willing to embrace a more comprehensive view and to fill the void and to suggest 'best practices' structures as candidates for adoption as standards in markets. The presentation of those candidates will take place in the registries of trust frameworks that are in the process of being assembled that will highlight the various solutions of IM professionals.

Applying systems engineering at large scale, in a distributed system, and including consideration of legal and policy engineering opportunities in those designs will help to bring these still-separate IM subsystems into ever-greater interoperability at all levels, including across current sectoral and jurisdictional boundaries. Law and economics offer external scaffolding for human and institutional choices that can help to hold previously siloed systems together while these interoperability connections are developing. Accomplishment of these cross-sectoral and cross-jurisdictional information flows, with adequate management of security, privacy and liability, is among the fundamental challenges of moving to the next stage of functionality and value creation on the internet; and is the work of the next generation of IM professionals.

Trust and reliability

An earlier section of this chapter set forth various unique challenges presented by emerging IM structures, including the challenges of trust and reliability in distributed IM settings. This section expands the discussion of the role of *trust* in building socio-technical systems, and how the measurable *reliability* of engineered systems offers a pathway to establishing trusted, distributed IM systems.

The need for reliability and trust

The development of future distributed IM will be hampered if IM systems are not perceived as reliable and trustworthy. Reliability and trustworthiness are also prerequisites to broad adoption, which is needed to manifest the network effects of broad consensus around operating rules, itself a precursor to risk mitigation at large scales. Trust and reliability are foundational to stable systems of interaction risk reduction through networked IM.

Under current system architectures and rules, cloud service providers, social networks and other online IM service providers find it difficult to accommodate all the varied expectations of users while at the same time avoiding conflicts between users in a multi-tenant environment and among their own internal policies. These variables, together with an inconsistent and uncertain global legal framework, lack of transparency, risk of lock-in and loss of direct control have, to date, limited trust in distributed IM systems and cloud computing. That lack of trust is limiting growth of these areas of critical information infrastructure. Without solutions to these problems the application of cloud computing and networked IM services could be limited to non-critical services or information; and the true potential of cloud services to enable us to address our most pressing problems will go unfulfilled.

The challenge facing IM professionals is to make distributed IM systems and cloud computing a suitable solution for services and information with high assurance requirements, and to do so at predictable cost, thus reconciling the open and multi-tenant nature of the cloud with the need to manage and process the entire spectrum of information, from the most highly critical and sensitive information to single data points.

For distributed IM systems to be reliable and secure, and therefore trustworthy, systems of accounting for these data flows need to be engineered simultaneously in technical, legal and economic domains. The term 'accounting' in this context means both 'tracking' and 'sharing benefits'. Realization of the promise of distributed IM systems in the cloud hinges on delivering data interaction reliability in the face of increasing relationship complexity so as to earn trust. As noted below, interactions are composed of 'actions', and the concept of 'data actions' is introduced as offering a set of universal landmarks for the development of hybrid technical, legal and economic standards and metrics to help achieve trust.

The relationship of trust and reliability

Trust is the foundation of reliable relationships among individuals and groups, and conversely reliability is a foundation of trusted relationships. Reliability and trust are tightly coupled, suggesting that addressing one can affect the other. This is a key starting point for approaching systems engineering of distributed IM systems. Even though the concept of directly engineering *trust* is elusive and awkward (and frankly a bit off-putting), the concept of engineering *reliable* systems is familiar and provides a hook for applying engineering solutions to human and institutional trust challenges.

Reliability and trust in socio-technical systems

Why is 'reliability' a good starting point? IM systems are socio-technical, meaning that their operation is dependent on the actions of people and technology. People and institutions make adoption and use decisions in IM systems based on their level of trust. Their level of trust is, in turn, affected by their perception of the reliability of those systems. The current lack of trust is expressed in the disparate languages of privacy, security and liability litigation concerns. Those issues create trust 'wastelands' in IM system landscapes – areas that cannot be developed to their maximum potential because of the shadows cast by those ambiguous (and currently unmeasured) concerns. How might those multiple concerns be simultaneously addressed, and trust enhanced, in distributed IM systems? How can socio-technical IM systems be made more reliable so that they can earn trust?

The technological elements of socio-technical systems such as IM are rendered reliable by conformity to standard specifications, with conformity demonstrated by the presentation of metrics of relevant performance criteria measured against the relevant variables set forth in those specifications. By contrast, the people (and by extension the institutional) elements of socio-technical systems such as IM are not rendered more reliable by conformity to technical specifications; they are rendered reliable by conformity to rules and laws, with their own set of metrics of conformity. Socio-technical IM systems can be made reliable only by the application of hybrid technology *tools* and legal/policy *rules*, documented in trust frameworks.

How can reliable tools and rules enhance IM reliability, trust and security?

There are many settings in which hybrid 'tools and rules' solutions already mitigate risk and enhance security, providing examples of these hybrid deployments. Consider that a stoplight combines technology (the light) and rules (stop on red) to reduce the risks of driving. In fact, the red light is a global standard that has had huge risk-mitigation benefits over the years in reducing the incidence of accidents, and huge cost benefits in eliminating the harms of expense and human misery that would have been caused by those avoided accidents. Reflection on the variety of everyday risks quickly reveals the familiarity of 'tools and rules' solutions. Consider that your car is currently safely parked in the parking lot, protected by tools (door locks) and rules (do not steal cars).

Tools and rules don't just reduce risk and offer security in the physical world. There are also examples of tools and rules operating together in the world of intangibles and various 'rights markets' (such as financial markets, commodities markets, insurance markets, etc.). For example, all of the world's financial, securities and commodities markets are based on standard rules that are integrated with information and identity technologies (i.e. for accounts and communications) to help convert a subset of unknown market risks into known, quantifiable risks that can be managed. Those markets cannot control all risks of complex markets; but the risk mitigation relating to market interactions that they can accomplish, presented to and referenceable by stakeholders in various forms of registries of interactions, permits stakeholders to allocate various unknown risks in those markets. For example, the normalization of trading in the orange juice futures market eliminates those trading variables, enabling participants to allocate the risks of uncontrollable weather affecting the crops.

Other markets that rely on tools and rules include those formal markets and informal supply chains of telecommunications, shipping, energy and a host of others. There are even examples of the application of tools-and-rules engineered systems in the online identity space, albeit primarily in the business-to-business context to date (such as the Transglobal Secure Collaboration Program, Safe Bio-Pharm, InCommon), or in carefully tailored business-to-customer space (such as the PCI-DSS payment card system rules). In each case, tools and rules come together to enable the reliable operation of systems that are built on the trust of their stakeholders.

How does law create reliability of the human components of IM?

'Engineered' legal rules and technology tools structures create enforceable duties imposed upon remote parties that other parties in the system can better rely upon and trust, thus enhancing the reliability and predictability of their behaviours in the future. The burden of law is called a 'duty' and the corresponding benefit of that duty is called a 'right'. Where those duties and rights are standardized across populations, the behaviour of multitudes can be made more predictable and reliable, eliciting trust by demonstration of an ability to mitigate the interaction risks of the erratic behaviours of others.

Duties (and their corresponding rights) are made possible through either compulsion or invitation, and both operate in legal systems to reduce interaction risk. In the case of compulsion, there must be sufficient authority (such as nation-state or other sovereign sub-part) and ability to coerce uniformity so as to render the system reliable. A sovereign might be defined, in this context, as having the monopoly of legitimate coercion in a system (legitimated by the deference of affected populations).

In the case of global challenges, however, the traditional forms of nation state-based compulsion are not available, since sovereignty is currently bound to nation-state structures, none of which covers the globe. The difficulties in addressing global problems like global warming, emerging diseases, energy policy, financial markets, resource usage, sustainable water practices and the like are evidence of the absence of meta-nation-state compulsory authority. By definition, sovereigns can make and break promises with impunity.

In the absence of global systems of compulsion to drive the imposition of duties, invitation for parties (including the nation-states themselves) to voluntarily 'self-bind' to duties is the only alternative strategy for constructing uniform, standard duties for trust and reliability. This means that each stakeholder must perceive it as being in their respective self-interest, without compulsion, to take on duties as a prerequisite to their being bound. For this to occur, they must perceive that self-binding will yield benefits in the aggregate that outweigh the burdens of the duties they assume as part of the arrangements, employing whatever calculus suits them so as to address the myriad considerations of that analysis.

Such a utilitarian analysis is engaged in by all individuals and institutions contemplating entry into a binding agreement. Each party (individual or entity) can be motivated by whatever sets of agenda suit them, but ultimately they must decide voluntarily whether they will join the effort, by whatever decision pathway leads them there. This analysis is different for every individual and entity, and the landscape of the aggregate of those many decision-making processes helps to trace out the recursive and paradoxical relationship of reliability and trust and how they affect security, privacy and liability mitigation. These myriad relationships are worked out at scale in markets, which form to address the shared risk of communities of interest.

The path from individual liabilities to governance systems, and from duties to rights

The identification and performance of standardized duties of 'obligated' parties (such as takes place in markets for services) creates corresponding rights in 'benefited' parties. Without enforceable duties, rights are just words on paper. Thus, the threat of imposition of penalties (aka 'good liabilities') on system actors can encourage reliable performance of duties that can give life to rights.

The types of rights that can be animated by duties include those rights that are currently at issue in the discussions of security, privacy and liability mitigation. Each of these concerns can be stated as involving the absence of a stakeholder right of some sort. Thus, by engineering duties, IM systems designers can indirectly engineer rights. The interrelationship of duties and rights among stakeholders in different roles, and the engineering of those relationships, is the substance of legal engineering for IM systems.

Once the duties/rights relationship is revealed by the consideration that rights are mere words if they are not respected with corresponding duties (to act or forbear from acting in a certain way in a particular context) that affect the behaviour of other parties, it becomes clear that we can engineer rights indirectly by engineering good liabilities to encourage system-friendly duties to be performed. Once we can indirectly engineer rights, it is simply a matter of knowing what rights we want to engineer. For that standard set of system rights requirements to be defined, along with their respective metrics to confirm performance, we need stakeholder participation-based rule making and governance processes that can operate across scales at multiple levels of population and group complexity. Those processes are anticipated in the Feedback/UI discussion below.

Standards

The preceding section described the role of reliability in fostering system trust, both prerequisites to broad system adoption and the proper functioning of distributed IM systems. In this section, the topic of standards is explored in greater depth, particularly with respect to its application in distributed IM systems. Standards are a stepping-stone to reliability, since the degree to which a system is standardized can help to establish the extent to which its operation will be reliable and predictable. Standards enable the measurement of system performance that provides evidence of reliable and predictable performance. Measurements and metrics are discussed in the next section.

Technical standards are already a familiar concept in engineering, which makes standards a leading candidate for inclusion in the systems engineering toolkit for enhancing IM system reliability and trust. Processes similar to those of technical standard setting, when applied to legal and economic elements of distributed IM systems, have the potential for delivering the same interoperability benefits for IM systems as they provide for other engineered systems. They can foster interoperability and scale, both of which are prerequisites to unleashing new forms of leverage and risk reduction.

This section starts with a very brief sketch of technical standard-setting processes and goals. Following the technical discussion, the socio-technical nature of IM is explored and the question of the potential for processes of legal standard setting is raised. The concept of legal standard setting is made more familiar by noting that various processes already occur through which uniform laws and rules establish uniform behavioural duties (aka 'legal standards'), promulgated by governments and private parties to reduce risk and increase leverage through legal interoperability.

The role of technical standards in interoperability

Ever since Eli Whitney developed the concept of interchangeable parts in manufacturing, standards have played a role in commerce. In the same way as standards enable individual parts of a product to be made uniformly, enabling the scaling of manufacturing, so too do standards enable the operation of engineered systems to be uniform, enabling their interoperability and the scaling of networks. As interoperability is a prerequisite to achieving scale in distributed IM systems, standards have once again become a centre of attention. The distributed technology called the internet is built on the interoperability of its parts, mapped by technical standards.

Traditional technical standard-setting processes

The role of standards and standard-setting processes is well known in technical circles. A technical standard is an established requirement for a system. Sometimes technical standards emerge as the natural result of the broad adoption of a product or service offering of a single company. This is called a *de facto* standard. Standards can also be created by agreement among multiple entities through standards processes (such as the myriad technical standards of IETF (Internet Engineering Task Force) and SWIFT financial messaging standards), or even by the compulsory requirements of law (such as electrical standards under building codes).

Where systems are built or operated by multiple entities, they must engage in processes to enable agreed-upon standards to be developed among those entities. In these processes a number of stakeholders (typically commercial enterprises, but also governments and occasionally civil society representatives) get together to identify core technologies in a system that are relied upon by multiple stakeholders in a system, and for which standards would therefore have broad benefits. These standards processes generally follow the pattern of the five stages of rule making (agenda setting–problem identification–decision–implementation–evaluation) set forth by Porter and Ronit (2006) and discussed further below.

The output of a technical standard-setting process carves out an intellectual property 'safe space' that enables technical interoperability to thrive. Specifically, the output includes a specification document and arrangements for patent cross-licensing (or similar arrangements). The specification document defines the scope of the standard and other details necessary for its implementation, and the patent licence (or other agreement) is an undertaking by each participating stakeholder to cross-license patents (or to not assert patents) that they hold that 'read on' the standard. In other words, the stakeholders agree not to sue each other for patent infringement for implementations built within the scope of the specification, and to make licenses available to one another on fair, reasonable and non-discriminatory terms (FRAND terms) for the implementations of patents within the scope of the standard. This is a risk-reduction safe space tailored to the risks of technical interoperability.

In effect, standards create intellectual property (IP) 'non-assertion zones' in which the development of each company's part of larger interoperable systems can take place with reduced risk of unexpected legal and economic consequences of IP infringement. This is critical in systems deployed within multiple inputs or extended supply chains (like mobile devices) and those that involve broadly distributed platforms (like online apps), where the 'patent thicket' (i.e. the complex cross-cutting rights of patents) would otherwise prevent system development. Distributed IM systems will continue to rely on standards.

What should distributed IM standards address?

IM systems are socio-technical systems, so IM standards should address technology and people issues, standardizing technology tools and people rules. As noted elsewhere in this chapter, systems of technology are made reliable by conformity to standard specifications. Systems of people are made reliable by assigning them specific duties so that their behaviour is in conformance with standard rules in contracts and public law and regulation, giving rise to rights. Rights are an emergent phenomenon of predictable duties.

When people in networked information systems handle data that is about other people or in which other people have an interest, they act as part of the socio-technical apparatus that comprises the networked information system. Their decisions affect system performance, and a lack of decision guidance in the form of enforceable legal standards can result in their exercise of discretion in a way that is inconsistent with overall system performance. This is what happens, for example, when an employee violates company policy by taking home unencrypted personal information on a laptop, and then leaves the laptop on a bus. Enforceable, standardized rules can provide support to technology tools built to standard specifications so as to enhance the reliability of overall socio-technical system performance, such as in IM systems.

Because they depend on the behaviour of people, distributed IM systems require both standard technology tools and legal rules in order to achieve overall reliability. The two must work together, hand in glove, along with input from other disciplines such as economics (for incentives and penalty structures), network theory (for evaluating emergent system properties), information theory (to integrate the disciplines) and other areas to design, develop and deploy effective data, information and identity infrastructures that are needed to support commercial, social and political infrastructures in the coming years. The development of networked information structures to date has not been characterized by collaborative work across domains, but has chiefly been viewed as a technical domain. Future IM systems will depend on IM professionals who can help to integrate these domains; focus on types of data actions can help to bring the needed disciplines together.

What do legal standards look like?

Technical standards were described above, but what might legal standards look like? The concept is initially strange, but legal standards are, in fact, quite familiar. They are part of our everyday lives in the form of laws, regulations and standard form contracts that guide individual and institutional behaviours in a variety of settings. Modern banking and finance, telecommunications, energy, transportation, resource and other systems are built on legal standards expressed in law and contract. Traffic rules, rules of commerce, rules of administration of educational and governmental institutions and myriad other sets of rules shape the behaviours of vast populations. Processes of law generate these artefacts of human efforts and processes to standardize and normalize human behaviour so as to reduce the risk inherent in interactions and increase the leverage of individuals acting in groups. Cohesive social, economic, political and other group structures are the result.

How do rules standardize human and institutional behaviour in IM systems?

Under legal analysis, generally speaking, a stakeholder is typically held responsible for the harms caused by their nonconformity to duties either placed upon them (by compulsory laws and regulations) or which they voluntarily took on (through contracts). The extent of nonconformity is typically the basis for liability and the payment of compensatory damages (and, in some cases, punitive damages that are meant to create additional disincentives for nonconforming behaviours).

The analysis of responsibility in law is determined by asking a simple set of questions. Was a party's right violated by another party failing to act in conformance with a duty owed to the harmed party? Did a particular party have a duty to do X action (or forbear from Y action)? Did they do X action (or forbear from Y action)? If they violated their duty and did not do X action (or did not forbear from Y action), did their failure to act (or failure to forbear) violate the right of another party, causing damage to that other party? How bad was the damage, and what should be the penalty? The answers to this series of questions inform the question of liability and are expressible as a legal algorithm:

Right + Legal Duty + Breach + Causation + Damages = Liability

Looking at the algorithm, it becomes obvious how legal engineering to support stakeholder rights might be accomplished through the engineering of sets of duties, since these are the roots of liability. There is no liability without a duty. There are no rights without duties. A quick glance at any legislation, regulation or contract quickly reveals that it is composed as a recitation of duties. Legal standards in contracts and legislation establish duties for people engaging in myriad interactions in a variety of settings as a way of creating a 'social network effect' that can help to mitigate risk and increase leverage opportunities. The larger the populations included, the greater the risk mitigation and leverage. Law (in legislation and contracts) is duty engineering to make people's behaviours more reliable and predictable.

Trust frameworks document hybrid standards to foster socio-technical system interoperability

As noted in the discussion above, standards documented in specifications can help systems to achieve technical interoperability. Hybrid trust frameworks that delineate standards for technical and user IM system behaviours act as behavioural specifications that can help to identify interoperability opportunities at both tools and rules levels, and provide additional guidance towards identifying potential interconnections with separate socio-technical systems as well. Trust frameworks have been helpful in the area of online federated identity systems, where the data associated with identity needs to be shared reliably among multiple systems. Those federations are linked together by both technology and policy standards documented in trust frameworks. What is an analytical construct through which engineers, lawyers and economists can be brought together to consider their varying definitions of risk in a setting of common concern?

Trust frameworks are data 'action' maps for navigating IM interaction risks

Engineers, attorneys and economists all care about the action of system components. The actions of components of systems are of interest to both engineers and attorneys, since both are responsible for making those actions among stakeholders (aka 'interactions') more reliable. Engineers design, develop and deploy systems to enhance the reliability of technology actions, and attorneys do so with respect to people's actions. Actions describe the responses of socio-technical system components to the dynamic environments in which systems operate, and the point at which conformity to performance criteria is measured.

Attention to data actions by both engineers and attorneys suggests that 'data verbs' may be a fruitful point of intersection for designing hybrid tools and rules in socio-technical systems; and a common focus of organizational design and operational measurement. This is confirmed by the tendency of the debates about privacy, security and liability to take place in the context of questions about various data actions such as collection, transfer, disposal, etc. Data actions are where the risk arising from interactions is spawned, and where it can be best addressed.

Reliable data actions taken by individuals, entities and devices reduce the risks of information interactions. Data actions are also the focus of data governance. Consider that both engineers and attorneys already have developed language and structures that seek to deal with data collection, data use, data transfer and data disposal, suggesting the relevance of such actions in both domains, but they have not yet done so in an integrated way. Trust frameworks offer that opportunity.

Metrics
The role of system metrics

If systems and subsystems are to be trusted by their stakeholders, they must be perceived as being reliable. The reliability of a system is based on the predictability of its performance as measured against standards of operation. Metrics are drawn from measurements of the performance of systems against standards. Reliability asks whether the system fulfilled expectations, typically with reference to specifications and rules upon which those expectations are founded. Those standards are established in specifications for technology and in rules and laws for people and institutions. Together, these tools and rules help to make socio-technical systems reliable. The feedback of those metrics to stakeholders, through accessible UIs, as a foundation of markets, representative political systems, observed norms of social and cultural behaviours, and other 'autocatalytic' systems of distributed governance is discussed in the next section.

The illness of lack of measurement at the root of IM challenges

Current distributed IM systems are perceived as being insufficiently private, insecure and risky from a liability perspective. The perception of a lack of reliability in each of these contexts is rooted in a lack of measurement of these system deficiencies against standards. How might the many facets of 'privacy' be measured? How can security be precisely measured?

In the absence of measurement and standards, it is not possible to evaluate relative levels of risk across multiple interactions, and not possible to negotiate allocations of liability among stakeholders, since the issues of context and stakeholder subjectivity overwhelm the analysis in the absence of a common set of measurements to guide the discussion. That is the current state of play in networked IM. The lack of standard measurements has the result that each of these types of risk cannot be evaluated from one transaction to another and across sets of related transactions (aka a 'market setting'). The lack of metrics prevents communication among stakeholders and evaluation of risk from one transaction to another. Systems engineering approaches that identify metrics that are relevant across multiple disciplines can help to address these challenges and to create the lines of communication that are necessary to render 'systems of systems' reliable.

If the system cannot be shown to act reliably, stakeholders will not trust the system and will not voluntarily join it, undermining the leverage and value propositions of system scale from the network effect that is at the heart of the value proposition of many global networked systems. Networks need virtuous cycles of measurement, reporting and adjustment so as to remain stable in dynamic environments.

The quantification of system performance baseline measurement in technology and law

System designers establish a variety of parameters that together form the baseline for evaluating system performance. Each performance parameter can be compared to the actual operation of the system, with the degree of conformity or variance to that parameter measured. Each such parameter establishes a dimension of system quantification; and the monitoring of those multiple measurement dimensions through feedback UIs enables governance of the system by and among stakeholders. Once system elements are quantified, stakeholders can apply the various metrics to monitor, value and create the social structures of markets. Law is not that different; system conformity is measured to establish responsibility and liability.

Consider, for example, that if a taxpayer miscalculates their taxes in the tax system, they are sent an assessment by the government for the balance (plus interest and penalties that vary with the severity of the variance). Similarly, failure to pay a monthly credit card balance in full leads to the imposition of interest (and possibly late-payment penalties). Note, however, that in the latter case the business model of consumer credit is based on the assumption that cardholders will not pay their entire balance on time, revealing credit cards as a convenient form of consumer credit. The US government doesn't have an interest in being a lender with respect to the amount of variance, but the credit card-issuing bank does. Thus, the exact same action (of not paying debts as they become due) is in one case (taxes) a variance from optimal system parameters, while in the other case (credit cards) it is essential to the business plan on which the system is based. Action is the common point of analysis in these different systems.

A similar paradox will be present in data interactions as well, and the paradoxes help to identify useful system metrics. Take the example of the current battles over privacy in online social networks and services settings. For example, the optimal system performance of a social network is geared to maximize its revenue. That revenue depends on advertising based on recordation of data about interactions, and the making available of that data to advertisers to inform them about future buying habits of consumers. The data has value to the advertisers because it helps them to more effectively target advertising. The better the data, the more accurate their inference about future buying behaviour. To pursue their business model, online service providers will be incentivized to extract as much data about as many intimate details as possible about individual people. That is optimal for monetization in the advertising model.

From the point of view of the individual data subject, however, the degree of inference that is made possible for advertisers with fine-grained data is perceived as an intrusion and is perceived to be inconsistent with optimal system performance from their perspective.

Thus, as in the 'failure to pay' example above, the single action of data collection yields two different and conflicting perspectives on optimal system performance. A single metric of the degree of value/harm of the information derived from data could inform both the advertiser and the data subject in their respective perspectives. The establishment of common measurements converts paradox into communication and can support the resolution of conflicts and establishment of markets in which the values of such interests are set. Metrics play a key role in this market negotiation, including allowing for the scaling of markets.

Shared metrics allow multiple parties with different interests to have a conversation. In the example above, if insight and intrusion are viewed as two ends of a single metric, that metric could support the negotiation of the parties about the issue. If they don't share a metric, that discussion cannot take place. The shared metric in this case might be the degree of intrusion/inference.

Objective metrics for elements of socio-technical systems

Metrics are most valuable when they are objective and repeatable. Metrics are familiar in engineering and useful in technical operations, where they are typically objectively measurable directly from system technical operation. But engineering has not traditionally provided comprehensive theories and analytical constructs or metrics to understand and evaluate human behaviours in socio-technical systems. Fortunately, those insights are available through economic and legal analyses and other emerging forms of applied social science that already embrace metrics, albeit often established based on correlations rather than causation, which can cause engineers some discomfort. For example, the economic analyses of transaction-cost accounting are applied to give a sense of stakeholders' respective motivations in complying with IM system rules. Legal analysis is typically associated with the measurement of stakeholders' performance of duties (against the duties standards set forth in laws, regulations and contracts).

Approaches to measurement

The hackneyed phrase 'what gets measured gets done' suggests the importance of measurement in motivating particular actions. In socio-technical systems, measurements are used to evaluate system performance against parameters to make sure that relevant aspects of the system, upon which stakeholders rely, get done. To date, most IM systems have generated separate sets of metrics associated with technical and individual performance. For more comprehensive integration of socio-technical IM systems, it is necessary to identify approaches to measurement that can more simultaneously address both technical and non-technical considerations.

Feedback/UIs
The role of feedback in systems

Feedback is the bane of acoustical engineers, where unwanted signals (aka 'noise') propagate and eventually drown out desired signals. That same propagation can be helpful where feedback involves desired signals, such as signals of risk-related metrics in statistically 'noisy' dynamic IM environments. The generation of metrics is of greatest use if the measurements are made available in accessible form to all stakeholders so as to help inform their interaction decisions in networks in real time, which in turn generates additional metrics, *ad infinitum*. Feedback/UIs are needed to feed and refresh the trust cycle for reliable and secure distributed IM.

Through mechanisms providing feedback on IM system performance, individuals and organizations can continuously refresh their understanding of the effectiveness of those systems in the myriad environments in which they are deployed. Feedback is not a new concept for organizations to understand their market environments, but it has quickly matured from the simple suggestion box, complaint department or market research of the last century's systems into sophisticated systems where organizations and individuals have access to broad and deep data about stakeholder behaviours, sufficient to convert detailed consumer feedback into 'feed-forward' systems that can predict consumer behaviour, rather than wait for it to occur. Individuals and organizations need access to feedback systems from data and identity systems and markets that can provide them with standard metrics of IM system performance in real time to help inform their interaction decisions in those same data and identity systems and markets.

Feedback is not new

Individuals are already experienced in using feedback UIs to interact with complex systems. Examples include the dashboard of a car for driving, apps on mobile devices for global communication and data sharing among their multiple communities of interest, or using tax-preparation software to complete a tax return. Feedback UIs are where standards, metrics and reliability/trust come together to reduce the stakeholder's risk in interacting with complex systems. It is where mediated interactions take place through dashboards, UIs and automated interfaces that deploy those standards and metrics in an effort to achieve and demonstrate reliability and hence earn trust and market share.

Feedback operates inside and outside of organizations

In distributed IM systems, feedback is an integral part of system operation both within and among entities. The former (feedback within organizations) is illustrated by the relationships among divisions in an organization. For example, the sales department will provide metrics of orders placed to inform the operation of the shipping department and the manufacturing department regarding product demand, and those departments will in turn inform sales about delivery schedules and availability. In the traditional model of business, these operational feedback loops took place within an organization, i.e. among the employees of an organization. The presumption (if not the reality) was that there was greater reliability if these feedback loops did not extend their dependencies outside of the business organization.

The outsourcing revolution of the past several decades has taken place because IM has improved to the extent that businesses and governments can access richer information demonstrating the operational reliability of other entities so that they can 'trust' third parties to undertake critical operations on their behalf. Outsourcing depends on reliable information feedback loops operating outside of organizations. Outsourcing is now the norm for various mission-critical processes such as shipping, payroll, data processing, advertising and other areas, each of which represents a business feedback process that is necessary for operations, but which is now outsourced.

IM is already being outsourced to the cloud at many levels of service (such as software as a service, platform as a service, etc.), and online identity (ID) functionality for organizations (called ICAM – identity, credentialling and access management) is being outsourced to federated identity systems. The maturity of this form of identity outsourcing is revealed by taking into account those *de facto* federated identity systems that are an incidental result of the broad use of online social networks, marketplaces, app stores, search and other online interaction mediation services from which a myriad data attributes can be collected to inform identity enquiries. At these early stages of that IM and ID outsourcing transition, issues of trust, risk and reliability are at the fore.

Outsourcing mechanisms involve feedback among organizations, which operates outside of individual operating entities, in the markets and supply chains in which they interact. The emergence of competitive markets for IM services (in the cloud and modern outsourced ICAM systems) gives rise to additional feedback loops that operate outside of the control of any one stakeholder, giving rise to new risks (and new leveraging opportunities) and calls for new standards and new metrics to capture emerging rights and duties. It is in these contexts that registries and contract analysis and construction tools can serve an important support function of identifying best practices of technology, law and business models as candidates for standardization *among* organizations.

Feedback UIs are needed for IM rules enforcement

Feedback UIs serve stakeholder needs by enabling rules enforcement. Engaged stakeholders can help to monitor system performance in a form of IM system 'neighbourhood watch' when they are provided with current updates of system performance against optimal rules. This is an important form of rules enforcement for distributed IM systems.

However, the fact that such crowdsourced solutions benefit all users can lead to new emerging challenges, such as the 'free-rider' problem (where some system stakeholders don't carry their fair share of the burdens of system operation). The interdisciplinary approach suggested in this chapter can better address these emerging system issues than a mere technical approach could standing alone. For example, in the case of free-rider problem, the economic analyses and metrics and the legal dispute-resolution processes can be engineered to shape the system so as to expose and reduce the incentives for free riders.

Feedback processes support governance processes that outline future IM institutions

Feedback processes relating to human and institutional behaviour in social settings are called rule making. Porter and Ronit (2006) posited that governance (rule making) systems share five basic steps in a feedback process similar to that described in this chapter. These steps include agenda setting, problem identification, decision, implementation and review. These line up nicely with the concepts of trust/reliability, standards, metrics and feedback/UIs. These five processes are engaged in by all organizations, whether commercial, governmental or otherwise, as part of their initial exercises in stating their business plan (for commercial entities) or mission statement (for civil society organizations) or scope of authority (for governmental organizations). They are also engaged in, more prosaically, any time that an organization starts a new programme, negotiates a new contract or takes other actions. The five steps trace out a rule-making feedback process that is relied on at many levels to help engineered and rules-based systems to evolve to meet dynamic operating environments.

If Porter and Ronit's five steps are considered in the context of broad IM services markets, they suggest how existing and new institutions and groups might fill various roles in those various steps, and how they might be loosely coupled in rules meta-structures to provide virtual feedback UI infrastructures in mature IM services markets. Trust frameworks are the documents that set forth the rules and tools for the operation of these data meta-infrastructures, and are the building blocks of future IM distributed service markets.

Trust frameworks structure feedback/UIs and anticipate IM governance structures

The rules of an organization or group of organizations relating to the use of data and identity are increasingly called a 'trust framework'. The trust framework is the constitutional document of an organization relating to data and identity handling and use. Most organizations have not yet constituted their data and identity policies in a single trust framework document, but they still have various policies and approaches to data and identity that are set forth in multiple documents and policies across the organization. The forcing function of regulatory compliance in some jurisdictions and market pressures in others is consolidating data and identity policies towards more coherent trust frameworks. Each trust framework details the technological and legal/policy rules that affect data flows that conform to that trust framework, frequently cross-referencing other relevant standards. For instance, online service providers frequently set forth their policies and rules for engagement with customers and suppliers in online terms of service and privacy policies, which are, in effect, trust frameworks. Trust frameworks operating at different levels provide the rules of data and identity flow within and among organizations, and hence provide a narrative map of their interaction structures. Since trust frameworks reveal the gross interaction anatomy of an organization, they can be seen as foundational governance documents for IM governance.

In fact, as information markets become more valuable and dynamic, and IM services more interoperable, they will test the limits of organizational internal operations, and an organization's 'fitness' will increasingly be a function of the quality of its information flows. This will make the trust framework (whether or not composed in a single document) as important as a company's articles and bylaws and other contracts. Each of these documents, in effect, 'programs' the organization, but it is the trust framework documents that define the feedback mechanisms for the interaction decisions that take place in real time, and in the ordinary course of business, such as movements of data and identity in the customer and supplier chains of relationships.

Given the emergence of IM challenges in the areas of privacy, security and liability mitigation, it seems clear that the future will see the emergence of standardized tools and rules as IM institutions address these challenges at scale. Today's feedback mechanisms at the contract level are all candidates for tomorrow's IM institutions.

Reference

Porter, T. and Ronit, K. (2006) *Self-regulation as Policy Process: the multiple and criss-crossing stages of private rulemaking*, Policy Sciences, Springer.

CHAPTER 6

Finding archived records in a digital age

Tim Gollins and Emma Bayne

Introduction

For an archive to be of real value, simply gathering and preserving records will never be sufficient; nor should it be. The ability for a user to find the records that answer their information needs must always accompany the task of keeping. Furthermore, presenting records in a way that allows understanding about the context of their creation is and remains essential to enabling users to interpret records and give them meaning. Preservation and findability truly go hand in hand – what real value does an archival collection have if it cannot be effectively used and interpreted?

This, in itself, is not a new challenge; the abstract problem of finding and understanding relevant records in a collection is as old as collections of records themselves. At The (UK) National Archives in London there are examples of 'finding aids' going back over 500 years, including one from 1575 which offers an early form of guidance on how to use complex Chancery records.[1]

The National Archives' catalogue had its genesis over 150 years ago in the annual reports that the Keeper of the Public Records provided to Parliament. These reports, beginning from the time that The National Archives (then known as the Public Record Office) was founded, quickly became the mechanism by which records could be found. Building on that legacy, generations of archivists developed a comprehensive printed catalogue with associated authority files and other finding aids.

As early as the 1980s computers began to be used to help archivists manage and structure the catalogue of hundreds of thousands of entries and produce it in paper form. These paper lists then became the basis for an electronic catalogue system used by National Archives staff to manage the collection. In April 2001, the first iteration of this electronic catalogue was made available online, revolutionizing the way users find records in the Archives. Since its release, The National Archives' catalogue has continued to grow and evolve as technology, the nature of the collection and users' needs and expectations have changed. It now holds many million entries, with more and more being added every week.

In this chapter we will discuss the latest evolution of The National Archives Catalogue, Discovery (http://discovery.nationalarchives.gov.uk/). We will discuss the ideas that underpin Discovery and illustrate how these can fundamentally change the users' perception of an archival catalogue. Finally, we will look to the future and speculate on the next steps in the Archives' transition to the digital, in so far as its catalogue is concerned.

The online catalogue

Did The National Archives' first online archival catalogue fulfil its apparent promise and enable easy access to the archive for all? Well no, not really.

The online catalogue did, very successfully, enable many more people to examine the catalogue in detail and get an impression of the vast array of holdings in the Archive. It did grant users on the internet the potential to find things in the Archive, and for many it did revolutionize their ability to actually find what they wanted. However, it also exposed a much deeper problem and, as a result, there were equally many more who were frustrated by the experience, unable to find what they wanted and left with the (often false) impression that the Archive did not contain what they sought.

To understand this problem we need to look much more closely at the nature of archival catalogues and understand how they may be perceived in the age of ubiquitous internet search.

The shape of the catalogue

The fundamental issue of representing the content of a library or archive holding in a catalogue is as old as libraries and archives themselves. The issue is beautifully illustrated in Umberto Eco's *The Name of the Rose*, in which the very layout of the labyrinthine medieval library is used to catalogue and find (or hide) the manuscripts that scholars desire.

Eco's library also illustrates another challenge: that the cataloguers themselves act as filters or projections on the collection. As William of Baskerville notes:

> the books are arranged according to the country of their origin, or the place where their authors were born, or, as in this instance, the place where they should have been born. The Librarians told themselves Virgil the grammarian was born in Toulouse by mistake; he should have been born in the western islands. They corrected the errors of nature.
>
> (Eco, 1983, 335)

Unlike Eco's library (or indeed any library with a more conventional catalogue), an archival catalogue is structured to reflect the context in which the records were originally created; this is done to enable the user to understand the purpose of the records in their historical context, and thus to aid accurate interpretation. This structure derives directly from the definition of a record, being the account of an event or activity conducted by an entity (organization or individual). This is quite distinct from a publication or a book in a library, which is catalogued by 'subject' or author.

As a result, the archival catalogue arrangement does not necessarily reflect the specific subject matter contained in the record; for example, the minutes of an organization's board meeting may discuss any number of subjects with which the organization is engaged but will all be catalogued together. Nevertheless, with experience, knowledge of the history of the originating organization and other domain knowledge, the traditional paper catalogue enabled the archivists to assist users in finding what they needed; and, of course, over time more regular users become skilled at understanding and using the paper catalogue themselves.

Putting the catalogue online did give more users access; but it also implicitly required them to learn how to use and understand the Archives' hierarchical information structure, in other words, to become to some degree experts in using archival catalogues. While a proportion of online users did learn these new skills, very many did not. Although putting the catalogue online did increase access, it did not necessarily increase either the findability of the content of the Archives or its interpretation. Many users were lost in the labyrinth.

The wider adoption of the internet led to increasing access and use of all things digital. As The National Archives placed more digital material online and exposed it to the internet, a more diverse and substantially larger community became aware of and began to use the Archives. As more material was available online, The National Archives had to look for new ways to explain how to understand the records, as users were no longer necessarily co-located with expert staff on-site, as they are when researching paper material in the Archives itself.

Some users found what they were looking for, especially if their research needs were simple. Unfortunately there are many examples of simple research needs that require complex searching – the path through the labyrinth may take many turns. Thus, many users were disappointed. They found the catalogue opaque, were confused by how it was arranged and were unable to find the answers they were looking for. In many cases they assumed that the Archives held nothing of interest, when in fact it may have been a rich source of very relevant but hidden information. A particular case in point are the Chancery records we have already mentioned that, from a catalogue perspective, look dry and uninteresting. However, in reality they contain a rich tapestry of human and political stories over many hundreds of years, as they record the activities of both the Crown and population as they take matters of dispute to law.

This is the challenge to which The National Archives continues to respond – how to make a vast, complex archival collection easily accessible and understandable to all. To do this we needed to start at the beginning with considering the core purpose of the catalogue.

The purpose of an archival catalogue

An archival catalogue has three roles:

1   to enable the archivist to manage, structure and arrange a collection and to know where to find the records in the repository
2   to enable interpretation of individual records in a clear context reflecting the circumstances of their creation
3   to enable finding (discovery) of records by the user.

A catalogue produced on paper has necessarily to fulfil all three roles with one structure and it does so by using a whole set of features including its layout and the structure of its referencing scheme. It may include specific authority files (which provide control and consistency for distinct topics such as place names and people), and finding aids designed and optimized for certain records or types of frequent enquiry.

When it comes to putting catalogues online for the first time, archives have in essence done exactly that; they have made the paper catalogue available digitally – in broad terms the structure and presentation of the material has remained largely unchanged. At the time this was of course the only reasonable approach; when doing something new, it is generally a good idea to at least start from something known and understood. However, after nearly ten years' experience of this approach and with understanding of its benefits and disadvantages, the opportunity to improve things arose.

Over time, in addition to 'The Catalogue', The National Archives made available a number of other catalogues, lists, finding aids and databases describing either new or specific parts of its collection in more or less detail. Unfortunately, while it achieved the goal of wider access by enabling more people to get to the resources, the result was fragmented and disparate systems which were hard for users to comprehend and exploit coherently.

In the remainder of this chapter we will discuss how a new approach has enabled The National Archives to deliver a cohesive discovery experience for the user, while retaining the capability to continue to efficiently and effectively manage and interpret the collection. In addition, a careful analysis has led to the realization that there is an underlying abstraction that can be used not only to unify the finding of all record resources, but also to provide direct access to content when this is in its various digital forms.

The collection

The paper holdings of The National Archives at Kew are over 1 billion paper pages (representing 1000 years of history).[2] At the same time there are now over 2.5 billion archived pages accessible from the UK Government Web Archive (representing less than 20 years of contemporary history) (The National Archives, 2013, 8).

As time goes by the nature of the record continues to change; for example, a recent high-profile public inquiry regards the digital video recording of its hearings as the definitive record of testimony, rather than the traditional text produced by the court stenographer (Leveson, 2014). These different types and representations of records are producing new challenges, not only for their presentation but also with regard to their cataloguing to enable users to find and understand them.

The paper collection

The National Archives holds one of the most complete international archives in the world, which contains government records from the Domesday book of 1086 to today. It covers the central government of the United Kingdom, which has changed extensively over the last thousand years. Some key examples are the medieval and later Chancery records already mentioned; the records of the Cabinet – the supreme decision-making body in British Government – which show why and how major decisions have been made since World War 1; extensive personnel and administrative records from both world wars; and large volumes of foreign relations material relating to the former British colonies.

Finding records in this collection is supported by a range of digital, on-site and remote services. Where material is not available digitally, users can remotely order copies on demand. Free access to all paper original and digitally available records is provided on site at The National Archives as a fundamental aspect of the Archives' role in supporting government transparency and accountability in our democratic society under the rule of law.

The digitized collection

The National Archives has been digitizing records in bulk since 2001.[3] As users' expectations to access material at home rose, it became clear that there was an opportunity to improve user experience and access by making material available online. The National Archives has done this via a number of routes. These include working with a range of commercial and academic partners, along with publishing some material itself. Using a variety of digitization solutions has enabled The National Archives to digitize millions of records at pace, and to provide a competitive online offering for finding archival records.

Many users expect everything to be digitally available immediately because so much of our day-to-day lives is now online. With over 1 billion pages in the collection, it would be unrealistic both economically and logistically to digitize it all. By choosing to digitize material with high interest and usage and with strong research potential, findability and access to the most popular content have increased. This also ensures the preservation of the paper originals – instead of thousands of people handling the original records, millions can download them from anywhere in the world. For example in financial year 2013–14, 204 million documents were downloaded by users (through direct online services or those of licensed associates).[4]

When records are digitized, key pieces of information found within them are transcribed and added to the descriptions. This value-added content is key to improving search and thus also improving access to this material.

Some may wonder why the technology of optical character recognition (OCR), which is now ubiquitously applied to cheques processed by banks and the books scanned by Google Books, is not applied to digitized records to enable them to be easily searched. The answer is threefold. First, the majority of records that have been scanned and the information of most interest are often handwritten (the printed sections are often the boilerplate of forms) and the efficient and effective OCR of handwriting in general (unlike cheques, which have a very limited vocabulary) is still a matter of deep research. Second is the nature of records, often disparate sheets with different structures and layouts and typing of poor quality on poor-quality paper, makes the application of OCR and interpretation of the results extremely challenging and again a matter for research. And third is the volume of text created and the errors that will still inevitably occur, these both presenting enormous challenges even for the most modern search systems, as we will discuss below.

The born-digital collection

The latest big challenge for The National Archives is born-digital records. This is a huge step change, probably the biggest challenge faced since first setting up the Archives. All current practices are based on paper, where there is extensive knowledge and experience, and now we must translate this into a digital model to support the Archives in the future. There is an initial period of dual running when hybrid sets of records containing both paper and digital must be added to the collection, catalogued, and made accessible too.

When paper records are added to the collection they are structured in a logical way based on the content; descriptions are manually provided based on a review of the records; and their references are manually created based on the content and structure of the material. This is a process which has been honed over hundreds of years. Fundamentally, there is a finite number of paper records that an institution can produce, manage and hold within the resource and space constraints it works with.

With digital records, many of these challenges are no longer relevant, nor apply. First, the volume issue changes significantly, as it is possible, as we all know, to fit huge amounts of data into a tiny physical space, and so the scale of the challenge has changed in terms of volume. The National Archives estimates that it will need 2 petabytes (equal to 2.1 million gigabytes) of storage for (non-Web Archive) born-digital records in its collection by 2020. This is simply an internal estimate created by one of the present authors for planning purposes in 2011.

The National Archives continues to handle more conventionally produced born-digital records separately from the UK Government Web Archive. This approach is a purely pragmatic one. The mechanisms and policies for selection, preservation and presentation of the UK Government Web Archive are quite distinct and the uniformity of the format of the data in that collection enables a much more automated process. As already remarked, the UK Government Web Archive represents a very substantial proportion of The National Archives collection in terms of both byte count and numbers of web pages archived. The UK Government Web Archive is crawled, preserved and hosted under contract with a commercial partner and is represented in the catalogue through a relatively small number of top-level descriptions. These descriptions then point to the sequence of periodic crawls (three or four times a year as a typical pattern) of each website concerned.[5] The UK Government Web Archive is indexed by Google and also has its own separate browse and search capability optimized for the particular volume and shape of that collection.[6]

For the more conventional born-digital records that represent the continuity from the papers, minutes and memoranda of the paper era, there are large-scale changes too in terms of both hierarchy and descriptions. Following a number of pilots with born-digital records, The National Archives has made a number of decisions about how to select and catalogue this material. Digital files are created on IT systems in government departments within native and local folder structures and these structures provide a natural hierarchy. The descriptions are provided by the file names and supplemented by any further information the creating institution can provide. An automatic referencing schema for digital records has been adopted which uses a randomly created sequence of letters and numbers to create a unique identifier. These decisions have been made to enable a pragmatic approach, moving forward. Using the same models as are used for paper records would not be sustainable as record volumes increase.

Born-digital records come in a wide variety of file types and formats. A record could be a website, a digital photograph, a presentation, an e-mail conversation, a Twitter feed, a YouTube video or a dataset in structured XML. These digital files offer lots of opportunities and challenges in terms of search, access and reuse. We will discuss some of these opportunities and challenges below.

Changing expectations

Archival catalogues were first conceived, designed and built by archivists for archivists, so a level of implicit knowledge was assumed. Putting a catalogue online for use by a mass audience is a very different proposition. To give an idea of the scale of the challenge of presenting a catalogue to this new audience, The National Archives' catalogue, Discovery, had over 5.5 million visits in 2014, and at the time of writing contains 21,724,000 entries for documents held at the Kew site and 10,726,000 entries for documents held at other archives. Discovery analytical data, available via an internal back-office application,[7] shows that there were 5,649,123 visits to Discovery from 1 January 2014 to 31 December 2014. Experience from providing advice and support to some of these users shows the huge variety of research needs and their varying complexity across the full spectrum of the collection.

In the past, the stereotypical user of the Archives was the academic historian sitting in the reading room. For The National Archives this pattern has now fundamentally changed, and the stereotypical user is now a family historian working online. However, services are not built just for the stereotypical user: they have to be built to support all users. To do this, The National Archives adopted a user-centred design approach and user personas, artificially constructed characters which represent common behaviours, goals and desires, to design a catalogue which meets a wide range of user needs from absolute novice to expert archivist. This approach is also used across all of The National Archives' digital services. Discovery provides a way of finding and accessing our collection, while the website provides much guidance and help to understand it. Considering services in a holistic fashion, beyond just the catalogue, gives much benefit and ensures a consistent user experience.

Research behaviours are constantly evolving as the types of records published and the supporting materials used change. Archives have moved from photocopies of documents available at their physical location to digitized copies and born-digital documents, datasets, images and e-mails available immediately online from anywhere; and from supporting explanatory printed paper leaflets to podcasts, online research guides, mobile apps and publishing catalogue data via an API (Application Programming Interface). It is an archival revolution. For all users the development of a society that is increasingly mediated through online and digital media results in new expectations of the service that an archive must deliver. As users' expectations increase, they fundamentally change the economics and make-up of the services archives must provide.

Search and its challenges

The difference between search and browse is one of the key changes in finding behaviours as archives move from paper to digital. Browsing through pages in a paper catalogue to find the records you need to consult, supported by a chapter list at the front and an index at the back, is the paper search model. Once online, this model is turned on its head. You search an index primarily, which is supported by guidance for particular topics (similar to chapters in the paper model) and browse the catalogue hierarchy. This completely changes the experience and skills needed by both the researcher and the archivist. It also adds a new skill-set – the digital tools themselves and the digital specialist who optimizes the underlying system. The archivist alone no longer provides the model for finding records: it is done by an electronic, automatic tool.

Users' expectations are set by their experiences of using online services. In terms of search, this generally amounts to the 'Google search model'. You type in what you want to find in your own terms and the search engine finds it immediately. Google holds nearly 90% of the search market and is currently considered the world leader in search solutions.[8] Google uses a number of methods to determine how results are ordered. The first and best-known algorithm is PageRank:

> PageRank works by counting the number and quality of links to a page to determine a rough estimate of how important the website is. The underlying assumption is that more important websites are likely to receive more links from other websites.[9]

http://en.wikipedia.org/wiki/PageRank

When doing archival research, you are sometimes looking for the most 'important' record related to a search term. A good example here is Jane Austen's will. If you search The National Archives' catalogue for this, we would make the assumption that you are searching for the famous author's will, due to the commonality of this name and the fact this will is in one of our collections. However, if you are searching for, say, your great-great-grandfather William Crooke's will you want to find the 'right' William Crooke, the one you are related to, not the most important one. The most important thing to you is that he is your ancestor. This means that The National Archives uses a custom search logic, iterated on the basis of testing and feedback, to combat its specific data challenges and try to make finding the record you need as easy as possible.[10]

There will always be issues around certain aspects of searching the collection. If your ancestor was named 'John Smith', you are going to face challenges.[11] The ancestors of 'Fawcett Hagbert Bugge' will be a little luckier![12] The National Archives is currently undertaking some research with the Institute of Historical Research, the University of Brighton and the University of Leiden into linking up individuals across different records using implicit facts such as name, date of birth, place of birth, individual's military numbers, etc.[13] Using these facts, we can analyse data and offer a percentage likelihood that the 'Samuel Michaels' mentioned in one record is the same as another. This could offer some interesting search solutions in the future.

Elements like advanced search help with these challenges, but the Archives' usage figures show that only about 5% of users use these facilities.[14] To help with this, The National Archives provides search tools designed for specific areas of research. This reduces the volume of records being searched, as it adds a number of limitations and also helps those users with less experience of using archives. Thirteen per cent of searches in Discovery are carried out using these tools,[15] so they clearly add much value to users and, in turn, improve findability of records.

Date is a very common piece of information held about a record, but dating practices have changed over the years and so they do offer a real challenge to archival users. An example is dating by regnal years, based on how long the monarch has been on the throne, which is common in archival material. Using a variety of date formats – especially obsolete and little-understood ones – when searching does not help users to find material. Discovery, The National Archives' catalogue, uses one date format in search and filtering, as all dates have been converted into the same formats using a range of complex conversion scripts. Using digital capabilities to normalize and improve data is one of the main ways of enabling users to find records. The original date formats are still maintained on the details pages of each record, as they are still an important part of that document's history.

One might naïvely expect that the issue of dating a document would be much simpler in the digital age. Unfortunately this is not the case; rather than the absence of date information, born-digital records often come with a plethora of associated dates within the document and in the metadata (so-called 'data about data') that accompanies it. For example, a simple Microsoft Word file containing the minutes of a board meeting held on 5 November 1997 could easily have the following dates:

• The date when the file was created (e.g. 7 November 1997) – recorded in the file system on which the document was first stored but also possibly in hidden data within the Microsoft Word document itself.
• The date when the file was last modified (e.g. 25 June 2004) – again recorded on the file system or also in hidden data (this because someone printed the document in 2004 and saved it afterwards by mistake).
• The date when the file was last read (e.g. 28 November 2014) – recorded in the file system where the document has been held in the department immediately prior to transfer because someone looked at the file to appraise it).
• The date of the meeting implicit in the title of the document (e.g. 5 November 1997 – board-minutes-97-11-05).
• The date in the footer of the document (e.g. 7 December 1997) –

recorded when the last 'real modifications' were made to the document following its approval at the following month's meeting.

This becomes a real challenge for processing born-digital materials, as the increasing volume of materials requires archives to automatically process such materials rather than have archivists use their experience and domain knowledge to establish a reliable date as they would with paper materials. In addition, archives now have to date all individual documents, as the registry systems that organized paper documents by date into files (the level to which most paper documents are catalogued) appear to have largely fallen out of use in the digital age. For different documents that have been created and processed by different systems during their life cycle and have had different patterns of use, none of the date sources discussed above is uniformly reliable. Further, research will be needed to develop heuristics that can be automated to enable scalable and reliable dating of born-digital materials.

Using tools like filters and subject taxonomies is a useful way of assisting with search, especially when dealing with such a large collection of material. Allowing the user to narrow down, based on topic, date or collection, can make a daunting task seem more achievable and guide the user to the right result. Subject taxonomies also help with challenges like the changing use of language over time or words with multiple uses or meanings. Customized subject taxonomies are utilized in Discovery to help with these challenges.

The creation of a folksonomy by allowing users to tag records in Discovery is now giving The National Archives more insight into language and the approaches people take to using an archival collection, as well as improving the users' ability to find records of particular interest. Using their own words, a user can create a set of records that directly relate to their interests and return to this collection again and again.

The searching and findability of automatically generated descriptions and references of born-digital records is one of the main challenges that The National Archives is currently considering. Inconsistency in the structure and language of descriptions makes searching harder and reduces findability, as we will explain later. Further work will be needed to establish the best techniques for automatically extracting descriptions that will maintain consistency with the human-generated descriptions of paper records created in the past. This will be a real challenge, considering the large volumes of born-digital records that we foresee coming to the archive in the future.

It is impossible to predict what the future will bring, but imagine the possibilities for improving findability to support users' needs. These might include using OCR tools (as discussed above) to extract knowledge and create a précis of a typed record; and taking it even further, using these tools to automatically index handwritten material; using different types of searching based on implicit knowledge held within the digital files, such as by colour, document type or searching the audio content in a video to find that exact moment you are looking for. All of these suggest significant threads of research into the management and presentation of digital archival material.

Information retrieval in the archive

Some of the earliest work on modern information retrieval systems was conducted in the late 1960s by Cyril W. Cleverdon (Cleverdon, 1970)[16] in the classic sequence of experiments conducted at Cranfield University Library. This was followed by the seminal work of Gerald Salton (Salton, 1989) and his successors. At this time the focus of research was on library catalogues, where the fundamental concept was of a document representative containing a summary or description of the objects of interest (the human-crafted catalogue entry) being matched to a user's information need expressed as a collection of words. As time and computer technology evolved interest moved to directly indexing digital materials by extracting their full text and algorithmically constructing the document representative, eventually leading to the ubiquitous internet search engines we see today.

In contrast, and only in some respects, the classic archival catalogue, reliant on short, human-crafted descriptions of the content of paper records, has not advanced far from those earlier times. This is not a reflection of the technology, nor of the archival community's need, but of (i) the fundamental nature of most archives still being that of collections of paper and (ii) the resources available for cataloguing.

There are a number of underlying and fundamental considerations which are inherent in modern search systems. One of these is the idea that the language (vocabulary) of the query (the set of words chosen by the user to describe their need) and the language (vocabulary) of the document representatives may not be the same. Although a number of techniques have been researched over time to overcome this challenge, in practice this issue is often largely ignored and the matching between query and document representative is remarkably simple. This works in most modern cases because the texts of documents are relatively long (compared to the query) and contain very significant redundancies along with many terms which may be used for the same thing. Thus, in the overwhelming number of cases there are overlaps between the query vocabulary and the document representative vocabulary (i.e. the full text of the digital object).

In the case of archival catalogues describing paper documents from earlier times, however, this may not be the case. As a matter of principle cataloguers are asked to reflect the terminology of the document in their descriptions – for example, the inquest into the death of the unfortunate William Roles who died of 'dropsy' – an old term for the swelling of soft tissues due to the accumulation of excess water (The National Archives, ref. HCA 1/107/7). As the documents are nearly always from such earlier times and the descriptions are necessarily short, this quickly reduces the likelihood of an easy match with users' queries (unless they are particularly skilled and already know the vocabulary of the time they are researching). This mismatch is further compounded by the effect of the era in which the descriptions of paper documents were produced. We cannot help but observe and describe the past through the lens of our present experience, and archival cataloguers of the last 150 years were no different. Thus, not only do the short descriptions reflect the language of the document described but they may do so through the language of the time of the description.

The transition to the digital then brings further challenges, both in the domain of the born-digital documents and in the context of OCR from digitized materials as discussed above. Naïvely, the approach would be to take the full text of new born-digital materials and OCR and welcome this as the better and enhanced document representative in the catalogue and expose this for matching to users' queries.

Unfortunately this compounds the problem: we now have the situation where not only are the older materials described in a different language (vocabulary) but the number of terms available to match with the query is small. In comparison, the new digital materials are in a much more similar language (vocabulary) to the query and there are vastly more terms to match. In practice all the returns for most searches return a list of almost exclusively digital documents and the paper documents are nowhere to be seen. This is not a problem that can be overcome by tuning the search system, the mismatch is just too huge.

This problem has yet to be solved. There are possible approaches, but the way forward is unclear. Should the archive construct 'artificial' descriptions of born-digital materials of about the same length as the average description of a paper document? What would be the consequences for search effectiveness? How should such descriptions be created, and at what level in the catalogue? After all, most paper documents are not described individually; often only a summary of description of the box or folder in which they are held is produced. What would be the equivalent for a born-digital collection? These questions and others concerning how to present and represent born-digital collections lie at the heart of the challenge facing archives as their materials transition from paper to digital.

However, the combination of the need to industrialize and the potential need for different types of archival description offers an opportunity as much as a threat. In principle, certain facts may be automatically extracted from digital records, including dates (discussed above), personal names and places. In principle, summaries could be created using tools developed from the decades of research into text processing and information retrieval. None of these issues is trivial, the challenges of applying these techniques to the heterogeneous and messy data that form the future archival record is significant. However, such tools are within reach and investment in pragmatic and practical research and development will undoubtedly succeed in providing archivists with the essential tools they need.

New abstractions

In constructing the new Discovery catalogue at The National Archives, and to unify the archive users' experience in finding the materials they are looking for, the team recognized that the rigidity of the classical hierarchical archive catalogue was too limiting. Equally, they recognized that, for the existing catalogue, that hierarchy was critically important, as it contained and represented core facts and knowledge about the collection.

The approach that the team took was to develop an abstraction of the archival catalogue that would enable the existing catalogue to be faithfully represented but that would also permit many other data to be equally well represented.

At the core of this abstraction was the concept of an 'Information Asset'. This concept enables the representation both of individual documents or records and of aggregations of the same. 'Information Assets' may have a parent that might represent the node above in the classic archival catalogue hierarchy, but that could also represent the archive in which one or more assets are held. Information Assets thus also may have children that might represent the nodes at the next level down in the archival hierarchy, or that might represent aggregations of objects held in an archive as a whole.

The concept of an 'Information Asset View' was created that allows a specific subset of the properties of an asset (or indeed its parent asset) to be exposed for a particular purpose (for example, for indexing in search, or for display to a user). This is particularly important when indexing the classical catalogue entries for the Discovery search function where 'facts' about a record may be documented in the description of assets higher up the hierarchy (for example, at series level) and (following the best archival cataloguing advice) are not repeated in the descriptions of each of the child assets.

Furthermore, the concept of a 'Replica' of an asset was created. This might be used to describe a digitized form of a paper record or the transformation of a born-digital record into an alternative format.

Finally, borrowing from the concepts of Open Annotations, the idea of an 'annotation' of an asset was created, to allow additional values to be added to the catalogue. This can be used to represent tags or other flexible structures to aid the finding and interlinking of assets.

How the abstraction helps

Taken together, these abstractions, and the concrete technical implementation of them, have been used to implement the Discovery catalogue. This brings together both the finding (Discovery) of records held by The National Archives at Kew, and also the collections held in other archives around the country. For the records held at Kew it also enables new online 'delivery' services to be realized, where users who are not on site can view and download digitized copies of the records they seek (where these exist) or pre-order documents for when they visit the Archives in person.

The generality of the Information Asset abstraction also enables new and extended services to be developed to begin to address some wider challenges as The National Archives' collection begins to become more digital. The abstraction allows these services to be built without breaking the existing capabilities and also without having to create a patchwork of specialist systems, as was the case in previous times. One example of this is the 'Discovery Video Player' that enables access to the video recordings that are the formal record of the hearings of the Leveson Inquiry into the culture, practices and ethics of the press (Leveson, 2014).[17]

Conclusion

Archiving itself and the ability to find/understand/access the archive are inexorably intertwined; without the archived record there is nothing to access, and if it is not accessible there is little value in keeping the record. The advent of digital technology, as is so often the case, has only exacerbated this interdependency and serves only to highlight fundamental issues and questions at the heart of the keeping and finding of records.

We have tried to touch on some of these issues and questions by drawing on the experience of conceiving and developing The National Archives Discovery catalogue system. As is the nature of such explorations, we have managed to scratch the surface, and indeed many of the issues we highlight do not yet have fully satisfactory solutions. The wide team of cataloguers, archivists (digital and paper) and technical experts at The National Archives, whom we must thank for being so generous in helping us with facts and figures, continue to strive to tackle these issues as they arise.

A great deal of further research is needed into understanding the fundamental challenges and opportunities that sit at the core of finding and accessing digital archival material. This research must be grounded in the actuality of born-digital and digitized records as seen by archives and the information needs that the real, operational users bring when they try to fulfil that very deep need to find out something about the past. This research must also not dismiss lessons from the past. The clerks of the medieval Chancery whom we have called on implicitly in discussing the records that they kept may, in their own indexes and approaches, still provide insight and inspiration that could solve some challenges of the digital archive.

Archives take the long view. Our new approaches to finding archived records in a digital age will need a similar perspective.

References

Cleverdon, C. W. (1970) *The Effect of Variations in Relevance Assessments in Comparative Experimental Tests of Index Languages*, Cranfield, http://www.iva.dk/bh/Core%20Concepts%20in%20LIS/Cleverdon_1970.pdf.

Eco, U. (1983) *The Name of the Rose*, Harcourt.

Leveson, Lord (2014) *Inquiry into the Culture, Practices and Ethics of the Press*, http://webarchive.nationalarchives.gov.uk/20140122145147/http://www.levesoninquiry.org.uk/ – Video of Seminar 1: The competitive Pressures on the Press and the Impact on Journalism: First Session – LEV 1/192 – http://discovery.nationalarchives.gov.uk/details/r/C14016465.

Salton, G. (1989) *Automatic Text Processing*, Addison-Wesley Publishing Co.

The National Archives (2013) *Annual Report*, http://www.nationalarchives.gov.uk/documents/annual-report-12-13.pdf (the latest set of audited figures available).

Notes

1 Chancery started as the medieval English state's (the king's) writing office, responsible for the production of official documents. In later times it expanded to become the official route through which petitions to the king were addressed; and, by an often obscure process of delegation, Chancery acquired a distinct role as a court of equity, in which the chancellor (or judges under him) dispensed justice in cases which were (allegedly) not amenable to litigation in the courts of common law. These and other roles continued until the late 19th century, generating a vast collection of records. (See http://discovery.nationalarchives.gov.uk/details/r/C43.)

2 Although the exact figure could never be realistically determined, there are approximately 10–12 million entries in The National Archives' catalogue at 'piece' level, which typically represent a box of records. Each box contains typically 100 or more individual sheets of paper (often many more). Thus, it is more than likely that the collection contains more than 1 billion sheets of paper.

3 One of The National Archives' first large-scale digitizations was the 1901 Census, released 100 years after it was taken.

4 See www.nationalarchives.gov.uk/about/our-performance.htm.

5 For example, see HO 472 – 'UK Border Agency – Working In The UK Website', http://discovery.nationalarchives.gov.uk/details/r/C17940 and the

list of crawls at http://webarchive.nationalarchives.gov.uk/*/http://www.
ukba.homeoffice.gov.uk/workingintheuk/.

6 http://www.nationalarchives.gov.uk/webarchive/.

7 See the 'select all' query on Discovery at
http://discovery.nationalarchives.gov.uk/results/r?_q=* for the latest figures
at any time. See note 15.

8 http://www.cnet.com/uk/news/googles-u-k-search-share-dips-below-90-
percent/.

9 The Wikipedia citation is to:
http://web.archive.org/web/20111104131332/http://www.google.com/
competition/howgooglesearchworks.html (4th paragraph).

10 The simple search 'William Crookes's will' returns 413 entries;
http://discovery.nationalarchives.gov.uk/results/r?_dss=range&_q=William+
Crooke%27s+will, but by using the specific tools available four wills can be
quickly identified as possible candidates; http://discovery.nationalarchives.
gov.uk/results/r?_d=PROB&_dss=range&_ro=any&_p=1800&_hb=tna&_q
=William+AND+%22Crooke%22+AND+will.

11 A search for John Smith returns 72,500 entries;
http://discovery.nationalarchives.gov.uk/results/r?_q=John+Smith.

12 A search for Fawcett Hagbert Bugge returns four entries; http://discovery.
nationalarchives.gov.uk/results/r?_q=Fawcett+Hagbert+Bugge.

13 The research project, 'Traces through time: Prosopography in practice across
Big Data', is funded by the Arts and Humanities Research Council;
www.nationalarchives.gov.uk/about/traces-through-time.htm.

14 Discovery analytical data, available via internal back-office application, shows
that advanced searches accounted for 5.49% of searches undertaken in
September 2014, 5.54% in October 2014, 4.84% in November 2014 and 5.75%
in December 2014, which averages at about 5%.

15 Analytical data, available via internal back-office application, shows there were
738,515 searches run from the structured searches within The National
Archives' guidance pages from 1 January 2014 to 31 December 2014. There
were 5,649,123 visits to Discovery in the same period.

16 This research is summarized at www.iva.dk/bh/Core%20Concepts%20in%
20LIS/articles%20a-z/cleverdon.htm.

17 An example video can be found in LEV 1/1
(http://discovery.nationalarchives.gov.uk/browse/r/h/C14018285?v=h).

CHAPTER 7

Security: managing online risk

Barbara Endicott-Popovsky

At least weekly we hear about significant data breaches or cyber attacks that threaten the financial health and privacy of millions of online users, or describe attacks by nation-states or terrorist groups with a political or propagandistic agenda. To the citizen observer, it must appear that those responsible for managing networks are helpless to do anything about rising online crime and threats.

How did we get here? How did our online interconnectedness, which has created so many benefits, result in so many challenges? Have we been so enamoured of creating the next new digital device or online service that we didn't take time to consider the unintended consequences that we've introduced into our lives (Endicott-Popovsky, 2008)?

Drawing on the field of cognitive psychology for an answer, I would suggest that we have outdated mental models that have blinded our perceptions. Drawing on systems dynamics, I suggest that we have relied too heavily on linear thinking and lack the skills in systems thinking to have foreseen this or to think through effective solutions to resolve the online crisis we're in. Drawing on theories of criminal justice, I suggest that we have not incorporated deterrence into the development of online systems; as a result, our systems unintendedly encourage bad behaviour – something like leaving our back doors unlocked and our wallets sitting in full view on the kitchen table! Each of these explanations will be examined in this chapter, ending with an admonition about how we should think of ourselves and our activities online in order to stay reasonably safe.

Drawing on mental models

The mental-model theory of reasoning was developed by Princeton University psychologist Philip Johnson-Laird (Johnson-Laird, 1983) and further enhanced by Ruth M. J. Byrne (Byrne, 2005). A mental model describes how an individual perceives that reality and functions in the world by thinking through conceptual representations of external reality. The Scottish philosopher Kenneth Craik suggests that the human mind constructs these models in order to anticipate and predict events so that we humans can function effectively in the real world (Craik, 1943). An individual will rely on these models to solve problems, assess the potential consequences of those solutions and gauge their actions accordingly. It becomes a personal algorithm for living.

Jay Wright Forrester, the founder of Systems Dynamics, goes further, describing mental models as

> The image of the world around us, which we carry in our head ... Nobody in his head imagines all the world, government or country. He has only selected concepts, and relationships between them, and uses those to represent the real system.
>
> (Forrester, 1975)

Viewing the transition to digital through the lens of the mental-model theory of reasoning, the rapid march into the information age is assaulting our existing mental models, destroying them and replacing them with others that are emerging, or are yet to emerge. In other words, as we watch the industrial age recede in the rear-view mirror the information age replacing it is transforming our lives in many ways, whether we consciously realize it or not, requiring that we replace old mental models that no longer work. To gain an appreciation of the enormity of these changes, reflect for a moment on Table 7.1. Consider how the context of living in each age impacted the individual's daily experiences. There have been profound shifts in mental models that have occurred with each shift in the paradigm – how we advance in the world, how we work, what is our sense of time, how we solve problems and how we learn.

Table 7.1 Transformative paradigms (adapted from Covey, 1990)

Attribute	Agricultural age	Industrial age	Information age
Wealth	Land	Capital	Knowledge
Advancement	Conquest	Invention	Paradigm shifts
Time	Sun/seasons	Factory whistle	Time zones
Workplace	Farm	Capital equipment	Networks
Organizational structure	Family	Corporation	Collaboration
Tools	Plough	Machines	Networked computers
Problem solving	Self	Delegation	Integration
Knowledge	Generalized	Specialized	Interdisciplinary
Learning	Self-taught	Classroom	Online

The engine at the heart of the transition to digital and the information age is the internet. We've developed a dependence on internet technology that is apparent from Table 7.2, taken from a moving statistical report, which demonstrates its pervasiveness and growth by world region. The next major innovation that is underway, ubiquitous use of virtual worlds, is even more mind expanding, as we become our avatars and enter into life-like digital environments to attend school, consult with our physicians, even take vacations! With approximately 30% of the world's population surfing the internet today, think how our lives will change as saturation increases and we move to virtual worlds.

But how did we miss this? I suggest that we have been clinging to mental

Table 7.2 World internet usage (Internet World Stats, 2014)

World regions	Population (2014 est.)	Internet users 31 Dec. 2013	Internet users Latest data	Penetration (% population)	Growth 2000–14	Users % of table
Africa	1,125,721,038	4,514,400	**240,146,482**	21.3%	5,219.6%	8.6%
Asia	3,996,408,007	114,304,000	**1,265,143,702**	31.7%	1,006.8%	45.1%
Europe	825,802,657	105,096,093	**566,261,317**	68.6%	438.8%	20.2%
Middle East	231,062,860	3,284,800	**103,829,614**	44.9%	3,060.9%	3.7%
North America	353,860,227	108,096,800	**300,287,577**	84.9%	177.8%	10.7%
Latin America/ Caribbean	612,279,181	18,068,919	**302,006,016**	49.3%	1,571.4%	10.8%
Oceania/ Australia	36,724,649	7,620,480	**24,804,226**	67.5%	225.5%	0.9%
World total	7,181,858,619	360,985,492	**2,802,478,934**	39.0%	676.3%	100.0%

models from the physical world and the industrial age that blind us to the changes around us. The embrasure of technology is moving so fast that it's difficult to keep up with the unintended consequences of what this has done to our daily reality and how society as a whole functions. In one sense, we are rapidly smashing our industrial-age mental models, where organizations are structured in hierarchies, knowledge is structured by discipline, our work is in discrete silos – departments and sectors: military, government, industry, academia – and replacing them with interconnectedness that, as a by-product, also enables online fraud, online voting scams, illegal downloads, continuing threats to network security and wrongful prosecution for misunderstood 'internet crimes' (Green, 2008; Itzkoff, 2009; Moscaritolo, 2009; Stevens, 2009). But who saw this coming, and how long did it take us to realize where we've got ourselves to? Like Mickey Mouse as the Sorcerer's Apprentice in *Fantasia* (Disney, 1940), we have assumed the wizard's powers without anticipating the risks! What was meant for good has ushered in unexpected problems. The internet has brought convenience, savings and productivity, but it also has created troubling dislocations that we didn't anticipate.

Drawing on systems thinking

As they were going digital, IT innovators focused primarily on developing functionality – the next great application that would revolutionize our lives – isolating their thinking from how that achievement fitted into the greater whole. It wasn't until 2002 that Bill Gates drafted the famous 'Trustworthy Computing memo'[1] that announced a sea-change in Microsoft's research direction to concentrate on cybersecurity. Getting away from a functionality focus, we must consider the context in which we are introducing technology. General systems theory assists in conceptualizing unintended consequences and can help to describe where we are.

Applying systems thinking to going digital, intuitively, we're in what could be described as an 'arms race' with online adversaries that, given our current thinking, we are destined to continue with no resolution. As our system defences get better, the adversaries' skills must get better if they want to wage successful attacks. As their skills get better, we must improve our defences so as to repulse their attacks. This only serves to inspire adversaries to acquire even better skills and abilities, which then stimulates us to improve the security of our systems even more, and so on, in a never-ending pattern of escalation with no obvious way out.

From general systems theory (Senge, 1990), a system is defined as 'a collection of parts, which interact with each other to function as a whole' (Kim, 1992). Using this definition, the adversarial arms race just described behaves as a system. All systems require energy to run and maintain. They are self-perpetuating and stable – resistant to change. A system can be described schematically using a simple drawing, called an archetype, that identifies system components and the feedback loops holding them together in relationship to one another. Simply put, it explains how a system functions (Senge, 1990). Kim has identified a small, finite number of these archetypes which, either singly or in combination, are sufficient to describe behaviour in all systems, whether it be the human body, an organization or a computer system. Discovering which archetype applies in any one situation is a process of discovery by analogy using an inductive reasoning approach (Kim, 1992).

For example, attackers and targets can be viewed as behaving as a system, locked in a pattern of escalating behaviour in response to one another. Intuitively, this is an arms race, best described by Kim's escalation archetype (Figure 7.1).

In this instance, the state of a target's computer security (on the left) depends on the state of a malicious intruder's capabilities (on the right). The arrows indicate that the system state will transition from more to less secure

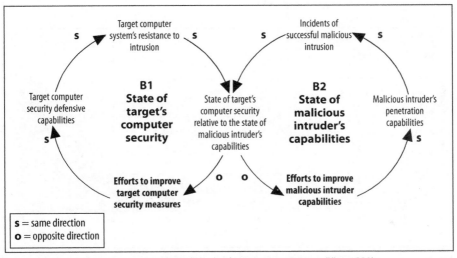

Figure 7.1 Escalation archetype applied to the hacker arms-race system (Kim, 1992)

and back again and, further, that the state of a malicious intruder's capabilities will transition from more to less capable and back again. In the language of systems, both sides are negative feedback loops, B1 and B2, meaning that they self-regulate, like a thermostat. When put together, they regulate against each other.

Several trends accelerate this escalation cycle, amplifying its effects, while at the same time our organizations are increasingly reliant on public networks, too often without tempering enthusiasm with a concern for security (Endicott-Popovsky, 2008).

1   **Increasingly sophisticated hacker tools.** With the advance of technology, it now takes less technical knowledge to launch increasingly sophisticated attacks using increasingly sophisticated hacker tools, fuelling the escalation cycle. This is an open invitation to those inclined towards online mischief or criminal behaviour.

2   **Increasing volume of attacks.** From 1998 to 2003, the CERT Coordination Center[2] for the Carnegie-Mellon Software Engineering Institute reported a dramatic escalation in cyber attacks (Byrne, 2005). By 2004, the use of widespread automated attack tools made tracking the numbers of incidents of little value, there were so many. The cumulative curve in Figure 7.2, derived from CERT data, provides visualization of this trend.

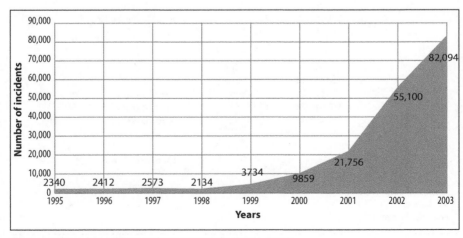

Figure 7.2 Cumulative CERT incidents 1995–2003 (Byrne, 2005)

With such a dramatic rise in incidents, one might ask why the situation continued unabated. Reports from organizations like PWC and Verizon continue to show increases in organizations' investments in security (PWC, 2014). Why, then, have these been so ineffective in stopping the escalation of the hacker arms race? Systems analysis offers answers.

All systems have vulnerabilities: built-in delays that make them 'wobble', reaction time limits and limits to the amount of change that they can endure before collapsing. According to systems theory, rather than directly 'attacking' a system, it is much better to analyse the way components are arranged, looking for vulnerabilities that can change the way the pieces interact (Covey, 1990; Itzkoff, 2009). To exit the hackers' arms race we must examine the system as a whole: identify its components, discover how the components interact and discover the system's vulnerabilities. This approach will lead to solutions for resolving any system, resulting in lasting change. Conversely, no matter how hard one pushes directly at a system, if no effort is made to change the way the components interact, any change will be only temporary. The system will eventually rebound to its original state.

Today the energy fuelling the system we've described originates with the intruders. Targets behave in response to them (Moscaritolo, 2009). Table 7.3 examines the conditions and characteristics of targets and intruders. Targets have an open-ended vulnerability in terms of the time and money they must invest to recover from attacks, while intruders can spend time at their discretion, incurring only nominal expenses, given that the hacker community generously shares its tools and exploits and all you need is a computer and access to a public network – both of which are inexpensive.

Table 7.3 Characterizing targets versus intruders

	Time	Costs	Consequences
Targets	Open-ended	Open-ended	Open-ended
Intruders	At their discretion	Nominal	None

Due to non-repudiation[3] in systems, few attackers are caught, and fewer still are ever prosecuted. The penalties for those who are caught are very minor compared to the damage they cause (Disney, 1940; Green, 2008; Kim, 1992; Schroeder, 2012; Senge, 1990). Thus, we have a system that benefits hackers at the expense of targets, resulting in an uneven playing field, essentially putting the hackers in charge! It's at their discretion how much time and money the targets are forced to spend on recovery. Hackers suffer few consequences for their actions.

As long as targets remain in a defensive posture, focusing on surviving attacks that are deemed to be inevitable, they will remain fully accountable for the outcomes of this arms race. Targets originally tolerated this inequality, recovering systems and patching them as intrusions have occurred, absorbing the consequences of intruder attacks. With the size and impacts of today's attacks this is increasingly intolerable (Kim, 1992; Schroeder, 2012). The following mathematical model, developed by H. R. Varian, describes hacker behaviour in terms of hacker motivation (Varian, 1998).

Equation 7.1 Mathematical model of hacker behaviour

$$M = f \, [P \, (v) - (c_1 + c_2)]$$

where:

M = hacker motivation
P = the probability of not failing to intrude
v = the value of success to the hacker
c_1 = the cost to the hacker
c_2 = the consequences to the hacker

According to this model, hacker motivation is a function of the *probability of not failing to intrude* (P), multiplied by the *value of success to the hacker* (v), less the sum of their *costs and consequences* ($c_1 + c_2$). Applied to the current situation, with the *probability of not failing to intrude* being high (given the easy accessibility of targets (PWC, 2014)) and with the value of success being prized by the attacker, P and v amplify the effects of each other. Additionally, with *costs and consequences* to the hacker being low, there is little to deter motivation to indulge in malicious and criminal online behaviour.

To change the outcome, we can either lower P, the *probability of not failing to intrude*, or *increase costs and consequences to the hacker*, represented by ($c_1 + c_2$). Previous security measures have focused on lowering P by increasing the defensive measures protecting systems. This appears to have fed a never-ending arms race. Raising the value of ($c_1 + c_2$) is an alternative. To do so, a target might adopt a policy of attacking back (active defence) designed to increase both costs and consequences, for example, disabling or crashing the attacker's system, thus rendering the attacker harmless or out of business for some period of time. The problem with initiating an active defence strategy is the unleashing of unintended consequences resulting from being linked to public networks, along with the legal ramifications (Baum, 2006; Endicott-Popovsky, Ryan and Frincke, 2005).

This makes active defence a less than desirable remedy – for now. As an alternative, targets might endeavour to incorporate strategies that increase the consequences of intruding behaviour. Increasing consequences means identifying the attackers and holding them accountable. Given the psychological profile of individual hackers (Baum, 2006; Endicott-Popovsky, Ryan, and Frincke, 2005; Suler, 2004), this might be the best choice. According to Suler, intruders find encouragement in their anonymity, which leads to a lack of accountability for their actions. For nation-states and organized crime, exposing them may also be a deterrent, as witnessed by the 2013 Mandiant report, which shed light on a major cyber nation-state protagonist (Mandiant Intelligence Center Report, 2013).

By deploying defensive measures such as firewalls and intrusion detection systems, targets have focused their defensive strategies on increasing the time penalty, in other words the costs (c_1), to hackers. Nevertheless, hacker response to these actions has been either to try the next, less defended, target or develop better skills. Thus, by focusing strategies on defending against attacks, targets only continue to fuel the arms race.

Examining consequences (c_2) as a potential candidate for intervention, developing strategies that focus on increasing the consequences to the intruder from 'none' to something more significant, would involve going outside the arms-race system to the legal system for intervention. This move is supported by general systems theory, which suggests that the solution to any system problem will come from outside that system (Covey, 1990; Forrester, 1975) to block the energy fuelling the system, thus limiting its growth.

While legal intervention appears intuitively obvious, in practice it is not happening with much frequency. Targets do not often pursue either civil action or criminal prosecution, and when they do the guilty parties are not often found guilty, or punishments are small (Disney, 1940; Green, 2008; Kim, 1992; Moscaritolo, 2009; Schroeder, 2012; Senge, 1990). In theory, introducing legal consequences through legal intervention should reduce hacker motivation (M) and should inhibit intruding behaviour, levelling the playing field between hackers and targets. However, this isn't happening as much as one might expect. The answer explains the third driver in maintaining the *status quo* of the hacker arms race – the criminal justice system, or rather, the lack of same!

Drawing on the criminal justice system

Holding online intruders accountable through the legal system is certainly not a novel idea. The criminal justice system is based on the concept that consequences for criminal behaviour are an effective deterrent. A more appropriate question is 'why haven't targets changed their focus from increasing costs in terms of the time an attacker spends breaking into a system, to a focus on holding them legally accountable?'

Part of the answer is that the legal system has been largely unsuccessful in prosecuting these criminals in the past, making the effort to track down and convict hackers not very cost effective for targets. There are other motivations as well, like the fear of negative publicity and the concern that needed operational personnel and equipment will be consumed in non-productive activities such as supporting the development of a legal court case (Department of Justice, 2009; Endicott-Popovsky and Frincke, 2006; Endicott-Popovsky, Ryan, and Frincke, 2005; Schroeder, 2012).

Inherent inertia is another reason. Systems have a tendency towards being self-sustaining. They return to their original structure unless the components of the system are altered in some permanent way. In essence, the hackers' arms-race system is resistant to change. Hackers are motivated to pursue targets as long as costs and consequences are insignificant, and targets have continued to play a defensive, reactive game in response.

Practitioners' models for developing strategies to prevent and inhibit malicious and criminal online behaviour that appear to institutionalize the hackers' arms race confirm the target mind-set. We will examine one well-known model and the suggested change, made several years ago, to attempt to alter the target mind-set – and thus permanently change the balance in the system.

The concept of a never-ending, escalating computer security arms race is reflected in the discipline of survivability, which had its moment in the early 2000s. Survivability was defined as the 'ability of a system to fulfil its mission, in a timely manner, in the presence of attacks, failures and accidents'. Computer Emergency Readiness Team (CERT) researchers Ellison et al. state that the discipline of survivability can help ensure that systems can deliver essential services and maintain essential properties including integrity, confidentiality, and performance despite the presence of intrusions. Unlike traditional security measures, which often depend on central control and administration, survivability is intended to address network environments [i.e., the internet] where such capabilities may not exist.

(Ellison et al., 1999)

While previous point solutions – such as 'PKIs [public-key infrastructures – encryption implementation], VPNs [virtual private networks] and firewalls' – focused on *blocking* attacks, the survivability approach reflects the inevitability of *experiencing* attacks (Ellison et al., 1999; Linger et al., 2000), suggesting that there is no resolution to the arms race. Introducing the survivability model, the authors assert that 'Despite the best efforts of security practitioners, no amount of hardening can assure that a system connected to an unbounded network [such as the internet] will be invulnerable to attack' (Ellison et al., 1999).

The survivability discipline was captured in CERT's 3R model for defining survivability strategies devised to secure computer systems (Linger et al., 2000). The three Rs – resistance, recognition, recovery – all reflect the inevitability of attack (Table 7.4).

Implicit in the survivability model is the assumption that the continual escalation of the hacker arms race is a given. It's not a matter of 'if attacks will occur', but 'when'.

To change intruder behaviour by increasing the consequences to the intruder, we must address the fact that few organizations pursue legal action,

Table 7.4 Strategies of survivable systems (Linger et al., 2000)	
Survivability strategy	**Tools**
Resistance	
Ability to repel attacks	• Firewalls • User authentication • Diversification
Recognition	
1) Ability to detect an attack or a probe 2) Ability to react or adapt during an attack	• Intrusion detection systems • Internal integrity checks
Recovery	
1) Provide essential services during attack 2) Restore services following an attack	• Incident response • Replication • Backup systems • Fault-tolerant designs

given some of the reasons listed previously. Were they to do so, it would necessitate incorporating into their computer security strategies a willingness to go to court and the ability to prevail.

This suggested a modification to the 3R model and the addition of a fourth R: redress was proposed (Endicott-Popovsky and Frincke, 2006), defined as the ability to hold intruders accountable. Initially, redress would be accomplished by pursuing accountability in the legal system. When the resolution of the legal and ethical implications of active defence occurred, then redress could also include the ability to retaliate when attacked. Both are included in the revised model.

Redress requires the incorporation of what Sommers called computer Forensics (with a capital 'F,'[4]) into the security strategies of the organization (Sommers, 1997; Sommers, 2002). While computer forensics with a small 'f' is assumed to be part of recovery, this activity is usually not carried out in a rigorous enough fashion, suitable for admitting evidence in a courtroom, and this is not the primary concern of technicians concerned about restoring service as quickly as possible.

This addition expands the duties of those responsible for securing a network to include adherence to the rules of evidence when investigating an intrusion (Endicott-Popovsky and Frincke, 2006; Sommers, 2002). This would likely require re-examination of current security measures, tools and techniques for compliance with more rigorous evidence collection and storage standards for courtroom admissibility (Endicott-Popovsky, Frincke and Taylor, 2007).

The proposed 4R model is presented in Table 7.5. While few hacking incidents have caused organizations to seek redress in a court of law, due to the many challenges of bringing a successful prosecution (Schroeder, 2012), as the severity of losses due to computer crime continues to grow the appetite to seek legal remedy will also grow. Since the 4R model was proposed we are already experiencing losses that organizations and the public appear no longer willing to tolerate, as well as an increase in the number of incidents for which legal remedies are being pursued (Kuntze et al., 2014).

As mentioned earlier, the requirements for gathering evidence suitable for admissibility in a courtroom are much stricter than those for simply gathering evidence in order to restore full function following an attack. This necessitates a re-examination of the mechanisms, methods, tools and procedures currently employed by security professionals during incident-response and recovery

Table 7.5 Strategies of accountable systems (Endicott-Popovsky and Frincke, 2006)

Survivability strategy	Tools
Resistance	
Ability to repel attacks	• Firewalls • User authentication • Diversification
Recognition	
1) Ability to detect an attack or a probe 2) Ability to react or adapt during an attack	• Intrusion detection systems • Internal integrity checks
Recovery	
1) Provide essential services during attack 2) Restore services following an attack	• Incident response • Replication • Backup systems • Fault-tolerant designs
Redress	
1) Ability to hold intruders accountable in a court of law 2) Ability to retaliate	• Computer Forensics • Legal remedies • Active defence

activities (Endicott-Popovsky, Chee and Frincke, 2007).

The additional requirements arising from the rules of evidence are not widely understood or followed by systems administrators or those setting security policy (Endicott-Popovsky, Chee and Frincke, 2007; Endicott-Popovsky, Ryan and Frincke, 2005). If the rules of evidence are not adhered to in the scramble to restore the system immediately upon an intrusion's being detected, any information collected that might lead to a courtroom victory may be invalidated as to its admissibility (Endicott-Popovsky, Chee and Frincke, 2007; Rudolph, Kuntze and Endicott-Popovsky, 2013).

How do we stay safe online?

Intrusions and data breaches are astoundingly large, compared to the script-kiddy intrusions of the turn of the century. The 2015 PWC Information Security Survey describes cyber risk now as a 'severe and present danger', with incidents worldwide estimated at totalling anywhere from '$740 billion to $2.2 trillion', depending on the study (PWC, 2014). In this time, the threat spectrum has escalated from teenagers with idle time on their hands to organized criminal activities, terrorism/hacktivism and nation-state involvement. In light of this context and the challenges that we face as a civil society in grasping the extent of our vulnerability and in applying legal redress to inhibit bad behaviour online, how should we think about online safety and security, and what are reasonable expectations of security?

First, if we harbour a valuable data object online, we must recognize that the probability of successful intrusion is 1. It's a function only of an attacker's time and resources before it's 'pwned',[5] because these are no obstacles to determined adversaries like nation-states and organized crime. Thus, those managing networks today, who understand the threat environment in which they are operating, have evolved to adopting a strategy of 'assumption of breach', which accepts that the attackers are already established within; have, unnoticed, established footholds in systems; and are quietly ex-filtrating data, or whatever their mission entails. This approach changes the mind-set of the target from one of keeping intruders out (a losing battle) to one of assessing the value of data objects and systems, ignoring some and layering defences on those most precious.

This doesn't resolve the hacker arms race, but at least it plants us firmly in the reality of where we are. As our systems have evolved from mainframe to desktop to distributed networks to ubiquitous connectivity, our concepts of security have lagged behind the functionality we have been creating. In the mainframe era, computer security, from a practical perspective, was synonymous with physical security. We placed our computing power behind cypher-locked doors with 24/7 guards (either guards or cameras watching who went in and who went out, carrying whatever!). As we gradually distributed processing into the workplace, we carried with us our mainframe mind-set. Physical perimeter defences became firewalls, and guards at the door became the software authentication systems that let us in.

As intrusions became more problematic we invented new ways to protect ourselves: intrusion detection systems (IDS) that would catch an intrusion even if our firewalls wouldn't keep them out. As these proved less effective, we added other types of technology: intrusion prevention systems; CAPTCHAs;[6] two- and three-factor authentication that requires not only a password but also perhaps a biometric (iris scan, fingerprint, face recognition, etc.) a chip-embedded card, a dongle that authenticates your access, and so on … the arms race played out on the defence side!

The classic approach to designing cybersecurity solutions remains:

Equation 7.2

Controls $= f$ (Threats + Vulnerabilities)

where:

Controls = human, process/procedure, technical mitigations designed in response to cyber risk

Threats = those actors arrayed against systems for malicious purposes; script kiddies, hackers for hire, organized crime, hacktivists, terrorists, nation-states

Vulnerabilities = flaws in systems that are subject to threat actors – these could be found in every node in the network, every wire, every human interface, every line of software code

In other words, risk-mitigating controls are developed from analysis of the intersection of online threats and system vulnerabilities. In today's organizations, that translates into a need to understand both the threat spectrum arrayed against it and their own organizational and IT vulnerabilities. According to Sun Tzu: 'If you know the enemy and know yourself, you need not fear the result of a hundred battles' (Tzu, 2009). This is a good mantra for today's chief information security officer and is the inspiration for the Know Your Enemy papers, written by the Honeynet Alliance, which shed light on the escalating threat spectrum we have been experiencing (The Honeynet Project, n.d.). This is a good source of information from which to begin to grasp the threat spectrum we are facing.

While the formula is simple, the execution is difficult. Organization networks have grown up over time, with many legacy pieces of equipment. Further, most organizations, if not all, have a difficult time identifying what is on their network and where it is. This makes assessing one's own set of vulnerabilities challenging. Further, the dynamic, changing nature of the threat spectrum requires cybersecurity practitioners to continuously learn. Professionals spend hours every day staying current, which is one of the most important skills someone in cybersecurity can have. Alvin Toffler, in *Future Shock*, claimed that 'The illiterate of the 21st century will not be those who cannot read and write, but those who cannot learn, unlearn, and relearn' (Toffler, 1971). This is certainly the case in the field of cybersecurity, where professionals are left behind quickly and exploit paradigms are shattered overnight.

To maintain currency, in addition to establishing a regular professional reading cycle, practitioners need to develop a 360-degree situational awareness, ever alert for anomalies. While technology provides monitoring of different kinds, the human in the system is still necessary and, according to most studies, the source of the most egregious and numerous attacks. This makes the insider threat more deadly than external threats. The alert practitioner suspects every node, wire, device on a network, and is particularly aware of the seams where elements in the IT system come together, including the human element.

Regardless of the nature of the threat, Mandiant generalizes the threat-actor's process to be the same, in spite of motivation (Figure 7.3). The intruder begins with reconnaissance in order to determine the most efficient and effective manner of gaining ingress, followed by the initial compromise and establishment of a foothold within the system. Once solidly inside, the threat actor escalates his/her user privileges and performs internal reconnaissance, determining when and where to move laterally. Once in the spot where they want to be, they maintain presence and cycle through the previous steps until the mission is accomplished, whether it is data theft, theft or damage to intellectual property online, etc. Stealth and persistence have led to the concept of the Advanced Persistent Threat (APT), which is a threat actor or action that requires long-term stealth and persistence in acquiring the desired targeted object. APTs are often governments exercising long-term national objectives.

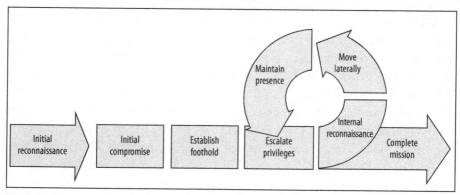

Figure 7.3 Same process regardless of threat actor (Mandiant Intelligence Center Report, 2013)

When determining vulnerabilities, the organization should be guided by the Flaw Hypothesis Methodology devised by Clark Weissman (1995) as a basis for security penetration testing. There are some general recommendations that should guide any vulnerability assessment, including ensuring against groupthink by bringing diverse views into the assessment process.

There are a plethora of third-party tools available for vulnerability and risk assessment exercises and programmes. Some are found at:

- International Organization for Standardization (ISO)
- National Institute of Standards (NIST)
- US Securities and Exchange Commission (SEC)
- Information Systems Audit and Control Association's (ISACA) CobiT (Control Objectives for Information and Related Technology)
- British Standards Institute (BSI)
- SANS Institute
- US Health Information Portability and Accounting Act (HIPAA)
- Peripheral Component Interconnect (PCI).

Most organizations with information-assurance programmes use one, or a combination, of these frameworks, depending on the stakeholders, internal and external, with whom they wish to communicate programme results. No matter what combination, frameworks provide only a structure for thinking through an exercise in determining system vulnerabilities and are not 'one size fits all'. In practice, they need to be modified to the organization, so there has to be a cultural and a mission/goals fit.

While frameworks are good guidance, they provide assurance of compliance, but not security. These are two different concepts. Compliance speaks to alignment with prevailing laws and regulations, which is challenging in multi-jurisdictional environments, but the issues of securing information in an organization require further steps: evaluating risks, balancing risk with cost and convenience, understanding the risk appetite of the organization, determining what controls to put in place once that has been done and continual monitoring as threats and vulnerabilities change and evolve.

Even so, there will always be residual risk; there will never be a 100% secure system, especially when there are humans involved! Technical controls can be designed well, but when humans disable them for convenience, or forget to patch, or post their passwords where someone could read them, they belie all of the controls we can devise. In the end, the human being is the weakest link and the most difficult element in the network to manage! Research is only beginning to touch the human element in the information system-security equation. We have a long way to go.

Conclusion

The unintended consequences that we are still dealing with as a result of having gone digital will be with us for years to come. There is an emerging body of knowledge describing cybersecurity like any other academic discipline, but we remain at a distance from converging on agreed-upon elements in a curriculum and body of knowledge. There have been national and international efforts to develop those standards, but the interdisciplinary nature of the field makes it a challenge to reach levels of agreement similar to those eventually seen in computer science. We will eventually get there, as we have in other practitioner-initiated fields; however, it is still a work in progress. Practitioners still remain at the tip of the spear, keeping back the hordes of intruders wanting in, and managing vigilantly among the insiders who might have intrusion in mind. The academics and researchers are running to catch up!

For anyone interested in getting in to the ground floor of an exciting field, the best way to stay current is to stay in touch with both academia and practice, even though they remain worlds apart still. More academic programmes are slowly appearing, research in this area is increasing, certifications for specific skills now abound, jobs remain plenty, even at a time when unemployment in many countries is high, and the long-term potential for a rewarding career is great. It is a nascent field, with much growth ahead and plenty of adversaries to continue to challenge our methods of defence, and we are a long way from ready answers to what we have done to ourselves!

References

Baum, J. (2006) Cyberethics: the new frontier, redOrbit, http://www.redorbit.com/news/education/345993/cyberethics_the_new_frontier/index.html.

Byrne, R. M. J. (2005) *The Rational Imagination: how people create counterfactual alternatives to reality*, MIT Press.

Covey, S. (1990) *The 7 Habits of Highly Effective People*, Franklin Press.

Craik, K. J. W. (1943) *The Nature of Explanation*, Cambridge University Press.

Department of Justice (2009) International Hacker Pleads Guilty for Massive Hacks of Retail Networks, http://www.justice.gov/opa/pr/international-hacker-pleads-guilty-massive-hacks-us-retail-networks.

Disney, W. (Producer), and Armstrong, S. (Director) (1940) Fantasia [Film]. (Available from RKO Pictures, 1270 Avenue of the Americas, New York, NY 10020.)

Ellison, R. J., Fisher, D. A., Linger, R. C., Lipson, H. F., Longstaff, T. A. and Mead, N. R. (1999) *Survivable Network Systems: an emerging discipline*, CMU/SEI 97-TR-013, May.

Endicott-Popovsky, B. (2008) Unintended Consequences of the Information Age: our children at risk. Paper presented at a workshop at the meeting of the Washington Library Media Association, Pasco, WA.

Endicott-Popovsky, B. E. and Frincke, D. (2006) Adding the Fourth 'R': a systems approach to solving the hacker's arms race. Presentation at the Hawaii International Conference on System Sciences (HICSS) 39 Symposium: Skilled Human-intelligent Agent Performance: Measurement, Application and Symbiosis, Kauai, HI.

Endicott-Popovsky, B., Chee, B. and Frincke, D. (2007) Role of Calibration as Part of Establishing Foundation for Expert Testimony. Paper presented at 3rd Annual IFIP WG 11.9 Conference, Orlando, Florida.

Endicott-Popovsky, B., Frincke, D. and Taylor, C. (2007) Theoretical Framework for Organizational Network Forensic Readiness, *The Journal of Computers*, 2 (3), 1–11.

Endicott-Popovsky, B. E., Ryan, D. and Frincke, D. (2005) The New Zealand Hacker Case: a post mortem. In *Proceedings of the Safety and Security in a Networked World: Balancing Cyber-Rights and Responsibilities Conference at the Oxford Internet Institute, the University of Oxford, Oxford, England*, www.oii.ox.ac.uk/research/cybersafety/extensions/pdfs/papers/.

Forrester, J. W. (1975) *Collected Papers of Jay W. Forrester*, Pegasus Communications.

Green, R. (2008) Connecticut Drops Felony Charges against Julie Amero, Four Years after Her Arrest, CTConfidential, November 21, http://blogs.courant.com/rick_green/2008/11/connecticut-drops-felony-charg.html.

Internet World Stats, http://www.internetworldstats.com/stats.htm.

Itzkoff, D. (2009) Student Fined $675,000 in Downloading Case, *New York Times*, 31 July, http://artsbeat.blogs.nytimes.com/2009/07/31/judge-rules-student-is-liable-in-music-download-case.

Johnson-Laird, P. N. (1983) *Mental Models: towards a cognitive science of language, inference, and consciousness*, Cambridge University Press.

Kim, D. H. (1992) *Systems Archetypes I: diagnosing systemic issues and designing high leverage interventions*, Pegasus Communications, Inc.

Kuntze, N., Rudolph, C., Schilling, H., Alva, A., Brisbois, B. and Endicott-Popovsky, B. (2014) Seizure of Digital Data and 'Selective Suppression' of Digital Evidence. Paper presented at 8th International Workshop on Systematic Approaches to Digital Forensic Engineering (SADFE) at IEEE/International Conference on Digital Forensics and Cyber Crime, 18–20 September, New Haven, Connecticut.

Linger, R., Ellison, R., Longstaff, T. and Mead, N. (2000) The Survivability Imperative: protecting critical systems, http://www.crosstalkonline.org/storage/issue-archives/2000/200010/200010-Linger.pdf.

Mandiant Intelligence Center Report (2013) APT 1: exposing one of China's cyber espionage units, http://intelreport.mandiant.com/Mandiant_APT1_Report.pdf.

Moscaritolo, A. (2009) Majority Think that Outsourcing Threatens Network Security, *SC Magazine*, **29**, http://www.scmagazineus.com/Majority-think-outsourcing-threatens-network-security/article/150955/.

PWC (2014) *Managing Cyber Risks in an Interconnected World: key findings from the Global State of Information Security Survey 2015*.

Rudolph, C., Kuntze, N., Endicott-Popovsky, B. (2013) Forensic Readiness for Cloud-based Distributed Workflows. Paper presented at the 1st Annual International Conference on Cloud Security Management, October, Seattle, Washington.

Schroeder, S. (2012) *The Lure*, Course Technology.

Senge, P. M. (1990) *The Fifth Discipline*, Doubleday Currency.

Sommers, P. (1997) Downloads, Logs and Captures: evidence from cyberspace, *Journal of Financial Crimes*, 5.JFC2, 138–52.

Sommers, P. (2002) Emerging Problems on Digital Evidence, Computer Forensics Workshop, University of Idaho, Moscow, September.

Stevens, T. (2009) Electronic Voting Outlawed in Ireland, Engadget, http://www.engadget.com/2009/04/28/electronic-voting-outlawed-in-ireland-michael-flatley-dvds-okay (retrieved 14 September 2014).

Suler, J. (2004) The Psychology of Cyberspace: the online disinhibition effect, www-usr.rider.edu/~suler/psycyber/disinhibit.html.

The Honeynet Project (n.d.) Know Your Enemy series, http://www.honeynet.org/papers.

Toffler, A. (1971) *Future Shock*, Bantam Doubleday Dell Publishing Group.

Tzu, S. (2009) *The Art of War*, trans. Lionel Giles, Pax Librorum Publishing House.

Varian, H. (1998) PBIs on Economics of Computer Security, School of Information Management, University of California, Berkeley, 10 November, http://www.ischool.berkeley.edu/~hal/Talks/security.pdf.

Weissman, C. (1995) Security Penetration Testing Guideline: a chapter of the Handbook for Computer Certification of Trusted Systems TM-8889/000/01, prepared for Center for Secure Information Technology, Naval Research Laboratory (NRL).

Notes

1   Trustworthy computing memo from Bill Gates, 15 January 2002, http://www.computerbytesman.com/security/billsmemo.htm.

2   CERT (Computer Emergency Response Team) statistical data was derived from government, academia, industry, security experts, law enforcement and vendors.

3   Non-repudiation in this sense refers to the inability of today's technologies to provide proof of the origin of data.

4   Sommers, a leading expert in digital forensics with the London School of Economics, makes the distinction between 'computer forensics', which is an investigatory activity to discover *what* happened prior to restoring computer systems that have been attacked, and 'computer Forensics' with a capital 'F', which implies that the investigation is not only for discovering what happened, but also to determine *who* did it by using techniques for gathering and preserving evidence that will be upheld in a court of law.

5   'Pwned' is a slang hacker term derived from the verb 'own', meaning to appropriate or gain ownership, and implies the humiliation of being defeated.

6   CAPTCHA stands for 'Completely Automated Public Turing Test to tell Computers and Humans Apart', which is a type of challenge-response test used for authentication that proves a human is on the other end of a transaction.

CHAPTER 8

Rights and the commons: navigating the boundary between public and private knowledge spaces

Gavan McCarthy and Helen Morgan

Introduction

For the 21st-century archivist, access to all archival materials is going to be one of the most complicated and difficult tasks. In the pre-digital world the number of variables that the archivist had to deal with was significantly fewer than that which they are confronted with in the networked digital age. As a rule, records in the pre-digital world were only in material form and in the custody of an archival service or repository. Access was provided physically through a research or reading room – the researcher had to go in person to the records. This physical containment of the records, the archivist and the researcher (or information seeker) in the one space enabled the negotiation of rules, restrictions and obligations associated with access to archival material. This containment facilitated responsible access to material not intended for publication that could, for example, contain information relating to third parties – in particular, other people – or information pertaining to national security or information of commercial interest. The research room was a frontier where the public were able to interact with private knowledge, whether those materials were generated by governments (in Western democracies these are often known as 'public records'), by businesses and organizations or by private individuals. In all cases these records have been kept by archives because they have been deemed to form a useful contribution to societal memory.

Differential access to records as determined, for example, by security or information privacy issues was managed through processes of restriction. This meant additional work for the archivist in preparing materials for release that might include redaction of third-party names or other information that might infringe the rights of others or compromise the role of government. In extreme cases highly secure research rooms were established purely to enable security-cleared individuals to access the most highly restricted materials. Similar conditions were set up for academic researchers wishing to consult medical or criminal records. With the passage of time the sensitivity of records diminishes. As a rule, for records over 100 years old, when the individuals concerned have died, commercial concerns are long passed and national security issues have become of historical interest only, access is less problematic. But, as we shall see, in a highly connected digital world even this rule of thumb is being challenged.

As with so many other aspects of life, the effectiveness of these access regimes was based on trust. This trust was built on the negotiated relationship between the archivist and the information seeker, on the presumption that the latter understood the nature of the materials, respected the rights of third parties mentioned in the records and would adhere to any non-disclosure obligations. Although this trust may have been formalized through a signed access agreement or a reader's ticket, it was ultimately built on the unwritten normative expectations of responsible citizenship and respect for our fellow human beings.

Access to digitized or born-digital materials via the web is increasingly expected by information seekers and this radically changes the topography of the public–private frontier. In this new, virtual space the archivist and the researcher do not meet face to face in a private environment controlled by the archival institution. The researcher may or may not have privacy and may indeed broadcast their interactions with the records more broadly, for example, via digital projection in a lecture theatre to students or colleagues. In this context, the normative expectations of behaviour cannot be established in the same manner as they are in a reading room. In addition, with a far broader geographic reach, a potentially much larger clientele and, as a rule, no increase in budget, the virtual reading room poses significant challenges for the 21st-century archivist. How will trust be negotiated in this new space?

This chapter will explore further what is meant by public and private knowledge spaces and the boundaries (or frontier) bridging the two domains that have traditionally been managed by archivists. It will look at issues around the intellectual rights and expectations of the public domain and assess why consideration of rights in relation to private-domain materials needs to encompass more than intellectual property and copyright and be more sensitive to moral rights, ethics and the rights of the subjects of records. In this regard, the chapter will reflect on the purpose and impact of various access regimes in the context of issues of ethical access, use and privacy, all of which is now framed by the International Council on Archives' (ICA) 'Principles of Access to Archives' (ICA, 2013). The key questions are how networked digital environments affect this frontier and how the role of the archivist might change. Through a series of case studies, with a particularly Australian flavour, this chapter will explore this new public–private frontier and propose a framework of four scenarios that might enable the emergence of a web-mediated Archival Commons Licence (McCarthy, 2012). Drawing on the experience and success of the Creative Commons Licence,[1] the proposed Archival Commons Licence would seek to establish clear statements of obligations that information seekers must agree to prior to gaining access to materials that were not created with the intention of publication.

Archival information seeking in the age of overabundance

The digital public domain is now awash with information in a plethora of forms and made available via an increasing range of services. While opinion differs as to just how much information is being created on a daily basis, the reality is that 'it's clear that no one really knows how much information is out there or how quickly it's actually being produce[d], but everyone is certain it's being produced increasingly quickly' (Finley, 2011). Eric Schmidt, former Google CEO, had been quoted as saying, 'There was 5 exabytes of information created between the dawn of civilization through 2003, but that much information is now created every 2 days, and the pace is increasing.' These new information services, for example, global search and indexing services and socially networked information-creation and -sharing platforms, work alongside older information-exchange mechanisms such as e-mail, facsimile transmission, telephony, postal services and face-to-face discussions. These technologies and those still to come change how we understand the concept of the public domain. For the purposes of this chapter the public domain could be understood simply as a place where information is located that was created with the intention of being made available to the whole community. For example, a book, newspaper, journal or indeed a sign on a shop are available to any member of society to access and utilize. The conditions of access and use are determined by law – for example, copyright – and by normative behavioural expectations.

The digital private (archival) domain is increasingly characterized by government departments, organizations and individuals creating vast amounts of documentary information in digital forms that are rarely managed in the ways that materials and records were documented, controlled and filed in the physical world (Moss, 2012). The same domain has also seen the emergence of new services and platforms to enable the citizenry to access archival materials. Bodies like Ancestry.com (http://www.ancestry.com.au) are using vast financial, professional and voluntary resources to digitize records and make them available for the purposes of family history, on a scale never seen before. Access to the service is via a payment and registration system that establishes the conditions of use and the obligations by which the information seeker agrees to abide.[2] It appears to be a model based on user rights, responsibilities and benefits that society has willingly adopted as a means of providing access to older third-party information that is of particular value to genealogists and family historians. The scale of the operation is extraordinary and has enabled the digitization of records and fine-grained indexing and documentation such as traditional archival practice has never achieved. Services like these change the expectations of the citizenry, who are increasingly questioning why archives and archivists are not able to deliver the same sorts of service across all the records they manage.

The pervasiveness of networked digital technologies in governmental agencies and private organizations and the consequent rampant proliferation of digital documents have radically changed the information landscape. As a consequence of the steady removal of back-office administrative support functions, the traditional processes of filing, records management and appraisal are now more likely to be highly distributed and under the idiosyncratic control of individuals.

The belief that search and indexing tools would be able to locate relevant materials of evidential value in unstructured and distributed systems has been shown to be misplaced. Without intentional record creation and preservation processes it is almost impossible to identify a genuine record providing evidence of a transaction amid a sea of 'false positives' – for example the drafts, the working documents, the widely distributed e-mails, documents and social media posts. In a context where information is uncontrolled and created on a scale that is uncontrollable, the identification of records and materials that can act as evidence becomes increasingly problematic.

Although it is outside the scope of this chapter to offer advice on how archivists might tackle the monstrous blobs of digital stuff that are likely to be the 'archival files' of the future, it remains essential that the 21st-century archivist has a clear understanding of the nature of the information objects they encounter and their associated information environments. Of particular importance are the purposes for which these materials were created, because it is this purpose – the intention that drives the creation – that determines how that material should be handled in the future, and how access should be provided to it.

Archival material and public knowledge spaces

Archivists deal with materials created and collected as the result of individual actions for personal, societal, governmental and business reasons. In contrast to material and other information created for the purpose of public exposure – published materials – archival records derive from materials that were created with a tacit understanding that they will not find their way into the public domain as published materials. This, of course, is not to say that the records could not be accessed by members of the public for acceptable purposes.

Once materials move from the realm of immediate use, from creator/custodian ownership and control, they enter a nebulous state where they are held on the presumption that they may be required for later use. Most of these materials remain in private hands or are destroyed without consideration that they might be accessed by others. Some of these materials move into places of deposit, such as galleries, libraries, archive repositories and museums, to meet social and cultural memory needs. It is these institutions that demarcate the frontier where archival materials from the private domain and the public meet. It is here that access to private-domain materials becomes policy driven and formalized.

Archivists manage access to archival materials, supported and guided by institutional and governmental access policies. Access may be open, or partially or fully restricted according to time limitations, cultural sensitivities and privacy considerations. In order to manage the archives in their care (to know where they are), to enable discovery and to facilitate access to them, archivists create inventories and descriptive metadata about materials. Although these are often only available in reading rooms, increasingly, as digital technologies have enabled, these guides and inventories are being published. This trend has been apparent from the early days of automated systems and since the earliest days of the pre-web. To begin with, a handful of archival repositories put up information about archival holdings on Gopher (pre-web) sites. The Australian Science Archives Project first contributed data about the archives of science in Australia to the National Library of Australia's OZLINE network in 1991 (multiple library databases were available to the public via OZLINE through AARNet or dial-up services). *Archives and Museum Informatics* published its first column on internet resources in spring 1994 (Wallace, 1994; Sherratt, 1994; Theimer, 2009; Wallace, 1995). However, the distinction between purpose and suitability for publication – moving into public knowledge spaces – of both archival materials themselves and the information about them is not always clear cut.

Working within the concept of the public–private information frontier, four scenarios can be identified that cover most cases of user interaction with information, based on the purposes underlying the creation of the materials:

1 Material/information is created with the intention of publication and is suitable for publication (published literature).
2 Material/information is created not with the intention of publication and is not suitable for publication (archives).
3 Material/information is created with the intention of publication but is not actually suitable for publication (time and cross-cultural sensitivities).
4 Material/information is created not with the intention of publication but is or becomes suitable for publication (for example, correspondence of deceased and notable scientists – Darwin Correspondence Project, University of Cambridge, and Correspondence of Ferdinand von Mueller Project[3]).

Scenario 1 is the one we live in every day. It is our shared societal space that provides the information fabric for daily activities, the functioning of markets, the exchange of goods and the provision of services. There are legislative tools, such as copyright and intellectual property rights, which surround the distribution of published materials and they have a long history. There is substantive understanding within the community around how citizens interact with published materials and what they can do with them, although this is under challenge. A citizen can buy a book, own it, sell their copy, and they are expected to respect copyright and not reproduce or distribute the work without permission. In the scholarly world there are guidelines for how a researcher can cite, use and reproduce content from within a published work.

In the networked digital age, the world wide web has added a profound and pervasive new dimension. The web defines a vast and ever-growing public knowledge space into which individuals and organizations are placing materials that were never intended for publication. The major search engines make an assumption as to purpose and suitability for publication and do not attempt to differentiate materials that do not meet those criteria. Naïve information seekers not aware that such distinctions exist between public and private materials may find themselves at odds with expected normative behaviour, as well as with copyright and other public information licensing laws.

Whereas Scenario 1 is characterized by the placement of materials in the public knowledge space, in Scenario 2 the individual user or information seeker is required to cross the public–private frontier. The individual has to depart from their everyday life in the public domain and traverse the boundary into the private world of the archive. Whether this is done physically, or virtually through web services, it should be clear to the information seeker that they have crossed that boundary and that they are in a world with different rules, obligations and expectations.

Scenario 3 defines an edge case where the intention of the creator was to produce something for publication but, through ignorance or intention, creates material that does not meet with community expectations and is therefore not acceptable for publication. In the networked digital world this has become more common, as it is easier to violate cross-cultural sensitivities. The process of publication has always been an ongoing negotiation with the citizenry in response to variations in contexts and sensitivities through time and across space. As a consequence, the location of the public–private information frontier is not fixed, but something dynamic and responsive to societal needs and desires.

Scenario 4 is perhaps the easiest to apprehend. As materials age that were not intended for publication, their sensitivities diminish to the point where they could be considered suitable for publication. In the pre-digital world this was the only means of increasing the availability of such materials to globally distributed communities of information seekers. The emergence of highly expensive scholarly print editions of the correspondence and records of the famous, infamous or notable, and the vast microfilming of archival collections characterized this form of dissemination.

The frontier, as defined above as a place where users, archives and archivists interact, is also where archives and publications intersect and can be interconnected. As both forms of material can be more meaningfully understood only in terms of the relationships they have with each other, the two-way citation of archival sources and publications is therefore a requirement for an effective information platform. Networked digital technologies provide the opportunity for a functionally interconnected information environment. As a rule, in the scholarly pre-digital world this interconnection was only one way – from the published article or book via a citation to an archival source. This has reinforced the public notion of the archive as a remote and inaccessible silo – a world apart.

This has been further compounded by the traditional boundaries of cultural purpose which have kept libraries, museums, galleries and archives relatively and functionally isolated. Although the Linked Data movement and the developing capabilities of the global search engines are working to break through the walls of the silos, this appears to be being done without due consideration of the natural boundary that exists between the private and public information worlds. As illustrated through the work of Aotearoa New Zealand Indigenous Knowledge Creative Commons and Local Contexts, this process is exposing the frontier and provides the impetus for the development of systems and services that will allow it to be responsibly navigated (Creative Commons, 2013; Local Contexts, 2014).

The following case studies examine how these issues have been playing out in practice. Although they draw on experiences from Australia and New Zealand, it is likely that they reflect situations in many countries.

Case study: Obligation in the academic sphere; some Australian examples

As an example of Scenario 2, Australian historian Stephen Garton, reflecting on the access situation in New South Wales, passionately articulated the problems facing academic users of archives at the beginning of the 21st century. He observed 'a shift in the culture of archivists and record managers. In a climate of privacy and data protection, they are becoming more conservative' (Garton, 2000). In earlier encounters with government archives he had been given access, as a doctoral student undertaking research, to restricted series of records relating to mental health. His thesis was eventually published and, Garton explained, 'I like to think that the results repaid the confidence' of the Health Commission's access officer who approved the access request. Twenty years on, Garton was finding that despite letters of support assuring the relevant authorities that no personal data in the records would be included in the research outputs, his doctoral students were being denied access to the archives critical to their research. He saw enshrining 'special access' – meaning access where the user's bona fides ('legitimate' researcher/user) and prospective use of the archive are taken into consideration – as 'the best means of safeguarding privacy, while promoting the historical research we need to understand the past'. His description of the relationship between the researcher, the custodian and content (subjects) of the archive being one of confidence, trust and obligation goes to the heart of what is required between creators, custodians and users of archives.

Founders & Survivors, an Australian project studying and recording the convict experience of the men, women and children transported to Tasmania in the 19th century, has also had to navigate issues of the seemingly far-removed privacy of the past in the digital realm of the 21st century. At first glance this would appear to be a straightforward example of Scenario 4. The project is 'a partnership between historians, genealogists, demographers and population health researchers' (Founders & Survivors, 2014). It brings together data gathered from archival material (registers, indexes, certificates) and involves data extraction and transcription, as well as digitization of the original sources and online publication of some of the material to preserve and make it more accessible. The data is personal, collected for the purpose of research into the health and lives of this group of people during their lifetimes and mapping the trajectory of this where possible via their descendants – for example, by connecting the founding group 'with those who served in the AIF [Australian Imperial Force] in World War 1 and compar[ing] the service records of the male descendants of male convicts to investigate changes in height, childhood diet and health, and resilience under stress'.

The project also accepted data about convict ancestry from the community. In taking custody of this data, the project wrestled with balancing its curatorial obligations to this community-contributed content – how much data should be made available (given back) to the public? – and the ethical obligations surrounding privacy. In inviting this, the project clearly states its position, governed by the requirements of universities, government funding bodies and legislation, in conjunction with its personal sense of obligation.[4] Data derived from the archival material, alongside the community-contributed content, is securely stored in databases accessible only to project researchers 'under strict access conditions for the purposes of linking names and entering the core data'. Only de-identified data (numbers replacing names) is made public. Privacy legislation constrained the publication of family trees from this data; however, the team was able to fulfil the obligation that it felt to the subjects of the data: we 'will endeavour to return to our donors any additional historical information we may find about their convicts and family history as far as 1920'. The project's home page explicitly states what it can and cannot publish and why (privacy legislation). Because, for example, death certificates were purchased for research purposes only, the cause of death cannot be published (released to the public domain) but basic metadata such as date and place of death can, along with registration numbers, enabling people to purchase certificates on their own behalf for the purpose of private research. Finally, the project's newsletter states:

> Neither do we believe we should provide links to AIF records as it is not our business to publicise people's convict ancestry without their permission. This also enables us to honour the privacy promises we make on the website to members of the public who contributed data on ancestors.
>
> (Founders & Survivors, 2014)

Founders & Survivors recognized the power of – and responsibility that should accompany – linking data to data in the digital realm. The act of linking entails a form of high-visibility public broadcasting that has ethical considerations. The decision late in the project to temporarily limit access to community-contributed content to registered users only speaks to this. Once a permanent home is found for this data and a secure data service is established around it, registration will be required for access. Who can register will not be restricted, meaning that the data will essentially be open – just not widely broadcast or easily discoverable via the web (McCalman, 2014).[5]

Case study: Trove and historic newspaper digitization – what's public is public

Launched in 2009, the National Library of Australia's Trove online discovery service, including digitized Australian newspapers, illustrates the challenges that highly tractable, findable and connectable information has raised in what had previously been the relatively stable worlds of Scenarios 1 and 3. The digitized newspapers range in date from 1803 (the earliest published newspaper in Australia) through to the mid-20th century and beyond. There are more than 14 million pages of digitized Australian newspapers available through Trove, a figure that, in keeping with digital formats generally, is multiplying rapidly. While the information in these newspapers was and is considered to be in the public domain, their original analogue form meant that over time their content retreated from the public eye. Now, digitization and fully text-searchable online publication has made the content highly discoverable – the majority of users arrive at Trove's digitized newspapers via external search engines.

As a consequence of this, and often enough to merit a section in the Trove FAQ, the public is finding 'surprising information about themselves or their relatives which is sometimes good and sometimes bad'. In addition to cultural warnings, the Library makes the disclaimer that 'Content which was published legally is not censored. The Library will consider removing content in cases where there is legal justification, e.g. proof that an individual has won a defamation case against the original publisher.' Under no other circumstances will the Library consider requests to remove information from Trove. Because the content has been legally published these decisions have been straightforward, even if, for some users, the consequences have been unsettling.

Opening up collections like these via digitization and web publishing opens up the potential for all kinds of use – and misuse. However, acknowledging this, Trove manager Tim Sherratt has observed that 'it also exposes that misuse to analysis and critique' (Sherratt, 2014).

Can the same approach be applied to digitized and digital material in archival collections – material not created with the intention of publication?

Case study: Large-scale digitization – what can be published?

Traditionally, access to archives has been managed through the reading room in the physical place of deposit, or via remote supply through on-demand copying (such as photocopying, microfilming and, later, digitization). The physicality of the reading room itself sets up expectations and norms of user behaviour (privilege, obligation, records of use) and creates barriers to the archives, such as distance (only local or determined distant users prepared to travel) and the granting (or not) of access based on the repository's access policies, framed around, for example, legislative requirements and donor agreements (Jeremy, Woodley and Kupke, 2008).

In an example of Scenario 4, the National Archives of Australia at the beginning of the 21st century began experimenting with digitization on demand for the purpose of access (rather than preservation).[6] This was primarily to meet its brief of enabling access to its collections, recognizing that not all researchers can travel to the reading room. Digitized material could be (and still is) delivered via CD, but web publication via the catalogue offered an easier means of delivery and a more accessible public-good outcome at the same time. All pages of a file and its container were digitized, and presented in an image viewer allowing paging through to 'replicate the reading room experience of reading a file from the top down' (Ling and McLean, 2004, 5).

Changing the means of access from the physical reading room to the web had no impact on what was made available:

> The Archives Act 1983 regulates public access to the collection and requires that
> we withhold a range of sensitive information, including some personal
> information, from every form of access. It is important to note that the archives
> only digitizes records that have been assessed as suitable for public release. The
> archives sought legal advice to determine if there was a distinction between
> releasing records to the public in a reading room or in photocopy form, and
> loading digital copies onto a website where they can be viewed by anyone with
> internet access. We were advised that there was no difference, so we were able to
> proceed.
>
> (Ling and McLean, 2004, 6)

As stated, this hasn't precluded all personal information and it is possible, for example, to find name-identified data and photographs of private individuals through the Archives' web catalogue. But these records – and the metadata about them – are discoverable only through the virtual reading room. The Archives' holdings are not currently discoverable via Google and lie buried in the deep web. No permanent identifier is given for the metadata records for citation purposes, although ways exist (if one knows how). On the one hand, this is problematic for the average user who wishes to provide a link to the metadata record and digitized material. If all digitized material (and its metadata) is deemed suitable for public release, then why is it hard to cite, and even harder to find outside the walls of the Archives? Should we be freeing finer-grained metadata buried in the deep web? On the other hand, this approach doesn't preclude anybody from actually accessing the digitized material; it only makes it harder to locate and reuse.

Should the Archives, like Trove, take a neutral position in relation to the material and its subsequent use? Is there any onus on institutions undertaking large-scale digitization to provide anything more than guidance on the citation of material, be it public information (Australian digitized newspapers) or formerly private (archival) material? Can all this simply be left to user education in conjunction with expectations of good will, as demonstrated by the position taken by researchers on the Founders & Survivors project in choosing not to link to AIF records in the National Archives of Australia's catalogue?

Conclusions

The question for the archivist in the 21st century is: what do they do? Where is their role in this emerging world that has many more variables in play? Perhaps we should also readdress the question of what sort of information people are looking for in the archive. It is often the case that they are seeking evidence that underpins the story of an event, on a small or large scale, that they are seeking to understand. It also needs to be noted that it cannot be predicted when those moments will occur in the life of an individual or the life of an organization. The motivation for both keeping and making materials accessible through time (archives) varies from place to place and time to time. In some Western democracies government accountability is the prime driver, in others this is less so. But whatever the circumstance, the need of individuals to understand their place in their society has long been important, which means that access to the private information world (the archive) and the negotiation of the boundary between the public information space and the archive will remain a societal need for the foreseeable future. And this means a continuing role for the archivist as facilitator, guide, negotiator and explainer.

It has been noted that the traditional archival processes of file management, appraisal and access do not meet contemporary needs. In a world of uncontrolled digital production, issues of sensitivity cannot be dealt with on a document-by-document basis and by redaction. The notion of restricted or controlled access may need to be replaced by processes that more formally describe/articulate the obligations a user must sign up to when given access to materials not intended for publication.

The global search engines have created a public knowledge space where all materials are treated equally, but do the same rights issues, restrictions and common archival usage norms apply in the digital public domain? In the interest of greater openness and equity of access is it appropriate to make private-domain materials available online with a 'no reader's ticket required' approach? What infrastructure do we need in place to manage the particular needs of the private domain in digital and networked environments?

Ultimately, the traditional archival work practices have proved problematic, often requiring the archivist to second-guess the interpretation of legislation and the requirements of national security and community expectations, all of which reflect a paternalistic relationship between the archive and the citizen. This has become all the more important after the decision of the US Senate in May 2015 not to renew the National Security Agency's permission to collect personal data, and the recent judgments against Google for breaching personal information rights (for example against Google Spain in 2014 (C-131/12)).[7] We propose a move away from 'restriction' being the guiding principle, to the recognition and codification of obligations and responsibilities that a user should sign up to before getting access to archival material.[8]

Arlette Farge, in *The Allure of the Archives*, captures the essence of all research and the interactions with cultural materials, those intended for publication and those not created with that intent, when she notes that these 'are elements of reality that produce meaning by their appearance in a given historic time' (Farge, 2013). If our goal is to build a societal knowledge fabric that respects that delicate interplay between meaning and historical context, and the two-way traversal of the public–private frontier, we contend that the archivist of the 21st century should have a prominent role in creating the enabling mechanisms and maintaining the environment in which they work.

References

Creative Commons (2013) Indigenous Knowledge, Creative Commons Aotearoa New Zealand, http://creativecommons.org.nz/indigenous-knowledge/.

Farge, A. (2013) *The Allure of the Archives*, trans. T. Scott-Railton, foreword by N. Z. Davis, Yale University Press.

Finley, K. (2011) Was Eric Schmidt Wrong about the Historical Scale of the Internet?, Readwrite, 8 February, http://readwrite.com/2011/02/07/are-we-really-creating-as-much.

Founders & Survivors (2014) The Future for Founders & Survivors, *Chainletter*, **16**, (April), 2, http://foundersandsurvivors.org/sites/default/files/newsletters/FASnewsletter_16_2014_large.pdf.

Garton, S. (2000) Shut Off from the Source: a national obsession with privacy has led to fears for the future of Australian social history, *The Australian*, **22**, November, 45. Quotations are taken from the published article. For the full, unedited version of the article see the archived post 'Privacy, Access and Evidence (long)' on the Aus-Archivists listserv, 30 November 2000, http://www.asap.unimelb.edu.au/asa//aus-archivists/msg00470.html.

ICA (2013) Principles of Access to Archives, http://www.ica.org/13619/toolkits-guides-manuals-and-guidelines/principles-of-access-to-archives.html.

Jeremy, J., Woodley, E. and Kupke, L. (2008) Access and Reference Services. In *Keeping Archives*, 3rd edn, Australian Society of Archivists, ACT.

Ling, T. and McLean, A. (2004) Taking It to the People: why the National Archives of Australia embraced digitisation on demand, *Australian Academic and Research Libraries*, **35** (1), 5, http://dx.doi.org/10.1080/00048623.2004.10755253.

Local Contexts (2014) www.localcontexts.org/.

McCalman, J. (2014) Corespondence with Helen Morgan, 6 November 2014.

McCarthy, G. (2012) Towards an Archival Commons Licence: managing access to the private domain in the digital universe, *Comma*, 2, 141–50, doi: http://dx.doi.org/10.3828/comma.2012.2.15.

Moss, M. (2012) Where Have All the Files Gone? Lost in action points every one, *Journal of Contemporary History*, **47** (4), 860–75, doi: http://dx.doi.org/10.1177/0022009412451291.

Sherratt, T. (1994) ASAP on AARNet, *History of Australian Science Newsletter*, 32, (March), http://www.asap.unimelb.edu.au/hasn/no32/feats32.htm.

Sherratt, T. (2014) Life on the Outside: collections, contexts, and the wild, wild web. Keynote speech at the Annual Conference of the Japanese Association for the Digital Humanities, 20 September 2014, Tsukuba, Discontents, http://discontents.com.au/life-on-the-outside/.

Theimer, K. (2009) Mini-contest: archives, history and the web – all your favourite things! (blog post), ArchivesNext, 26 August, http://www.archivesnext.com/?p=335.

Wallace, D. (1994) Basic Navigation and Resources, *Archives and Museum Informatics*, **8** (1), 13–23), http://www.archimuse.com/publishing/ AMInewsletters/AMInewsletter1994_8-1.pdf.

Wallace, D. (1995) The Internet: archival repositories on the World Wide Web: a preliminary survey and analysis, *Archives and Museum Informatics*, **9** (2), 150–75, http://www.archimuse.com/publishing/AMInewsletters/AMInewsletter1995_ 9-2.pdf.

Notes

1   Creative Commons Corporation, 'About [Creative Commons]', https://creativecommons.org/about.

2   www.ancestry.com/cs/legal/termsandconditions.

3   http://www.darwinproject.ac.uk/; http://www.rbg.vic.gov.au/science/herbarium-and-resources/library/mueller-correspondence-project.

4   Become Involved: Ethics and Privacy, http://foundersandsurvivors.org/plans.

5   McCalman, J., notice on home page of Founders & Survivors website, http://foundersandsurvivors.org/, 'We regret that owing to worsening technical and security problems we have had to close part of the FAS website to public use. You can still search for a convict and read the transcriptions of his/her records, but, at present, ONLY REGISTERED VOLUNTEERS can access the Community Contributed material. You can still access the FAS newsletter 'Chainletter' via the website. WE ARE NO LONGER ACCEPTING REGISTRATIONS. When the project is transferred to an official, long-term site, all users will again be able to access Community Contributed material. By this time the data will have been cleansed, sorted and verified by the volunteers.'

6   Digitization on demand was introduced as a free service by the National Archives of Australia in 2001. See 'Our history – National Archives of Australia', www.naa.gov.au/about-us/organisation/history/; see also 'The National Archives Digitisation Service – Fact Sheet 249', http://www.naa.gov.au/collection/fact-sheets/fs249.aspx.

7   C-131/12 - Google Spain and Google
    http://curia.europa.eu/juris/liste.jsf?num=C-131/12.
8   Trove manager Tim Sherratt frames this in terms of user education
    around responsibility: 'What's important is not training users to
    understand the context of our collections, but helping them explore
    and understand their responsibilities to the pasts those collections
    represent.' And: 'Bad people will do bad things, but by asserting a social
    and ethical framework for the use of digital cultural collections we
    strengthen the resolve and commitment of those who want to do right.'
    (Sherratt, 2014).

CHAPTER 9

From the Library of Alexandria to the Google Campus: has the digital changed the way we do research?

David Thomas and Valerie Johnson

Introduction

Reading about the future of digital humanities in London is a curiously illusory experience. Sit at a terminal in the London Library and you will read about digital manifestos and urgent discussions of the need for more training, better education and the need for a whole new approach to the humanities. Go outside and walk towards Piccadilly Circus, and you will see hundreds of ordinary Londoners engaging with the digital even as they walk along the streets or wait for underground trains. This is a profound change from 1989, when a short book, *The Allure of the Archives* (Farge, 2013), was published. An excellent book, it was republished in 2013. Though its historical and conceptual approach still strikes the reader as entirely modern, indeed postmodern, the world of research that author Arlette Farge outlines is from a different age. She describes sitting in cold and silent search rooms, ordering documents via paper slips and copying them out in long-hand. No present-day researchers would recognize this picture. From the institutional side, digitized catalogues, digitized and born-digital documents have transformed access; whilst on a personal level, digital cameras, laptops and tablets have transformed research capture.

The authors will explore this shift to a new digital space, and its implications for research, researchers, research resources and research methodologies. Following the authors' experience, it will deal mainly with the humanities.

Content and access

The digital era has seen an explosion in the number and diversity of sources available to the researcher. This growth is manifest in multiple permutations. Whilst in 2009 Jisc (the Joint Information Systems Committee) announced its E-books for Further Education project to support the higher and further education sector,[1] individual companies are releasing digital resources for research by all. For example, the New Connections project, which ran from 2011 to 2013, saw half a million images from the British Telecom (BT) archive catalogued, digitized and published online, representing 165 years of the history of 'the world's oldest and most established communications company' (Hay, 2014, 29). Significantly, the internet has also enabled access to hitherto 'secret' content, as individuals and groups upload material to the web from Freedom of Information requests, legal discovery and, in some cases, leaks. One has only to think of the information released to the world by Edward Snowden or Julian Assange via WikiLeaks to see evidence of the impact of this data, the rapid world wide dissemination of which could simply not have happened before the advent of the internet.

But it is not simply a case of *more* sources. Alongside this, indeed, *part* of this increased access is due to another fundamental change to research and sources: the sheer speed with which material can be searched and accessed. Moreover, new and different types of sources are now emerging which have no physical equivalent – for example, tweets and web archives – to challenge researchers with new forms, content and context. However, this increased access can be poorly organized, even random. Information can be hard to find. There is no central index of the internet, apart from various search engines which are not well suited to academic research. In addition, reliability can be a real challenge. Is the information genuine? Can it be trusted? Charles Seife reported in his book, rather tellingly entitled *Virtual Unreality: just because the internet told you, how do you know it's true?* that up to a third of online reviews are fake (Seife, 2014).

With digitized rather than simply web-based search information, poor-quality sources are certainly an issue. Early digitization projects tended to photograph the pages. These could be badly reproduced, itself an issue. Worse was the decision, or ignorance, that resulted in projects that reproduced not data (which is searchable), but photographs of text (which is not). Though projects such as these do increase access – the material is available online – the missed opportunity to make the information into data renders some of these projects of little help to researchers.

A considerable amount has been written, and concern expressed, that in an age of digital search of documentary sources, their context, or provenance, is being lost. Searches that take the researcher straight into the document from the search page can leave the user lost, and also with no idea of where the information they are looking at is situated – both physically and intellectually. Yet, this loss of context can also be seen as liberating and enlightening. Certainly, online search technologies do not distinguish between format, and a single search will return results from books, DVDs, journals, artwork and so on, breaking down the boundaries of format and encouraging the bringing together of multiple sources in new and exciting ways. New archival and library theory now emphasizes the need for fluidity: for information professionals to allow, indeed to encourage, multiple approaches and paths to information systems so as to enable different communities with different cultures equal access and equal rights to control and interpret information, rather than being constrained by traditional pathways (McKemmish, Gilliland-Swetlund and Ketelaar, 2005; Dervin and Nilan, 1986). Technologies that facilitate this shift away from a prescriptive approach to organizing and interpreting information are to be applauded.

Digitized records

Initially, the digitization of primary resources for humanities was a slow-burn process, with some writers tracing its origins back to the early work of the Cambridge Population Group and the publication in 1980 of E. A. Wrigley and R. S. Schofield's *The Population History of England, 1541–1871, A Reconstruction.* Things began to hot up in the year 2000 with three separate initiatives: the establishment of the then Arts and Humanities Research Board's (AHRB) Resource Enhancement Scheme; the New Opportunities Fund; and the project by the then Public Record Office (now The National Archives) to digitize the 1901 Census.

Not all these projects were successful: few of the New Opportunities Fund projects had sustainability plans and some were never completed. Sustainability has now become much more of a concern across the breadth of the information field (Chowdhury, 2014). Nevertheless, there were some successes – the Old Bailey Online project and the Charles Booth Archive being notable examples (Hitchcock, 2008).

Since 2000, three separate strands have emerged in resource digitization. Academic and research funding bodies have produced a range of digital resources which, with a small number of exceptions, are freely available to the public and scholarly users. At the same time, a number of commercial publishers have begun to offer collections of digitized resources for sale to libraries. These include copies of newspapers, historical archives, as well as theses and dissertations, all of which are aimed at the academic and education markets. There are also a small number of companies which focus on delivering digitized records to the family history community. The biggest of these is Ancestry.com, a US company whose majority owner is the Permira private equity fund; and it is huge. Ancestry has 2.1 million subscribers, generates over half a billion dollars in annual revenue and has made 14 billion records available online.[2] A slightly smaller, British rival is D. C. Thomson Family History, which owns a range of family history resources, including Genes Reunited, Find My Past and Mocavo, and has made 1.8 billion records available online.[3]

'Amateur' historians or the academy?

As a result of these initiatives, local and family history were amongst the first areas to move online, with commercial companies and larger archives providing large-scale resources to a growing body of 'amateur' historians. This resulted in a rather unexpected outcome: family historians pioneering the way in using digital records. Sources online remain dominated by huge sets of name-rich data, mined for local and family history. The authors' experience is that the standards of digitization and metadata created by these companies are as good as the best scholarly examples, but the resources which they make available are little discussed by scholars. The only reference we have found to the potential value of non-scholarly resources is by Brian Maidment, who states that

> scholars need to show a certain humility in the face of the levels of information and understanding available outside the narrow confines of the academy – it is easy to assume that websites devoted to the enthusiasms of collectors such as Yesterday's Papers will not be sufficiently scholarly to support academic study yet there is much here of use to the researcher.
>
> (Maidment, 2013, 116)

There has also been concern that the increasing use of new digital research tools, such as Geographic Information Systems (GIS) research or data mining, which requires some level of technical sophistication, militates against greater collaboration between the two groups. However, as with the issue of context, there exist forces pulling in the opposite direction, empowering public historians and bringing them a new respectability in the academy. The democratization of source material, combined with a move towards impact and inclusion, has spawned the new sub-discipline of Public History.

There has been a small coming-together of the academic and non-academic resources with the development of the British Newspaper Archive. The core of this collection was funded by a grant from the academic funding body Jisc and was made available freely to UK higher education organizations. Subsequently, the British Library developed a commercial partnership with a subsidiary of D. C. Thomson Family History Limited to establish the British Newspaper Archive.[4] This has been able to fund the digitization of many more out-of-copyright newspapers and to work with some newspaper groups to include more recent material. It offers subscriptions to individuals and also has a package for libraries and institutions.

Sadly, there are issues with digitized resources which limit their value to the researcher. One rarely acknowledged issue is that digitization is itself a transformative process. Writing about the use of digital images, Brian Maidment states that 'Digitisation adds yet one more process to the complex of socio-cultural and aesthetic transformations through which empirically gathered understanding of the world is represented on the image' (Maidment, 2013, 123). The same argument applies to the digitization of newspapers and other documents.

There is also the problem of scope: it is not always clear what is the scope of any digital resource, and it is easy to make false assumptions as a result. One example comes from the digitization of newspapers. Some 19th-century newspapers, such as *Lloyd's Weekly Newspaper* or *Reynold's Newspaper*, printed several editions of their Sunday editions to take account of geographically dispersed readers and late-breaking news. However, this does not seem to have been in the mind of those responsible for producing the digital edition of 19th-century British newspapers. Some stories which are found in the microfilm edition are not found in the online copy. There is a danger that if researchers are unaware of this issue, they could make important but false conclusions based on assumptions about the readership or dissemination of a particular piece of news contained in an edition (Crone and Halsey, 2013, 102). Similar issues have been found with 19th-century American periodicals, where Antebellum periodicals from the South are less thoroughly represented than those from the North or Midwest (Cordell, 2013, para. 9).

Technical issues and sources of bias

There are also technical problems with digitizing and indexing certain types of material, notably fragile or damaged manuscripts. As a recent workshop on imaging and processing historical records pointed out, 'as digital repositories become the primary focus for future scholars, we are in danger of limiting access to pieces that can be digitized and indexed using currently available technology' (Landon, 2014).

The technical problems of indexing material have become apparent with the Nineteenth Century British Library Newspaper Database, which has been subject to careful analysis. This has found problems with the quality of the optical character recognition (OCR) and indexing. In order to get a reasonably reliable index, the OCR software needs to accurately identify more than 80% of the significant words on a page (significant words exclude stop words such as 'the', 'he', 'it', etc.). If an accuracy level of above 80% can be achieved, then search engines which use fuzzy logic can ensure that 95% to 98% of words on a page can be retrieved. Sadly, the researchers found that only a quarter of newspapers had a significant-word accuracy of above 80%, and the overall significant-word accuracy was 68.4%. The quality of accuracy of the digitized version of the Burney Collection was even worse (Tanner, Muñoz and Hemy Ros, 2009).

Even when the indexing was accurate, some users have expressed concerns because the technology for finding articles in digital versions of newspapers privileges search above browse, and this may decontextualize the material. For example, it might be important to see where in a newspaper a particular article was found – this could provide information about the value and importance attached to the item by the paper's editor (Weller, 2013, 7).

There are also other possible sources of bias because of the way in which material is selected, or in the nature of the digital material itself. Even scholars can produce 'unscholarly' projects or be deceived by forgeries, notoriously the Hitler diaries. The Reading Experience Database is an online collection of evidence of people's reading of print or written material, covering the period 1450 to 1945. It contains over 30,000 entries taken from diaries, correspondence, commonplace books, etc., and each entry contains a small snippet from the source of information. It is an immensely interesting and valuable source, and it is fortunate that two of the scholars involved in the project have been quite open about the biases that it contains. One is that some of the material comes from crowdsourcing, and some writers have a greater fan base than others. For example, the [Robert Louis] Stevenson Society added 405 entries about the reading habits of its author, while there is only one entry for Arthur Conan Doyle. However, it is known from his autobiography that Conan Doyle was a voracious reader.

There are other possible biases in the material. For example, 78% of the 19th-century evidence for reading printed materials concerns books, whereas only 7% shows people reading newspapers; but newspaper reading was probably more common than book reading in this period (Crone and Halsey, 2013). Equally, there are few references to servants or other working-class readers: the large volume of evidence from the diaries and letters of famous people – Elizabeth Barrett Browning, George Eliot and Lord Byron – tends to overwhelm evidence from sociological surveys, criminal court records and observational surveys (Crone and Halsey, 2013, 99 and 105–7).

Rosalind Crone and Katie Halsey, who wrote about the Reading Experience Database, drew attention to the need for rigorous care when using online resources: 'The skills of evaluation and interpretation are crucial to understanding material discovered online but are generally under-deployed in a culture that values fast information in the same way that it values fast food' (Crone and Halsey, 2013, 98.) Perhaps the best place to start would be to provide researchers with more information about the digital resources they are searching. Publishers should be much more open about the sources they have used, and allow researchers to have access to the OCR transcript of the text, which would allow them to make a full assessment of its scope and limits. The alternative is to continue to behave in the way Tim Hitchcock describes: 'We use the Burney collection regardless – entirely failing to apply the kind of critical approach that historians have built their professional authority upon. This is roulette dressed up as scholarship' (Hitchcock, 2011).

The paradox of the book

Through all this discussion of the digital text, one important thing stands out: the book is still the currency of humanities scholarship. Money is regarded as having three functions – a means of exchange, a store of value and a unit of account. Books provide a means of both storing and exchanging ideas and information. They are also a unit of account: the production of monographs is a way of measuring academic achievement.

According to some writers, this currency is rapidly being debased. Tim Hitchcock has argued that history was organized to be written from 'books', found in hard copy libraries; the whole academic apparatus of provenance, edition, transcription, cross-referencing, footnotes and textual analysis is centred on the book. However, he believes that the book is dead because digital books are no longer books, they are simply electronic text. He says that 'Modern humanities scholarship is a direct engagement with a deracinated, Google-ised, Wikipedia-ised, electronic text', and claims that 'the transformation of books to texts forces us to question the methodologies of modern history writing' (Hitchcock, 2011).

So, are we at a tipping point, with people who share Professor Hitchcock's views on the prophets of a new age; or are those who believe in some sort of continued dialogue between the book and the digital in the right? It is hard to be certain, but, if books really are the currency of humanities, then there is at least one economic factor which means they are being debased. The issue is that, increasingly, there is a tension between funding bodies, commercial publishers and learned societies. Funding bodies are anxious that research which they pay for is made available freely through the means of institutional repositories. Publishers see little value in producing books which merely duplicate material which is freely available. Learned societies, which might be thought to be in favour of free access to information, generate substantial sums from publications. In 2012–13, the Royal Historical Society had a total income of £293,000; of this £88,000, came from royalties (Royal Historical Society, 2013, 289). Some academics are having to rewrite material to make it sufficiently distinct from their theses or other funded pieces of research, while there are discussions about re-establishing university-based publishing companies. In the long term, these tensions may have an impact on the future of the academic book as the currency of research.

The digital library

Hitchcock's view is at one extreme, but the impact of the shift to digital in specialist research libraries has been undeniable. Mark Brown describes how 'the "library without walls" now includes digitization and discovery for research collections, advice and support for authors on citation and impact, fostering digital skills, shaping research data management strategies, managing research outputs and research metrics, digital preservation, institutional repositories, digital publishing and Open Access' (Brown, 2013, 158). The same was found by a Research Libraries UK (RLUK) report from 2012, *Re-Skilling for Research* (RLUK, 2012). Expectations from users are high and increasing, whilst library budgets are tending in the opposite direction. Librarians from universities described to the authors how students expect information immediately, libraries were open 24 hours a day and were indeed used during all of that time.

The library is in a hybrid state, and this means that the transitional stage for information resources is having varied impacts on different institutions as they travel the road from paper to digital at different paces. One university library described to the authors how it now no longer has any reference books, and few hard-copy journals. Manual cataloguing is disappearing, the cataloguing being provided automatically as metadata by the publishers (interview with John Tuck, Amy Warner and Dace Rozenberga, Royal Holloway University Library, 14 August 2014). One of the most important British special collections libraries, the Wellcome Collection, is generously and well funded, but is still facing unexpected issues with the shift to digital. E-books and e-journals serve as a useful example.

Economic implications

In the paper world, libraries purchased the physical article, which they then owned. In the digital world they merely own a licence. This has implications which were perhaps not anticipated. For example, the Wellcome Trust is a charity aimed at opening its collections to as wide a public as possible. If it therefore owns a collection of documents or special collections books it can (subject to copyright) digitize them and allow access to all. In the digital world, if Wellcome offers online access to e-journals and e-books to all, the journal and book publishers' economic models will collapse.

This is not the only issue. The Wellcome Library used to purchase only the journals it needed. They were in a defined area, and were not commonly held by other libraries. This gave Wellcome a unique selling point: a particular niche in medical history. Now publishers are 'bundling' journals into packages, so universities receive journals that they previously did not purchase, and Wellcome receives lots of journals that it does not want. This is damaging Wellcome's unique selling point, as its core academic audience can now access journals from their home university (interview with Simon Chaplin, Head of Libraries at the Wellcome Library, 30 July 2014). Ironically, this point was also reflected by a university librarian, who stated that she did not want 'the irrelevant stuff' which comes as part of bundled packages either (interview with Darlene Maxwell, Librarian of the Royal College of Art, 19 August 2014).

Wellcome's response is to offer *different* digital content: digitized copies of its own archival and special collections holdings, and access to collections of other digitized content, such as digitized books, in its specialist field. In fact, Wellcome has recently announced a major initiative in partnership with Jisc, the Higher Education Funding Council for England and a number of university partners to create a huge online resource, the UK Medical Heritage Library, the basis of which will be Wellcome's own collections.[5] However, the Wellcome Library is generously funded, and this kind of approach is not an option for many other library services. The librarian at the Royal College of Art felt that digital sources worked via economies of scale; and that smaller institutions such as hers could not compete. Yet, interestingly, she too had come to the same conclusion as the Wellcome Library: to focus on the institution's specialism. Although, clearly, authors' rights have always been important and should be respected, the additional problems of online copyright created by the online library may result in libraries privileging material that they have paid for and own, and lead them to become more insular and focused on their own collections, to the detriment of the overall offer to researchers and scholars.

Long-term implications

There are, then, a number of conflicting pressures. There are moves that seem to increase access (more academics can view material from their institutions), yet at the same time the economic pressures of current publishing models may act to reduce it (libraries are able to offer better access to historic and old collections than to newer holdings). With publishing models in flux, there was a view that journals themselves will disappear, to be replaced by the publication of single articles, the so-called 'nano-publication' (interview with John Tuck, Amy Warner and Dace Rozenberga from Royal Holloway University Library, 14 August 2014). Open Access policies only add to a complicated picture.[6]

It may be that there will be a slower shift to digital print. At the Royal College of Art, only two of its top 20 or 30 titles were available as e-books (interview with Darlene Maxwell, Librarian of the Royal College of Art, 19 August 2014). In addition, it is by no means the case that researchers prefer the online library. At the Royal College of Art, the librarian described how students could have an e-book on loan within 24 hours, but preferred to wait two to three weeks for the hard copy. Other non-university libraries, such as the London Library, found the same. The Wellcome Library has experienced no drop in the numbers of its on-site visitors, despite the shift to digital. It may be that certain disciplines, such as art, which is not well suited to e-readers or small-scale reproduction, may reject the dominance of the digital. Many special collections and original archival materials remain accessible on site only. Importantly, it is also true that students and academics value the library as a quiet place for work and study. This was confirmed by the librarians of the Royal College of Art and Royal Holloway, University of London.

Conversely, one university library stated that it has students who have never used a library before, and it considered that, over time, there will be an impact on research from the fact that digital-only students had no experience of using books. As an example, it told of a student having to be shown how to use paper clips! The librarian stressed that this shift would not necessarily be detrimental, simply a question of different mind-sets, contexts and culture feeding into the research outputs (interview with John Tuck, Amy Warner and Dace Rozenberga from Royal Holloway University Library, 14 August 2014).

The London Library, an independent lending library founded in 1841, still sees the book as core to its mission and has over a million volumes in its collection. It offers its members access to a substantial digital library of reference works and online journals and newspapers, but it sees its digital resources as reflecting, enhancing and speaking to its core book collection. It does not see conflict between the physical book and digital resources but, rather, a mutual reinforcement full of new possibilities, in much the same way as radio was not killed off by television, nor cinema by video. This view was expressed by Helen O'Neill, Archive, Heritage and Development Librarian, London Library (interview, 21 August 2014; Edgerton, 2007).

However, the pace of digitization may have a serious impact. In 2010, Google estimated that just under 130 million individual book titles had been published since book publication began (Taycher, 2010). It is not beyond anyone's imagination that within a decade or so a significant number of these will have been digitized; as long ago as 2010, Google had digitized 12 million books, while a number of other institutions have also created huge collections – the Internet Archive, for example, has made more than two million books available online (Jackson, 2012). If a situation is reached where a substantial proportion of the books used for humanities research are available as digital texts, then we may well have reached a tipping point and the visions of a digital-heavy, book-light future may become more of a reality.

The full implications of this have yet to be fully envisaged. It is, for example, becoming more evident that one reads electronic resources with a different mind-set. Recent research showed that people read more slowly on e-readers; and that reading on electronic readers 'promoted more deep reading [when the reader is highly immersed in the text] and less active learning' [making notes, cross-referencing] (Baggini, 2014, 10). Concern has also been expressed about the loss of materiality of the book. Books are physical things, and their size, weight, design, cover art and so on affect our interpretation. Divorcing the text from its physical form has effects which have not yet been well studied. Jisc is currently running the Digital Student project, looking at the expectations and experience of students in a digital environment.[7] More research in this shifting space is clearly needed.

Research and tools

With all this digital source material flooding the digital research space, one of the key questions is whether the digital has made it possible to ask new research questions. At a superficial level, it seems that fairly crude tools have allowed researchers to do things which were impossible in the pre-digital world. One concerns the issue of 'close and critical reading', long trumpeted as the prime research method of the humanities. However, close reading has its limits. As Franco Moretti pointed out in 'Graphs, Maps, Trees', 'what a minimal fraction of the literary field we all work on' in literary studies, drawing claims about literature and culture after reading 'less than one per cent of the novels that were actually published' (Moretti, 2003, 67). Similarly, Jim Mussell (Mussell, 2013) talked about the tendency of researchers to focus on individual, exceptional texts, rather than focusing on the whole corpus.

Analytical tools

Google has a solution to this problem – the Ngram Viewer, which allows researchers to trace the frequency of words and phrases across the Google Books database. It is possible to select books from different date ranges and from different categories – English, British English, American English, English Fiction, Chinese, French, German, Hebrew, Italian, Russian and Spanish. The Ngram Viewer exemplifies Moretti's solution to the problem of close reading by allowing 'distant reading': scholars can track trends in language across millions of books rather than selecting evidence from a few representative works. The Ngram Viewer may be able to offer broad insights into the concerns of a historical period and generate the kinds of questions that drive close analysis.[8]

However, there are real dangers that the use of tools such as the Google Ngram Viewer may simply confirm what is already well understood. As Tim Hitchcock observed, 'most stabs at distant reading seem to tell us what we already know" (Hitchcock, 2013). To take a trivial example, if you search for references to the word 'Sputnik' in Ngram Viewer, you will find a dramatic rise from 1952 to a peak in 1961; this is hardly surprising, since Russia's first artificial satellite, Sputnik-1 (Спу́тник-1) was launched in 1957, with the third and final satellite in the series launched in 1958, whilst the programme had been under discussion for a few years before.

Where tools like the Ngram Viewer really come into their own is where it is possible to explain their results in a literary or historical context – to zoom in from the digital to the textual. A good example of this process comes from Ryan Cordell's work on the Antebellum religious press. Google Ngram Viewer told him that use of the word 'sectarian' in the American-English corpus spiked during the decades just before the Civil War. It appears in approximately 0.000025% of the books and periodicals that were published in the United States in 1800. Its use steadily increased over the next decades. By 1850, 'sectarian' appears in 0.000375% of those books in Google's corpus which had been published in the US. In other words, in 1850 books and periodicals used 'sectarian' more than ten times more frequently than in 1800 (Cordell, 2013, 32).

Cordell was able to explain this phenomenon in the context of changes in religious denominations in the US in that period. By the 1840s and 1850s, the nation's largest denominations – Methodist, Baptist, etc. – were breaking into sub-groups, each with its own particular social, political or theological opinions. Perhaps most importantly, in 1845 the Baptist and Methodist denominations in the United States split into northern and southern conventions over slavery. The increased use of the word 'sectarian' was a consequence of these splits and divisions.

Colin Jones makes a similar use of such tools in his *The Smile Revolution in Eighteenth Century Paris* (2014). His thesis is that until the late 18th century smiling was frowned on in polite French society. If an aristocrat smiled, it was disdainful rather than humorous. This refusal to smile was partly to emphasize their social superiority and distance from the Rabelaisian culture. Mostly, however, it was aesthetic – the increased use of sugar in their diet had given everyone from the king downwards the worst teeth in any period in French history. In the second half of the century, a number of factors came to make the smile acceptable among the bourgeoisie. There was the influence of cheerful writers, notably the English writer Samuel Richardson, whose works, *Pamela*, *Clarissa* and *The History of Sir Charles Grandison*, were available in translation in the 1740s and 1750s. Most important was the growth of scientific dentistry, based on the conservation of teeth rather than tooth pulling. As a consequence, people's teeth were in better condition – whiter and with less decay. Even if they did all fall out, teeth could be replaced by the newly developed dentures. Smiles were simply more attractive and more acceptable to those smiled at (Jones, 2013).

Scholarly histories of dentistry are rare, and histories of smiles even more so. However, Jones was able to confirm his thesis by a careful analysis of the digital textual evidence. He used the digital corpus ARTFL/Frantext, which contains over 3500 French-language texts from the 12th century onwards and is particularly strong on canonical works of French literature and culture. He was able to show that the use of the word 'sourire' was rare in the late 17th and early 18th centuries, with no occurrences between 1700 and 1710. When the word was used, the adjectives used with it included 'forced', 'disdainful', 'bitter', 'mocking', 'proud' and 'ironic'. The smile was used by aristocrats and courtiers condescending to and inwardly laughing at their inferiors.

From the 1730s, and in particular from the 1740s and 1750s, there was a massive increase in the frequency of use of this word, and from the 1740s and 1750s smiles were more likely to be 'enchanting', 'sweet', 'good', 'agreeable', 'friendly' and 'virtuous'. Similar results are achieved by using the Google Ngram Viewer, but the rise in the use of 'sourire' is not quite as sharp from 1750 to 1800. Jones puts this down to the fact that the Google corpus is less literary than the ARTFL/Frantext one (Jones, 2013, 62, n. 196).

Jones also uses this technology to trace the rise of the Gothic style in France. The works of Gothic writers such Matthew 'Monk' Lewis, Anne Ratcliffe and William Beckford, whose *Vathek* was written in French and published in 1786–7, had begun to attract attention even before the Revolution. These writers described a world of crumbling castles, underground passages, suspense and horror; and a new and different sensibility as regards the smile developed. French literary works began to describe smiles that were 'chilling', 'ogre-like' and 'frightful' (Jones, 2013, 164 and 214, n.). The advantage of this approach is that it is infinitely repeatable. The phrase 'sourire affreux' first appears in the French corpus in 1798 and reached its peak in 1833.

It is possible to achieve the same results by searching the Google Ngram Viewer (https://books.google.com/ngrams) using the phrase 'sourire affreux', the French language corpus and the date range 1700–1900.

Is the digital transformative?

The use of analytical tools is entertaining, and a valid way to confirm historical theses or to indicate new avenues of research. However, what the digital really seems to have contributed to the research by both Ryan Cordell and Colin Jones is that it provided them with a huge corpus of material on which to base their research. Cordell's work was on the reprinting and re-authorship of Nathaniel Hawthorne's *Celestial Railroad* in the Antebellum religious press. The story is unusual because it was favoured for its doctrinal orthodoxy and power of religious instruction, whereas Hawthorne is traditionally seen as a religious outsider. The standard bibliography of Hawthorne lists 22 reprintings of the text in the 19th century, but by using digital archives Cordell was able to find another 25 and to find about 100 references to characters, themes and settings in contemporary articles and books. By using the Juxta collation tool he was able to compare different printings of the same text and to identify excisions and changes. Equally, it was possible to show how different sects used the text to bolster their own beliefs. Cordell's research shows some of the difficulties of accessing historical texts online – he did not have one source to go to; rather, he had to search nine different databases (Cordell, 2013, paras 4–5, 21, 31, 63). Jones was luckier, having one major source – the Bibliothèque Interuniversitaire de Santé has a large database of medical texts, including over 100 historical dentistry works (Jones, 2014, 184).

Cordell is clear about the nature of what he is doing in his research:

> The discoveries I enumerate here are theoretically quite traditional. Were I to remove references to my methodologies, this essay would outline a new historical account of Hawthorne's early career drawn from a range of primary sources: contemporary books and periodicals. The witnesses and paratexts I have accumulated *could* have been amassed through trips to archives and interlibrary loan. In practice, however, this study emphasizes the great benefits of working in a digital scholarly mode. To build a bibliography like mine for 'The Celestial Railroad' without digital book and periodical archives would require … unacceptable expenditures of time and labor.
>
> (Cordell, 2013, para. 8)

Cordell's observation raises the question about whether the digital has been truly transformative in the traditional humanities. Clearly it has made it possible to do things much more quickly and to undertake research which would not be practically possible in a world where a good publications track record is required. Jones and Cordell could have analysed hundreds of texts, but not in a realistic timeframe. As we have seen, there are other limits on the use of the digital to analyse texts. There are problems with the scope of material which has been digitized and the way in which it is indexed. There are concerns that the digitization process leaves material decontextualized and that it might introduce biases. At a higher level, there is a belief that the use of distant reading might simply confirm what is already known.

More subtly, there appear to be a few concerns that applying large-scale digital processes to humanities might not always be appropriate. Writing about the Reading Experience Database, Crone and Halsey explain that the database contains references to over 10,000 titles for the 19th century. However, there are fewer than 50 examples of each title being read. On the one hand, Crone and Halsey believe, this might be confirmation of the trend in studies of reading to emphasize the great diversity of reading diets in the 19th century. Or it might simply expose significant problems with using essentially quantitative methods to analyse qualitative sources (Crone and Halsey, 2013, 105). A related point is made by Cordell when he talks about the need to abandon the quantitative universe and use the historical and literary context to explain changes in the use of the word 'sectarian' (Cordell, 2013, para 34). Some scholars have gone further, questioning the use of data and quantitative methods in the humanities as being at odds with the principles of humanistic enquiry such as context-dependent interpretation and the inevitable 'situated-ness' of researchers and their aims. Others have pointed out that because data is manufactured for use, it is not an observer-independent fact (Schöch, 2013).

Radical approaches

If the analysis of digital texts has its limitations, are there other more radical approaches? One approach is to move from the textual, in Sayeed Choudhur's words, to move 'from a document-centric view of scholarship to a data-centric view of scholarship' (Choudhur, 2010, 194). There has been a huge move among research funding bodies to fund research in this area. Since 2010 a group of international funding bodies have funded three rounds of research into using a range of tools to analyse different large bodies of data. The research has allowed academics to experiment with a range of approaches across a large number of disciplines. Indeed, funding has driven large-scale collaborative interdisciplinary projects. Subjects range from an analysis of the Old Bailey Records to a project to map dialect variation and human migration patterns in the United Kingdom and the United States and to understand the extent to which migration patterns explain regional linguistic variation. In 2014 the Arts and Humanities Research Council announced an investment of £4.6 million on 21 projects in the field of Big Data.

So, is Big Data the way to transform humanities research? And what is Big Data? There are two definitions worth considering. One is simply that Big Data is concerned with ways of creating new insights or forms of value which can be done at a large scale but cannot be done at a small scale. The second definition points to the three Vs: volume, velocity and variety. Some of the projects we have described fall into the volume category – because they involve searching large collections of data. The second V (velocity) is concerned with real-time analysis of data which is being constantly generated – for example by sensors or by people interacting with online systems (Schöch, 2013, section 3). At the moment there seems to be little use made of this sort of data in the digital humanities, but this may change because some of the large social media sites do offer analysis tools which might have a value to humanities researchers, although some, such as Google Analytics, seem to be aimed mainly at the corporate market.

The third 'V' (variety) may well be the most powerful vector for change in the way in which humanities research is done. Variety refers to the use of heterogeneous sources and formats of data to allow all kinds of inferences. Some of the recently funded research projects fall into this category. For example, one project which was funded under the 2013 Digging into Data funding call aims to understand how linguistic variation is shaped by migration in both the past and present. Two sorts of Big Data will be collected, cleaned and analysed for spatial patterns: tweets will be used to document regional linguistic variation, and family trees to describe the large-scale migration patterns that might explain this variation. An earlier Digging into Data project was concerned with the railroads and the making of modern America. It used a whole range of disparate data sources – unstructured text from books, newspapers and railroad-related periodicals and ephemera, alphanumeric census and non-census data sets, GIS data sets and maps.

Some data can be used without any modification, but a number of collections need enriching to ensure that more-intelligent queries are possible. Some can be improved by automatic annotation, but in other cases human intervention is required. A number of projects have been established to allow members of the public to contribute to data analysis. The most famous ones are run by Zooniverse, the Citizen Science Alliance which allows people to help identify the shapes of galaxies, or wild animals in the Serengeti. It supports two humanities projects: one from Oxford University for transcribing fragments of papyri found in the ancient town of Oxyrhynchus, and one from The National Archives editing war diaries from World War 1. Another UK project is Transcribe Bentham, which allows volunteers to transcribe pages from Jeremy Bentham's papers. In 2012 the project had 1726 registered users and by October 2014 nearly 11,000 manuscripts had been transcribed. However, the bulk of the work was done by a small number of the volunteers – seven users had worked on 70% of the transcribed manuscripts and one had worked on 28% (https://www.zooniverse.org/; Causer and Wallace, 2012).

If Big Data is to be truly transformative, then the probability is that it will have to move away from the purely textual. Most of the projects we have discussed and, indeed, most of those funded by the funding councils are text based: French dentistry books, Antebellum religious books, war diaries, Jeremy Bentham's papers, even tweets and family trees. But, as Tim Hitchcock says, 'As long as we are using digital technology to re-examine text, we are going to have a hard time competing with two hundred years of library science and humanist enquiry.' He says that there is a danger of giving ourselves over to a form of what sociologists refer to as 'problem closure' – the tendency to reinvent the problem to pose questions that available tools and data allow us to answer (Hitchcock, 2013).

So, the genuinely radical shift in humanities research might come by combining other forms of data with the purely textual. David J. Bodenhamer paints an enticing picture of a world in which GIS become part of the toolkit of humanists. He refers to the possibility of developing 'deep maps', first imagined by the French Situationist Guy Debord in the 1950s and defined by Mike Pearson and Michael Shanks (2001) as:

> Reflecting eighteenth century antiquarian approaches to place, which included history, folklore, natural history and hearsay, the deep map attempts to record and represent the grain and patina of place through juxtapositions and interpenetrations of the historical and the contemporary, the political and the poetic, the discursive and the sensual; the conflation of oral testimony, anthology, memoir, biography, natural history and everything you might ever want to say about a place …

A good example of the sort of thing which Bodenhamer imagines is Locating London's Past, which provides an intuitive GIS interface enabling researchers to map and visualize textual and artefactual data relating to 17th- and 18th-century London against John Rocque's 1746 map of London and the first accurate modern OS map (Bodenhamer, 2013; Pearson and Shanks, 2001).

Turkel, Kee and Roberts have written positively on new approaches to 'navigating the infinite archive' and how a multiplicity of methods can open minds and encourage innovative research (Turkel, Kee and Roberts, 2013). However, it is possible to detect a sense of nervousness about the possible implications of this digital turn for humanities scholars. Toni Weller argued that 'Historians do not need to learn new technologies or computer codes; they do not need to become computer scientists. Indeed, I would argue that part of the problem thus far has been too much emphasis on historians becoming something they are not; to the detriment of the fundamental skills and expertise that is the craft of the historian' (Weller, 2013). On this point, at least, Professor Bodenhamer offers some reassurance when urging the adoption of GIS technology by historians: 'The goal is not to sacrifice the rational, logical and empirical approach to knowledge that has been the hallmark of the humanities since the Enlightenment, but rather to complement it with different ways of discovery' (Weller, 2013).

Conclusion

Information services and research methodologies are still heavily influenced by the paper world and are not yet fully digital. We are in a hybrid age. John Tuck, University Librarian from Royal Holloway University, quoted a professional colleague who stated that 'the printed page is still at the heart of the e-book' (interview, 14 August 2014). Yet, at the same time, digital resources *are* doing something different. An article in the *Financial Times* of 11 April 2014 described how a group of investigative reporters working to expose corruption in the Ukraine had their offices raided by masked gunmen. They rang the Internet Archive, desperate to have the website archived so that their reports could be kept. Within ten minutes of the call, the Archive started to harvest their web pages. Brewster Kahle, founder of the Internet Archive, described the internet as a 'blessing', and 'an opportunity to transform the study of history'. He went on: 'It is a golden age for librarians, historians and scholars ...' (Kuchler, 2014, 1–2). We are so far only at the dawn of that age – a golden future awaits.

References

Baggini, J. (2014) Ways of Reading, *Financial Times*, 21/22 June.
Bodenhamer, D. J. (2013) The Spatial Humanities: space, time and place in the new digital age. In Weller, T. (ed.), *History in the Digital Age*, Routledge.
Brown, M. L. (2013) The Role of the Research Library. In Shorley, D. and Jubb, M. (eds), *The Future of Scholarly Communication*, Facet Publishing.
Causer, T. and Wallace, V. (2012) Building a Volunteer Community: results and

findings from Transcribe Bentham, *Digital Humanities Quarterly*, **6**, 2, http://www.digitalhumanities.org/dhq/vol/6/2/000125/000125.html.

Choudhur, S. (2010) Data Curation: an ecological perspective, *College and Research Libraries News*, **71**, 4.

Chowdhury, G. (2014) *Sustainability of Scholarly Information*, Facet Publishing.

Cordell, R. (2013) 'Taken Possession of': the reprinting and reauthorship of Hawthorne's 'Celestial Railroad' in the Antebellum Religious Press, *Digital Humanities Quarterly*, **7**, 1, para. 9, http://www.digitalhumanities.org/dhq/vol/7/1/000144/000144.html.

Crone, R. and Halsey, K. (2013) On Collecting, Cataloguing and Collating the Evidence of Reading: the 'RED movement' and its implications for digital scholarship. In Weller, T. (ed.), *History in the Digital Age*, Routledge.

Dervin, B. and Nilan, M. (1986) Information Needs and Uses, *Annual Review of Information Science and Technology*, **21**, 3–33.

Edgerton, D. (2007) *The Shock of the Old: technology and global history since 1900*, Oxford University Press.

Farge, A. (2013) *The Allure of the Archives*, trans. T. Scott-Railton, Yale University Press. (See also review of the book by Valerie Johnson in *Archives and Records*, **35** (2), 169–71.)

Hay, D. (2014) New Connections: the BT Digital Archives project, *Business Archives*, **108** (May 2014), 29–52.

Hitchcock, T. (2008) Digitising British History since 1980, Making History, http://www.history.ac.uk/makinghistory/resources/articles/digitisation_of_history.html.

Hitchcock, T. (2011) Academic History Writing and Its Disconnects, *Journal of Digital Humanities*, **1**, 1 (Winter), http://journalofdigitalhumanities.org/1-1/academic-history-writing-and-its-disconnects-by-tim-hitchcock/.

Hitchcock, T. (2013) Big Data for Dead People: digital readings and the conundrums of positivism, blog post, 9 December, http://historyonics.blogspot.co.uk/2013/12/big-data-for-dead-people-digital.html.

Jackson, J. (2012) Google, 129 million Different Books have been Published, *PC World*, 6 August, http://www.pcworld.com/article/202803/google_129_million_different_books_have_been_published.html, https://archive.org/details/texts.

Jones, C. (2014) *The Smile Revolution in Eighteenth Century Paris*, Oxford University Press.

Kuchler, H. (2014) History Rebooting, *Financial Times*, Life and Arts supplement, 12–13 April.

Landon, G. V. (2014) Report on the 2nd International Workshop on Historical Document Imaging and Processing (HIP 13), *D-Lib Magazine*, **20**, 3–4, http://www.dlib.org/dlib/march14/landon/03landon.html.

Maidment, B. (2013) Writing History with the Digital Image: a cautious celebration. In Weller, T. (ed.), *History in the Digital Age*, Routledge.

McKemmish, S., Gilliland-Swetlund, A. and Ketelaar, E. (2005) 'Communities of Memory': pluralising archival research and education agendas, *Archives and Manuscripts*, **35** (May), 146–74.

Moretti, F. (2003) Graphs, Maps, Trees: abstract models for literary history, *New Left Review*, **24** (November–December).

Mussell, J. (2013) The Proximal Past: digital archives, and the here and now, Manchester Metropolitan University Digital Transformers Conference, 2013, http://jimmussell.com/2013/05/23/the-proximal-past-digital-archives-and-the-here-and-now/.

Pearson, M. and Shanks, M. (2001) Theatre/Archaeology, pp. 64–5, http://www.locatinglondon.org/.

RLUK (2012) *Re-skilling for Research*, Research Libraries UK.

Royal Historical Society (2013) Statement of Financial Activities for the Year Ended 30 June 2013, *Transactions of the Royal Historical Society*, sixth series, 23.

Schöch, C. (2013) Big? Smart? Clean? Messy? Data in the humanities, *Journal of Digital Humanities*, **3**, 2 (Summer), http://journalofdigitalhumanities.org/2-3/big-smart-clean-messy-data-in-the-humanities/.

Seife, C. (2014) *Virtual Unreality: just because the internet told you, how do you know it's true?* Viking.

Tanner, S., Muñoz, T. and Hemy Ros, P. (2009) Measuring Mass Text Digitization Quality and Usefulness, Lessons Learned from Assessing the OCR Accuracy of the British Library's 19th Century Online Newspaper Archive, *D-Lib Magazine*, **15**, 7–8 (July/August), http://www.dlib.org/dlib/july09/munoz/07munoz.html.

Taycher, L. (2010) Books of the World, Stand Up and Be Counted! All 129,864,880 of you, blog post, 5 August, http://booksearch.blogspot.co.uk/2010/08/books-of-world-stand-up-and-be-counted.html.

Turkel, W. J., Kee, K. and Roberts, S. (2013) A Method for Navigating the Infinite Archive. In Weller, T. (ed.), *History in the Digital Age*, Routledge.

Weller, T. (2013) Introduction to History in the Digital Age. In Weller, T. (ed.), *History in the Digital Age*, Routledge.

Notes

1 https://www.jisc-collections.ac.uk/Catalogue/Overview/Index/1999.
2 http://corporate.ancestry.com/about-ancestry/.
3 www.dcthomsonfamilyhistory.com/about.
4 www.britishnewspaperarchive.co.uk/help/about.
5 http://www.timeshighereducation.co.uk/news/wellcome-and-jisc-take-19th-century-medical-archives-online/2014935.article.
6 See www.rcuk.ac.uk/research/openaccess/policy/.
7 www.jisc.ac.uk/research/projects/digital-student.
8 https://books.google.com/ngrams.

Index

WITHDRAWN
GLASGOW
LIBRARY

WITHDRAWN